FEB 06 2012

Best Bike Rides
Chicago

Help Us Keep This Guide Up to Date

Every effort has been made by the author and editors to make this guide as accurate and useful as possible. However, many things can change after a guide is published—roads are detoured, phone numbers change, facilities come under new management, etc.

We would love to hear from you concerning your experiences with this guide and how you feel it could be improved and kept up to date. While we may not be able to respond to all comments and suggestions, we'll take them to heart and we'll also make certain to share them with the author. Please send your comments and suggestions to the following address:

Globe Pequot Press
Reader Response/Editorial Department
P.O. Box 480
Guilford, CT 06437

Or you may e-mail us at:
editorial@GlobePequot.com

Thanks for your input, and happy riding!

BEST BIKE RIDES® SERIES

Best Bike Rides
Chicago

The Greatest Recreational Rides
in the Metro Area

TED VILLAIRE

FALCONGUIDES

GUILFORD, CONNECTICUT
HELENA, MONTANA

AN IMPRINT OF GLOBE PEQUOT PRESS

FALCONGUIDES®

Maps by Trailhead Graphics Inc. © Morris Book Publishing, LLC
Photos by Ted Villaire unless otherwise indicated

Text design: Sheryl Kober
Layout: Kevin Mak
Project editor: Gregory Hyman

Library of Congress Cataloging-in-Publication data is available on file.

ISBN 978-0-7627-4689-7

Printed in the United States of America

10 9 8 7 6 5 4 3 2 1

Contents

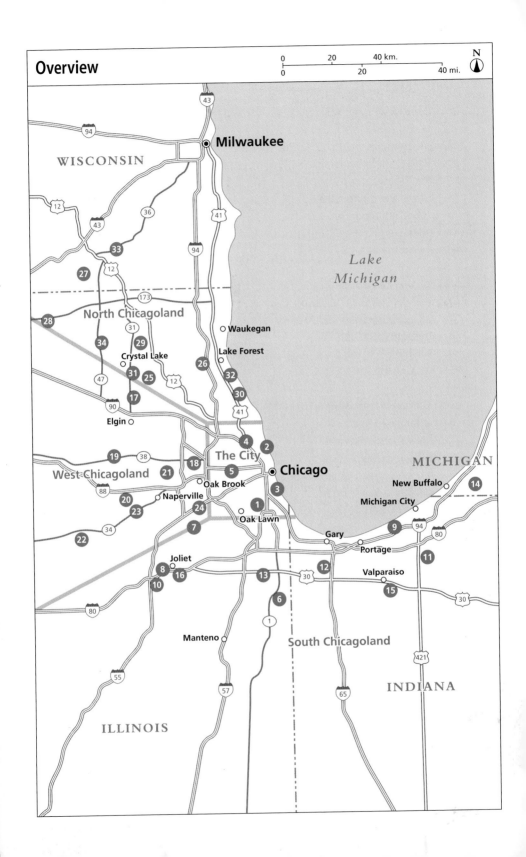

Overview

0   20   40 km.

0   20   40 mi.

N

WISCONSIN

94

94

43

● **Milwaukee**

12

43   36

41

33

94

27   12

173

28   North Chicagoland

31

34   29

Crystal Lake

31   25

47

17

90

Elgin ○

12

Lake Michigan

○ Waukegan

Lake Forest

26   32

30

41

4   2

19   38

The City

West Chicagoland   21   18

88   5

Oak Brook

20   3   ● **Chicago**

Naperville

23   24   1

22   34   Oak Lawn

7

MICHIGAN

New Buffalo ○   14

Michigan City

9   94

Gary   80

8   Portage   11

Joliet   16

10   13   30   12   Valparaiso

6   15

INDIANA

1

Manteno ○   **South Chicagoland**

421

55

57   65

ILLINOIS

Acknowledgments

Whether they know it or not, a number of people helped me with gathering the information contained in this book. I want to thank the local cycling organizations that provided route suggestions, such as the McHenry County Bicycle Club, the Oak Park Cycle Club, and the Calumet Crank Club. I'm grateful to the organizers of local fund-raising rides that inspired rides in this book, particularly the Alliance on Mental Illness of Racine County Bike 'n Hike and the Apple Cider Century.

This book would have been much more difficult to produce without the Active Transportation Alliance's Chicagoland Bicycle Map. As an employee of the organization, I have some inkling of the countless number of hours that Active Trans staff and many dozens of volunteers put toward creating the map's fifth edition. Thanks to Ed Barsotti and the League of Illinois Cyclists for its excellent advocacy work and its growing collection of maps. Thanks to all the grassroots groups throughout Chicagoland that maintain trails and advocate on behalf of cyclists and rail trails in their community. And let's not forget the efforts of the state park and county forest preserve staff throughout the region who maintain the many local trails, despite strained budgets.

I also wish to thank friends who joined me on rides as I explored and documented these routes: Doug Burk, Kari Lyderson, and Timothy Merello. They were extremely patient with me as I stopped to snap pictures every 100 yards and constantly interrupted our conversations with notes dictated into my voice recorder. Thanks to my family for support and encouragement. This book is dedicated to Christine. I look forward to our future rides together.

Introduction

The Chicago region is well suited for pedaling. The gentle terrain, the lakeshore, the abundance of bike paths, and countless distinctive neighborhoods and communities all make the region a great place to explore on a bicycle. Outside of the city, you'll find scores of county forest preserves featuring rivers, woodland, wetlands, and restored prairie. If you know where to look, you can uncover quiet farm roads, charming little towns, and diners and ice cream parlors that have been in operation for decades. Whether you're new to the area or a native, you'll never exhaust the array of interesting museums, restaurants, and parks in the region.

The landscape of the Chicago area seems like it was fashioned with the cyclist in mind. While a gently rolling landscape appears now and then, flatness generally dominates. Particularly in Chicago, most of the inclines you'll encounter are the ones leading over bridges spanning expressways and rivers. Chicagoland cyclists consider the local topography a great gift. No need to adjust a route to avoid big hills or walk that bike up a steep slope. Instead of huffing up a hill, our attention can be focused on more important ventures like admiring the skyline and architecture, exploring the neighborhoods and parks, and looking for the next fantastic restaurant. That's not to say the terrain in the region is completely uniform. Hills exist, but you have to look for them. They're tucked away in places like Barrington, southern Wisconsin, and southwest Michigan.

What could be more enticing to cyclists than Chicago's official motto of "Urbs en Horto" or "City in a Garden," which calls attention to 20 miles of lakeshore parkland and the elaborate system of leafy boulevards that connect a series of mega-parks throughout the city? Coupled with the stellar parkland is an ever-expanding cycling infrastructure featuring more than 100 miles of bike lanes, thousands of bike racks, an automated bike rental program, and the Millennium Park Cycle Center, which offers showers, secure bike parking, and a cycle shop.

Thanks to former mayor Richard M. Daley's interest in making two-wheeled travel easier and a well-organized biking advocacy community, the city of Chicago has become one of the best large cities for cycling. One major triumph for local cyclists is the ability to take bikes on trains and buses. This program allows cyclists to expand their local range exponentially. (Directions for rides in this book will indicate if the ride is easily accessible via public transit.) And not to be overlooked is the rich assortment of local bike club activities, racing events, and charity rides that bring cyclists together in the city and suburbs. Whatever your interest in cycling, you'll find it in Chicagoland.

The North Branch Trail is one of the most well-loved trails in Chicagoland. See Ride 4.

This rich tapestry of cycling culture is nothing new for the Windy City. As far back as the late 1890s, cyclists were seemingly everywhere. Chicago hosted more than fifty bicycle clubs that claimed some 10,000 members. Cyclists constituted a major political force, pressuring elected officials to create bike paths and improve road surfaces. At about this time, Chicago became the bicycle-building capital of America, manufacturing two-thirds of the nation's bikes and bike accessories. This was also the time a German immigrant named Ignaz Schwinn helped form a Chicago company that dominated bicycle sales for most of the twentieth century.

Chicago's heritage as a transportation hub has reaped huge rewards for local cyclists. The Illinois Prairie Path, which runs between the Des Plaines River and Wheaton, was one of the first linear trails in the nation converted from a railroad line. Since that trail was built in the late 1960s, local governments have transformed several hundred miles of railroad into regional trails, making it the most extensive collection of rail trails in the Midwest, perhaps the nation.

Like most other big metropolitan areas around the country, the Chicago area has been growing by leaps and bounds. People move here for jobs, for social connections, and for the rich cultural benefits. These factors and others turned several northeastern Illinois counties into some of the fastest growing counties in the nation during the past decade. The six counties of northeastern Illinois are expected to surpass ten million people by 2030, and that's not counting the growing populations of northwest Indiana and other areas beyond Chicago's traditional collar counties.

So what does this steady growth mean for local cycling? Typically, it means more traffic congestion. It means more subdivisions sprouting up overnight, and it means that you have to look harder to find quiet roads for recreational riding. The good news is that more and more local communities are learning from the mistakes of unchecked growth and growth that is hostile toward cyclists and pedestrians. Fortunately, more communities are seeing that slowing traffic down, adding bike lanes and shoulders to roads, and building bike trails and bike racks makes a community a healthier, better place to live.

The Rides

I chose rides for this book for a variety of reasons: location, length, historic and natural attractions, and traffic and road conditions being the primary considerations. I discovered the rides through a variety of channels, including local cycling clubs, friends and acquaintances, Internet posts, cycling maps, and my own exploration. I'm happy to report that I've ridden most of the routes in the book multiple times, at different times of the year and different times of the day. I hope readers will forgive the fact that some of the rides also appear

A short walking path takes you from the Stone Bridge Trail to the local landmark for which the trail is named. See Ride 28.

in my other books *Best Rail Trails Illinois* and *Road Biking Illinois*. This is due to the simple fact that there are only so many great destinations an area has to offer.

Since we have rail trails shooting out in just about every direction within the region, it made sense to devote an ample number of pages of this book to their exploration. With the metro-area population heading toward ten million, and far too many of those people driving automobiles, the local landscape sometimes resembles a big parking lot. To put it bluntly, Chicago-area traffic can suck. Local trails provide a perfect means to escape the traffic and still put some mileage under your tires. A handful of the rides offer the enjoyable combination of rail trails and road riding. For you roadies who look down your nose at rail trails, I urge you to widen your horizons and give them a try. Similarly, for the people who religiously avoid riding on roads, I encourage you to check out some of the rides that explore the many bike-friendly roads of the region.

The local trails offer a fairly equal amount of pavement and crushed gravel. The crushed gravel is surprisingly smooth; those with road bike tires will have little trouble. Crushed gravel trails will even accommodate the slick spaghetti-thin road bike tires. It's true, your average speed goes down a mile or two an hour on crushed gravel surface. If you're training for a race, this may be an important factor. If not, why should the need for speed surpass all other considerations?

Safety and Equipment

For most of the road routes contained in this book, traffic will be minimal. In some places, the amount of traffic will depend on the time of day you're riding and the day of the week. Quiet suburban roads sometimes get swamped with traffic during the afternoon commute. In other places, traffic jams can occur on Saturday afternoons.

If you've never cycled in heavy traffic, riding a bike through constipated traffic in Chicago initially can be daunting. To stay safe, the first order of business is being predictable. This means that when motorists have a good sense of what to expect from you, you'll be safer on the road. Riding with traffic, signaling turns, and generally obeying the same rules that apply to motor traffic are great habits to take up. For the novice, riding through congestion in Chicago will be easier than you think. Part of the reason for this is that drivers are accustomed to sharing the road with you.

Being predictable and eliminating your own bad cycling habits will go a long way in helping you minimize the chances of a collision. Still, that won't prevent you from being on the receiving end of the foolishness of others. Avoiding bad spots caused by the ineptitude and carelessness of drivers means being able to anticipate potential problems before they happen. A couple of the biggest dangers to watch for are drivers opening car doors and drivers making left turns. The door zone—the area where car doors swing open—should be avoided like the plague, even if that requires riding farther into the traffic lane than some motorists would like. Let them honk. Better to quietly endure a car horn than getting doored. Similarly, when avoiding potholes or other obstacles on the roadside, you have the right to take the lane. Again, drivers will honk. Your job is to keep a level head and then move back to the right side of the road when your pathway is clear. Seasoned cyclists (meaning, those who have had some scrapes of their own) know that one of the most common collisions occurs when oncoming cars turn left. A lawyer friend of mine who represents cyclists and pedestrians says this type of crash accounts for about half of his cases involving cyclists. Bikers are advised to use special caution around these problem areas; this means not assuming that drivers see you, and not assuming drivers will stop for you.

In some cases, drivers present less of a problem than do pedestrians and other cyclists. Busier local trails—such as the Lakeshore Path and the North Branch Trail—can be just as hazardous as the road. While you may be tempted to abandon your laser-like focus while pedaling along a trail, don't. Be prepared to act quickly when stray children, dim-witted Chihuahuas, and disco-dancing Rollerbladers suddenly appear in front of you. As pocket-size electronic doo-dads multiply, cyclists must be even more watchful for squirrelly behavior among those they encounter on the road and on the trail.

If you're just learning the ropes of riding in traffic, a bike safety class can offer a big leg up. Beginners will become more self-assured if they know basic skills such as riding predictably, being visible, and keeping a safe distance from parked cars. People who participate in a good bike safety class consistently express how much safer and more comfortable they feel riding in a variety of traffic conditions. Cycling courses also typically touch upon other topics essential for novices, such as bike selection and fit, basics of bike handling, and maintenance.

So what should you bring on your ride? This list varies a great deal depending on the season, the length of the ride, and how prepared you like to be. First, pack a pump and spare tube or patch kit. A small multitool will help with adjustments and minor repairs. Bring lights for front and back if there is even a slight chance that you'll be riding after dusk. Bring water, something to snack on, and one more layer than you think you'll need. Cell phones have proven to be handy in case help is needed; a few dollars stuffed in your pocket will score you some freshly baked cookies along the way to replace your burned calories.

Summer presents perfect weather for cycling in the Chicago region. It's the time of year when you can combine a ride and swim at the beach. It's the time when all you may need for a short ride is a patch kit and a helmet. Spring and fall offer months of good cycling opportunities, too. Most often, a light layer of nylon or fleece is all you'll need: a jacket, light gloves, a thin cap, and comfortable pants will do the trick. If it's a long ride, take an extra layer. Be mindful that the temperatures can fluctuate substantially depending on your proximity to the lakeshore.

Suiting up for winter gets a little more complicated and involves a certain amount of trial and error. The basic approach is the same as any cold-weather outdoor physical activity: use layers that can be peeled off easily and pay special attention to keeping your hands and feet happy. Those new to cold-weather cycling will be amazed by how little insulation is actually needed. (Check out the website www.bikewinter.org for tips and activities focused on winter riding in Chicago.)

How to Use This Book

When choosing rides in this book, the mileage will provide a pretty good idea of the difficulty of a particular ride. There are exceptions—most notably the Southwest Michigan Loop, the Walworth/Racine Counties Loop, and the Barrington Loop—which are hillier rides and therefore more difficult. For the most part, though, the landscape on these rides is a gentle companion. When a ride is not predominantly flat or slightly rolling, the text will let you know.

Taking a look at the Rides at a Glance section at the back of this guide, you'll see that the ride distances are weighted toward the 20- to 30-mile range. This bias can be chalked up to a few factors. First, most people are able to carve out time for a 25- or 30-mile ride far more often than they are for a 50-mile ride. Busy people will concur: taking a several-hours-long ride is far better than taking no ride at all. Second, there are a lot of new cyclists in our midst lured to two wheels for the purpose of getting in shape, saving money, and doing their small part to battle pollution and climate change. These people need encouragement and lots of options to keep them rolling forward. Third, many of the shorter rides can be combined to create longer rides. This is true of both road rides and rail trail rides. In many cases, opportunities for extending rides will be mentioned in the text. In other cases, the Active Transportation Alliance's Chicagoland Bicycle Map may give you some good ideas on how to add more miles. I have some friends who regularly extend their rides by taking two laps on a particular route.

GPS coordinates: Readers who use either a handheld or car-mounted GPS unit can punch in the coordinates for each starting point, and have the GPS lead the way. All coordinates were generated using mapping software, rather than taking readings "in the field."

Mileage markers on the map: While charting the routes described in this book, I used a GPS device to continuously track my progress via satellites. While I have found this procedure accurate in determining mileage covered, it unfortunately doesn't mean our numbers will match up precisely. Don't be alarmed if the distances provided in the book don't match up with distances provided by existing trail maps or your own bike odometer. If you're using a bike odometer, keep in mind these have to be calibrated carefully; just changing to a larger tire can make a noticeable difference. While GPS devices are generally accurate, they too can lead you astray. If you backtrack or pursue a side trip and forget to subtract this distance from the total mileage covered, that of course will create a different mileage reading. The best policy is to use the mileage markers on the maps in this book as a rough guide that provide you with a close—but not exact—determination of distance traveled.

Ride No.	Ride Name	Best Rides for River Lovers	Best Rides for Lake Lovers	Best Rides for Families with Children	Best Rides for Great Views	Best Rides for Nature Lovers	Best Rides for History Buffs	Best Urban Rides	Best Rides from Public Transit	Best Rides for Solitude	Best Rides for Hills
1	Beverly/Oak Lawn Loop								•		
2	Chicago Lakefront and Boulevard Loop		•		•		•	•	•		
3	Chicago South Side Loop		•				•	•	•		
4	North Branch and Green Bay Trails Loop	•	•			•			•		
5	Salt Creek Trail/Oak Park Loop	•				•		•	•		
6	Cedar Lake Loop		•							•	
7	I&M Canal/Centennial Trails	•		•			•			•	
8	I&M Canal Trail	•		•	•	•	•			•	

#	Trail									
9	Indiana Dunes/Porter County Loop					•	•		•	
10	Joliet Area Trails Loop				•					
11	LaPorte Loop	•					•	•		
12	Oak Savannah/Prairie Duneland Trails									
13	Old Plank Road Trail			•				•		
14	Southwest Michigan Loop	•	•			•	•			
15	Valparaiso Loop		•							
16	Wauponsee Glacial Trail		•							
17	Fox River Trail			•		•	•	•		•
18	Great Western Trail: DuPage County		•	•				•		

Ride No.	Ride Name	Best Rides for River Lovers	Best Rides for Lake Lovers	Best Rides for Families with Children	Best Rides for Great Views	Best Rides for Nature Lovers	Best Rides for History Buffs	Best Urban Rides	Best Rides from Public Transit	Best Rides for Solitude	Best Rides for Hills
19	Great Western Trail: Kane and DeKalb Counties			•						•	
20	Illinois Prairie Path: Aurora and Elgin Branches			•					•		
21	Illinois Prairie Path: Main Stem			•					•		
22	Plano Loop									•	
23	Virgil Gilman Trail			•						•	
24	Waterfall Glen Trail			•	•	•					•
25	Barrington Loop								•		•

#	Trail	1	2	3	4	5	6	7	8	9	10
26	Des Plaines River Trail			●			●	●	●		●
27	Lake Geneva Loop	●				●		●		●	
28	Long Prairie and Stone Bridge Trails		●				●		●		
29	Moraine Hills State Park Trail						●		●		●
30	North Shore Loop			●							
31	Prairie Trail		●	●					●		
32	Robert McClory Trail			●							
33	Walworth/Racine Counties Loop	●	●					●			
34	Woodstock Loop		●	●							

Map Legend

Transportation

Interstate Highway ═══(55)═══

Featured U.S. Highway ══(41)══

U.S. Highway ══(14)══

Featured State, County, or Local Road ━━━━━━

State Highway ──(20)──

County/Local Road ──────

Featured Bike Route ▪▪▪▪▪▪▪▪▪▪▪▪▪

Bike Route ▪▪▪▪▪▪▪▪▪▪▪▪▪

Hydrology

Lake/Reservoir/ Major River ⬭

River/Creek ∿

Marsh

Land Use

Large State Park/ Large Wildlife Area ▭

State Line ─ ─ ·· ─

Symbols

Trailhead (Start) **10**

Mileage Marker 17.1◆──

Small Park ♠

Airport ✛

Bridge ⏑

Campground ▲

City ◉

Direction Arrow →

Historical Site 🏛

Museum 🏛

Parking 🅿

Park Office 👫

Picnic Area ⊼

Point of Interest/ Structure ■

Restroom 🚻

Town ○

University/College 🎓

Visitor Center ❷

Wildlife Area 🦅

The City and Environs

With a population greater than most states in the union, Cook County offers a bit of everything, from the heavy industry of Calumet Harbor to the south to the opulent Victorian homes on the North Shore. Residing within some 130 incorporated Cook County municipalities are about 5.3 million people, the lion's share of whom call the city of Chicago home.

When people think of cycling in Chicago, they often picture the glorious Lakefront Path as it winds through nearly 20 miles of parkland on the Lake Michigan shoreline. Running between Bryn Mar Avenue and 71st Street, the path takes you by beaches, world-class museums, piers, grassy parkland, and harbors containing acres of moored boats—all underneath an exquisite Chicago skyline. The lakeshore is where the city comes together; it's the city at its best. Fortunately, the city has begun embracing the shoreline more fully, making it more accessible and giving it proper status as the city's front yard. Now that Chicago planners have taken up an interest in the lakeshore, the rest of the city has followed suit. Cyclists beware: On summer afternoons, the north half of the path gets thoroughly congested.

The Lakefront Path is the jewel in the crown, to be sure. It's a great place to turn your pedals, but it's not the only place. A multitude of great Chicago cycling destinations will give you fascinating local history, stunning architecture, and scenic wooded pathways.

While touring the neighborhoods of Chicago, you'll have an opportunity to gawk at dazzling nineteenth-century architecture in the Prairie Avenue District, Pilsen, Pullman, Logan Square, Hyde Park, and South Shore. You'll explore the great parks of the city—Washington, Douglas, Garfield, Jackson, Lincoln, and Humboldt—all connected like pearls on a string by the city's system of grassy boulevards. Within these big parks are lagoons, wetlands, flower gardens, and grand park buildings. On the far south side, you'll have a chance to see old industrial areas, such as Calumet Harbor and Calumet Lake.

On the far northwest side of the city, the North Branch Trail gives Chicago cyclists an opportunity to trace the route of the Chicago River's North Branch as it wends its way through a series of densely wooded forest preserves. The trail takes you through the Skokie Lagoons and then ends at one of the best botanical gardens in the nation. On the return trip, you'll follow the Green Bay Trail as it sweeps through the North Shore towns of Glencoe, Winnetka, Kenilworth, and Wilmette.

An equally attractive—but lesser known—trail takes you through another series of Cook County forest preserves situated alongside Salt Creek. After exploring the Salt Creek Trail, you'll ramble through a series of leafy suburban communities that grew up alongside the rail line that ran between Chicago and Aurora. In the village of Riverside, which was designed by the famous landscape architect Frederick Law Olmstead, you can gawk at a series of attractive public buildings and huge Victorian homes.

The lakeside walkway near North Avenue Beach offers a primo view of the city skyline. See Ride 2.

Best Bike Rides Chicago

Beverly/Oak Lawn Loop

This ride opens with a short stint on a heavily wooded section of the Major Taylor Trail, one of the newest trails in Chicago. The route in Beverly takes you by a collection of historic mansions, including one that was modeled after an Irish castle. From Beverly, you'll head west through the quiet streets of Mount Greenwood and pass some of the local cemeteries for which the area is known. After tours of the suburban towns of Oak Lawn and Evergreen Park, you'll return to Beverly to gawk at more of the sprawling mansions.

Start: Dan Ryan Woods Forest Preserve, parking lots 15 and 16, near the intersection of Western Avenue and 83rd Street

Length: 17.9 miles

Approximate riding time: 2 hours

Best bike: A road bike or hybrid bike

Terrain and trail surface: The Major Taylor is paved and flat. The on-road sections of the ride take you through flat urban residential neighborhoods, with occasional small hills in the Beverly area.

Traffic and hazards: Most of these streets are quiet; a few short sections of the route follow busier roads.

Things to see: Dan Ryan Woods Forest Preserve, historic homes and mansions in Beverly, and residential neighborhoods within Oak Lawn and Mount Greenwood

Getting there: By car: Take I-94 south from downtown Chicago. Exit at 79th Street and head west to Damen Avenue. Turn left onto Damen Avenue, then turn right onto 83rd Street. Park in the Dan Ryan Woods Forest Preserve's parking lots 15 and 16, located on the right. **By public transportation:** Take the Rock Island Metra Line to the 91st Street station in Beverly. The Major Taylor Trail runs along the east side of the railroad tracks. GPS coordinates: 41 44.613 N / 87 40.717 W

THE RIDE

Known for its historic homes, tree-lined streets, and racially integrated population, Beverly is one of the most likeable neighborhoods in Chicago. The large lawns, hilly topography, and close-knit community atmosphere give the area an unusual appeal. Along Longwood Drive, you'll encounter a progression of mansions built in various styles, many with wooded surroundings and landscaped yards and gardens.

Before arriving in Beverly, though, you'll follow the first leg of the Major Taylor Trail as it gradually curves along an old railroad embankment on the eastern edge of the Dan Ryan Woods Forest Preserve. Dense stands of trees rise high above the trail and lean overhead, creating a tunnel of branches and shrubs. When the trail leaves the 20-foot-high embankment and returns to street level, the forest preserve continues to sprawl on the right, occasionally dotted with wetlands and marsh grasses.

On Longwood Drive in Beverly, take note of the small ridge that runs parallel to the street on the right. This several-mile-long glacially deposited moraine is called Blue Island. Some 14,000 years ago, at the tail end of the last ice age, this ridge was actually an island when Lake Michigan's water level stood 60 feet higher and the shoreline meandered farther inland.

The hilly topography provides a pleasing environment for the well-kept historic mansions along Longwood Drive. The first block heading south takes you past a couple of houses built in the Prairie style, one of which was designed by Frank Lloyd Wright (9914 South Longwood Dr.). At 10200 South Longwood Dr. sits a mansion built in 1890 in the Colonial Revival style by Horace E. Horton, founder of the Chicago Bridge and Iron Co. Probably the best-known community landmark, the Castle, at 103rd Street and Longwood Drive, is a replica of an Irish castle built in 1886 by real estate developer Robert C. Givins. As the story goes, Givins built the limestone castle in an effort to woo a bride from Ireland. Owned by the Beverly Unitarian Church since 1942, the structure has an assortment of ghost stories attached to it.

In the neighborhood of Mount Greenwood, you'll pass a couple of large cemeteries. The Mount Greenwood Cemetery at 111th Street and California Avenue happens to be where Major Taylor is buried. Major Taylor, whose name was given to the trail you encountered earlier, was an African-American track cyclist who dominated the sport at the turn of the century—at a time when it was the most popular spectator sport in the country—winning world championships in 1899, 1900, and 1901. Mount Greenwood has long been a popular spot for the dead: The community is sometimes called Seven Holy Tombs in honor of seven large cemeteries in the area. In his book, *Geology Underfoot in Illinois*, Raymond Wiggers explains that the abundance of local cemeteries around Mount Greenwood is no accident: Gravediggers preferred to dig in the sand and gravel of the Blue Island Moraine versus the poorly drained soil so common elsewhere in Chicago. Local historians say that some commercial areas in Mount Greenwood developed because funeral-goers needed nearby places to eat and drink after the burials.

Crossing the Chicago city limits takes you into Oak Lawn, one of the largest suburbs in Cook County. The town was fairly small until about 1960, when it started to swell with whites fleeing Chicago during the era of white flight. In recent years, the complexion of the town has become more varied. The route passes a few of Oak Lawn's many commercial areas, as well as its huge hospital complex, which employs some 3,500 people.

At 107th Street and Laramie Avenue, you can traverse a pedestrian bridge to Wolfe Wildlife Refuge and then follow a 0.5-mile-long bike path through forty-five acres of wetlands surrounding Stony Creek.

As you return eastward, the route zigzags through Evergreen Park, known as the "Village of Churches" on account of the thirteen established congregations serving a community 4 square miles in size. Another detail to know about Evergreen Park is that it's the hometown of the Unabomber. Up until he left for Harvard University at age sixteen, Ted Kaczynski spent most of his youth in Evergreen Park.

> ## Bike Shop
>
> **Beverly Bike and Ski: One of the few bike shops on the far south side; 9121 South Western Ave., Chicago; (773) 238-5704; www.beverlyallseasons.com**

The last leg of the ride takes you again to the tree-laden streets and stately homes of Beverly. A string of impressive mansions pop up along Pleasant Avenue, including another designed by Frank Lloyd Wright (9326 South Pleasant Ave.). The Queen Anne–style house at 9319 South Pleasant Ave. was the residence of Impressionist artist John H. Vanderpoel. (His works can be seen in the Vanderpoel Gallery at the Beverly Art Center.) The Colonial Revival–style house at 9203 South Pleasant Ave. was built by the first director of the Art Institute of Chicago and designed by the museum's lecturer in architecture.

A short trip through the forest preserve brings you back to the starting point at the north end of the Major Taylor Trail.

MILES AND DIRECTIONS

0.0 Head north on the Major Taylor Trail from the parking area and then follow it as it takes a sharp turn right, heading south.

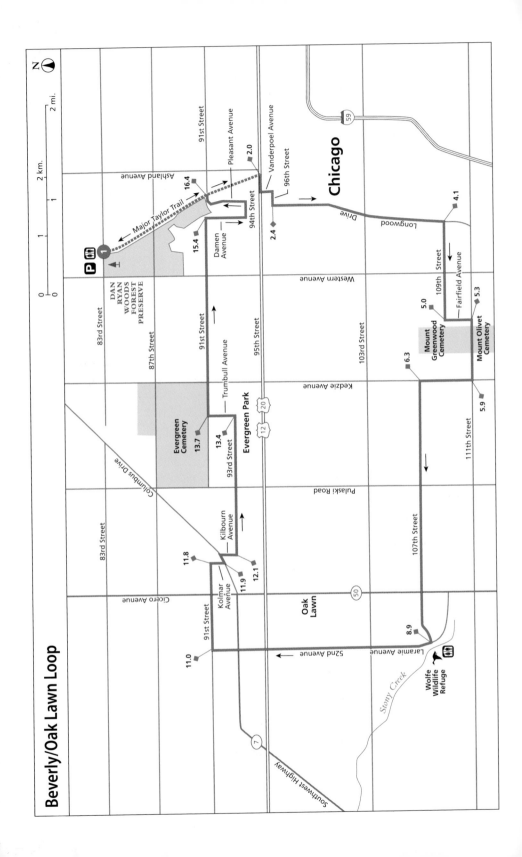

Beverly/Oak Lawn Loop

2.0 Where the trail abruptly ends at the fence, continue south through the grocery store parking lot. At 95th Street, turn right. Proceed with care: 95th Street is busy.

2.2 Turn left onto Vanderpoel Avenue.

2.3 Turn right onto 96th Street.

2.4 Turn left onto Longwood Drive, lined with many of Beverly's famous mansions.

4.1 Turn right onto 109th Street.

5.0 Turn left onto Fairfield Avenue.

5.3 Turn right onto 111th Street.

5.9 Turn right onto Kedzie Avenue.

6.3 Turn left onto 107th Street.

8.9 Turn right onto Laramie Avenue. Take the bike path over the bridge to follow a half mile or so of bike trails that run through Wolfe Wildlife Refuge.

9.4 At 103rd Street, Laramie Avenue becomes 52nd Avenue.

11.0 Turn right onto 91st Street.

11.8 Turn right onto Kolmar Avenue.

11.9 Turn left onto Columbus Avenue and then immediately turn right onto Kilbourn Avenue.

12.1 Turn left onto 93rd Street.

13.4 Turn left onto Trumbull Avenue.

13.7 Turn right onto 91st Street.

15.4 Turn right onto Damen Avenue.

15.8 Turn left onto 94th Street.

16.0 Turn left onto Pleasant Avenue.

16.3 Turn right onto 91st Street.

16.4 Turn left onto the Major Taylor Trail.

17.9 Arrive at the parking area at Dan Ryan Woods Forest Preserve.

RIDE INFORMATION

Local Events/Attractions

Beverly Arts Center: Features gallery exhibitions and a gift shop; hosts films and live music; 2407 West 111th St., Chicago; (773) 445-3838; www.beverly artcenter.org.

Beverly Hills Cycling Classic: Held in July, this annual 100K criterium bike race through Beverly is paired with the annual Tour de Beverly Family Ride; organized by the Beverly Area Planning Association; (773) 233-3100; www .bapa.org.

Restaurants

Franconello's: Italian cuisine; located in an old storefront at 10222 South Western Ave., Chicago; (773) 881-4100.

Koda Bistro and Wine Bar: Well-regarded upscale eatery; 10352 South West-ern Ave., Chicago; (773) 445-5632; http://kodabistro.com.

Major Taylor: champion bike racer

Major Taylor, an African-American bike racer in the early 1900s, was lauded for his strength and speed—particularly for his tactical abil-ity and his dazzling last-minute sprints. He made triumphant tours of velodromes in Europe and Australia, defeating everyone he com-peted against. The title of his autobiography, *The Fastest Bicycle Rider in the World*, was no exaggeration: It cites the many speed records he set and the world championship races he won in 1899, 1900, and 1901. Despite regular harassment and frequent attempts to ban him from cycling because of his race, his prowess on a bike made him the wealthiest African-American athlete in America. Taylor lived in Chicago during the final years of his life after he had sadly lost all his wealth on bad business deals. He died in 1932 while living at a YMCA in Chicago's Bronzeville neighborhood. Taylor initially was buried in an unmarked grave in the Mount Greenwood Cemetery, but in 1948 a group of Chicago bicycle racers convinced local bike manufacturer Frank Schwinn to donate money for installing a proper headstone and moving Taylor's grave site to a more respected spot in the cemetery.

Millie's Ice Cream Shoppe and Deli: Old-style place with a soda fountain; located right on the route; 5172 West 95th St., Oak Lawn; (708) 423-9293.

Southtown Health Foods: Offers groceries and a smoothie bar; 2100 West 95th St., Chicago; (773) 233-1856; www.southtownhealthfoods.com.

Restrooms

Start/finish: Dan Ryan Woods has restrooms and water.

Mile 8.9: A portable toilet is located at the Wolfe Wildlife Refuge (turn left onto Laramie Avenue from 107th Street).

Mile 10.5: The intersection of 52nd Avenue and 95th Street has a selection of chain restaurants.

Maps

USGS: Blue Island quad

DeLorme: *Illinois Atlas & Gazetteer*: Page 29

Chicago Lakefront and Boulevard Loop

Enjoy a classic Chicago bike ride along the Lakefront Path as it winds past harbors, beaches, the dazzling skyline, and the big blue mysterious lake. After passing the museum campus and Soldier Field, you'll leave the well-beaten biking path and head into the neighborhoods of Pilsen and Little Village and then meet up with the Chicago boulevard system. The boulevards guide you through three large Chicago parks sprinkled with gardens, lagoons, and elegant park buildings. The final section of the route tours several of Chicago's North Side neighborhoods.

Start: Montrose Harbor, located where Montrose Avenue meets Lake Michigan in Chicago

Length: 29.6 miles

Approximate riding time: 3 hours

Best bike: Road bike or hybrid bike

Terrain and trail surface: The Lakefront Path is paved. The terrain is flat throughout the ride.

Traffic and hazards: Most streets on this route do not have heavy traffic. During the summer, the north section of the Lakefront Path gets congested. For lighter crowds, go earlier in the day. The route follows a few one-way streets, which need to be avoided if following the route in reverse. You'll encounter speed bumps on a few streets. While riding in any urban area, keep aware of your surroundings.

Things to see: Parkland along the Chicago lakeshore; the city skyline; beaches; Soldier Field; the Field Museum; the Shedd Aquarium; the Alder Planetarium; the Chicago Boulevard system; Douglas, Garfield, and Humboldt parks; and assorted Chicago neighborhoods on the North and South Sides.

Getting there: By car: From downtown Chicago, head north on Lake Shore Drive. Exit at Montrose Avenue and turn right toward the lake. Park in the large lot. Catch the trail as it heads south along Lake Shore Drive. **By public transportation:** To reach the starting point, catch bus 78 heading east from either the Montrose station on the Brown

Line "L" Train or the Wilson station on the Red Line. The bus will bring you to the corner of Marine Drive and Montrose Avenue. From this intersection, head under Lake Shore Drive. GPS coordinates: 41 57.986 N / 87 38.694 W

THE RIDE

It's no mystery why Chicago cyclists love the Lakefront Path: The views of the skyline, the grassy expanses, the boats lined up in the harbors, and the big lake make for unparalleled riding. While the lakeshore is indeed one of the best places in Chicago for riding, it's certainly not the only good place to ride in the city. This route follows the much-loved trail along the lakefront, but it also leads you to less-trodden destinations such as the Prairie Avenue Historic District, the Pilsen neighborhood, and the city's boulevard system.

Heading south from Montrose Harbor, the path winds through many acres of grassy parkland scattered with trees. There's also a golf course, an attractive brick clock-tower park building, and dozens of boats moored in Belmont Harbor. The greenway goes on hiatus at the Fullerton Pavilion, a Prairie-style structure built in the early twentieth century as a "fresh air sanitarium" to promote good health among the infirm. (The building is now home to a cafe and a summer theater.)

South of the pavilion, the path squeezes between Lake Shore Drive on the right and North Avenue Beach on the left. At the south end of North Avenue Beach sits a beach house designed to look like an ocean liner that has been parked in the sand. Getting closer to the Loop, the path continues to be wedged—sometimes uncomfortably—between a traffic-choked six-lane thoroughfare and the lake.

In the warmer months, Oak Street Beach has plenty going on, whether it's jugglers, BMX trick riders, or in-line skaters whizzing through a slalom course. After passing Navy Pier (the largest tourist trap in the state) and making an awkward crossing of the Chicago River along the lower level of Lake Shore Drive, you'll roll along acres of boats docked in Chicago Harbor. Across Lake Shore Drive in Grant Park, you can't miss the 150-foot geyser shooting from Buckingham Fountain.

From the fountain, the route passes along the backside of the John G. Shedd Aquarium. The paneled glass wall facing the path contains the largest indoor saltwater pool in the world, home to a family of beluga whales and a handful of performing dolphins. To the right is the huge marble structure of the Field Museum. The building contains a vast collection of natural science exhibits, as well as the skeleton of the largest and most complete T. rex ever found.

South of the Field Museum is Soldier Field—the Chicago Bears' home turf—built in 1922 and the recipient of a unfortunate face-lift in 2003 when a glass-and-steel addition was dropped on the top of the existing neoclassical structure. Soldier Field is where you'll head west away from the lake and over the new pedestrian bridge that crosses the train tracks.

Bike Shops

Boulevard Bikes: Knowledgeable staff and friendly atmosphere; located on the route in Logan Square; 2535 North Kedzie Blvd., Chicago; (773) 235-9109; www.boulevard bikeshop.com

Irv's Bike Shop: Small neighborhood bike shop; located on the route in Pilsen; 1725 South Racine Ave., Chicago; (312) 226-6330; www.irvsbikeshop.com

The west end of the bridge drops you off at the Prairie Avenue Historic District, which became the city's most fashionable neighborhood following the Chicago Fire of 1871. Although many of the rambling Victorian mansions were demolished in the mid-twentieth century, the remaining buildings provide a sense of the neighborhood's former character. Two of these sumptuous multilevel brick homes are now museums: the Clarke House and the Glessner House.

Continuing along 18th Street takes you over the South Branch of the Chicago River, under the Dan Ryan Expressway, and into Pilsen. Once home to a large population of Eastern Europeans, many of whom were Czechs, it's now home to the largest concentration of Latinos in Chicago. Visitors will enjoy the lively shopping district along 18th Street, the delicious smells from local restaurants, the many murals, and the attractive nineteenth-century architecture.

In the Little Village neighborhood, you'll connect with Marshall Boulevard, which is part of a system of boulevards that were designed to connect Chicago's major parks. Here on Chicago's west side, the boulevards connect three great parks: Douglas, Garfield, and Humboldt—each to be visited on this route. William Le Baron Jenney—a landscape designer, architect, and engineer now considered the father of the skyscraper—originally designed all three parks in the late nineteenth century. The renowned Prairie-style designer Jens Jensen oversaw a second phase of improvements for these parks during the early twentieth century.

Douglas Park has gardens, lagoons, paths, and an eye-catching open-air structure designed by Jensen called the Flower Hall. As you head west from Douglas Park, you'll pass attractive gray stone houses overlooking the leafy boulevard. In Garfield Park you'll find more quiet lagoons with islands, as well as several notable park buildings, including an elegant bandstand and a gold-

The bandstand is one of the hidden gems in Garfield Park.

domed field house with a wildly ornate facade. Garfield Park's most impressive building, though, is the glass-and-steel structure that houses one of the largest publicly owned conservatories in the world. Some 5,000 plant species grow within six enormous glassed-in rooms. Jensen designed the structure, built in 1908, to resemble a giant haystack.

At Division Avenue, in Humboldt Park, sculptures of bison stand inside a formal flower garden on the left side of Sacramento Boulevard. On the right, the graceful arches of the Prairie-style Humboldt Park Boat House create a pleasant spot to look over the lagoon fringed with cattails and walking paths.

At one time, many of the city's boulevards were bordered by stately brick mansions like those along Logan Boulevard. Built by wealthy people attracted to the boulevards' greenways, most of the mansions on the other boulevards fell into disrepair and were demolished to make way for newer homes.

After crossing the Chicago River again, the route cuts through the Julia Lathrop Homes, built in 1938 as the first Chicago housing project designated strictly for elderly residents. The lightly ornamented brick apartment buildings and row houses, the grassy lawns, and the curving riverbank create an atmosphere more pleasant than most city housing projects. Despite pressure from residents and local preservation organizations to save it, a plan is now under way to tear down the Lathrop Homes and redevelop the land.

The route along Ravenswood Avenue takes you between a string of old brick warehouses and a set of train tracks perched on an earthen embankment landscaped with trees, rocks, small gardens, and occasional benches. After reaching the Lakefront Path, you'll pass Foster Avenue Beach and Wilson Skate Park, and then arrive at Montrose Harbor, where the ride started.

MILES AND DIRECTIONS

0.0 Head south on the Lakefront Path as it parallels Lake Shore Drive.

7.7 Turn right onto Woldron Drive, which runs along the south end of Soldier Field.

7.9 Bear left on the pathway that goes under Lake Shore Drive. Follow the ramp over the railroad tracks.

8.1 Head west on 18th Street, then take a quick tour of the Prairie Avenue Historic District by going a block south of 18th Street on Prairie and Indiana Avenues.

9.5 Turn right onto Halsted Avenue and immediately turn left onto 18th Street.

10.8 Turn left onto Wood Street.

11.0 Turn right onto 21st Street.

12.5 Turn right onto Marshall Boulevard.

13.1 Turn left onto Douglas Boulevard.

14.0 Turn right onto Independence Boulevard.

15.2 Turn right onto Music Court Drive.

15.4 At Woodward Drive, bear left toward Central Park Avenue. Head north on the pathway that runs on the left side of Central Park Avenue.

16.2 Turn right onto Franklin Boulevard.

16.9 Turn left onto Sacramento Boulevard.

17.8 North of Division Avenue, continue north on the path on the right side of Sacramento Boulevard/Humboldt Drive. Use the pathways to explore Humboldt Park's lagoons.

19.1 Turn left onto Palmer Boulevard.

19.4 Turn right onto Kedzie Boulevard.

19.9 Turn right onto Logan Boulevard. Stay on Logan Boulevard as it curves to the left.

21.2 Turn right onto Diversey Avenue. Cross the Chicago River.

21.3 Turn left onto Leavitt Street.

21.6 Turn right onto Wellington Avenue (a one-way street).

22.0 Turn left onto Wolcott Avenue.

23.0 Turn right onto Grace Street.

23.1 Turn left onto Ravenswood Avenue after passing under the train tracks.

25.9 Jog left onto Peterson Avenue, then immediately turn right onto Ravenswood Avenue.

26.0 Jog right onto Ridge Avenue, then immediately turn left onto Ravenswood Avenue.

26.2 Turn right onto Granville Avenue.

27.0 Turn right onto Winthrop Avenue (a one-way street).

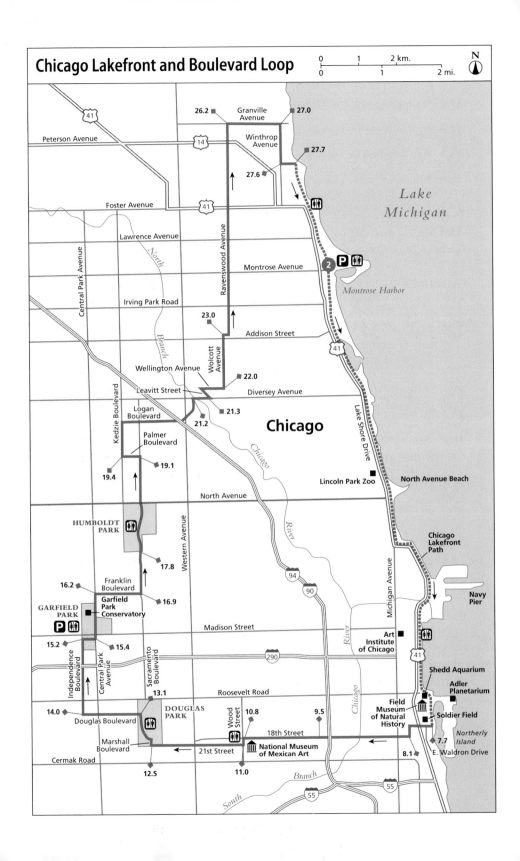

Chicago Lakefront and Boulevard Loop

0   1   2 km.
0   1   2 mi.

N

US 41
14

26.2   Granville Avenue   27.0
Winthrop Avenue   27.7
27.6
Peterson Avenue

Lake Michigan

Foster Avenue   US 41

Lawrence Avenue

Central Park Avenue

Ravenswood Avenue

Montrose Avenue   **2** P
Montrose Harbor

Irving Park Road

23.0

Addison Street

US 41

Wolcott Avenue

Wellington Avenue   22.0

Leavitt Street   Diversey Avenue

Logan Boulevard   21.3
Kedzie Boulevard   21.2

Palmer Boulevard   **Chicago**

Chicago

19.4   19.1

North Avenue   Lincoln Park Zoo   North Avenue Beach

HUMBOLDT PARK

Western Avenue

River

17.8

94
90

Franklin Boulevard   16.2
Garfield Park Conservatory   16.9

Chicago Lakefront Path

GARFIELD PARK   P

Navy Pier

Madison Street

Michigan Avenue

15.2   15.4

Independence Boulevard

Central Park Avenue

Sacramento Boulevard

290

River

Art Institute of Chicago

US 41

Shedd Aquarium

Adler Planetarium

13.1   Roosevelt Road

14.0   **DOUGLAS PARK**

Wood Street   10.8   9.5

Field Museum of Natural History

Soldier Field

Douglas Boulevard

Marshall Boulevard   21st Street

18th Street   7.7

Northerly Island

8.1   E. Waldron Drive

Cermak Road   12.5   11.0   🏛 **National Museum of Mexican Art**

Branch

South   55   55

27.6 Turn left onto Ardmore Avenue.

27.7 Head south on the Lakefront Path.

29.6 Return to Montrose Harbor.

RIDE INFORMATION

Local Events/Attractions

The Field Museum: 1400 South Lake Shore Dr., Chicago; (312) 922-9410; www.fieldmuseum.org.

Garfield Park Conservatory: 300 North Central Park Ave., Chicago; (312) 746-5100; www.garfield-conservatory.org.

Glessner House Museum: A stately English Arts and Crafts home that now contains a world-class collection of nineteenth-century decorative arts; 1800 South Prairie Ave., Chicago; (312) 326-1480; www.glessnerhouse.org.

John G. Shedd Aquarium: 1200 South Lake Shore Dr., Chicago; (312) 939-2438; www.sheddaquarium.org.

National Museum of Mexican Art: Perhaps the best small museum in the city; free admission; 1852 West 19th St., Pilsen; (312) 738-1503; www.national museumofmexicanart.org.

Navy Pier: Contains the Chicago Children's Museum, a 3-D IMAX theater, the Chicago Shakespeare Theatre, a concert venue, a museum of stained-glass windows, a monster-size Ferris wheel, and oodles of obnoxious tourist-oriented shops and overpriced mediocre restaurants; 600 East Grand Ave., Chicago; (800) 595-PIER; www.navypier.com.

Restaurants

Joy Yee's: Various types of Asian cuisine; huge menu with pictures; located in Chinatown at 2159 South China Place, Chicago; (312) 328-0001; www.joyyee .com.

Lula Cafe: One of Chicago's great small neighborhood restaurants; eclectic fare; 2537 North Kedzie Blvd., Chicago; (773) 489-9554; www.lulacafe.com.

Mundial Cocina Mestiza: Latin American cuisine with a Mediterranean influence; 1640 West 18th St., Chicago; (312) 491-9908; www.mundialcocina mestiza.com.

Oak Street Beachstro: Good selection of sandwiches and salads; seasonally located where Oak Street Beach meets the Lakefront Path; 1001 North Lake Shore Dr., Chicago; (312) 915-4100; www.oakstreetbeachstro.com.

Spacca Napoli Pizzeria: Authentic Neapolitan pizza made in a wood-burning pizza oven; 1769 West Sunnyside, Chicago; (773) 878-2420; http://spaccanapoli pizzeria.com.

Restrooms
Start/finish: Montrose Beach House has restrooms and water.
Mile 6.2: Restrooms at the north end of Chicago Harbor (just south of the Chicago Yacht Club).
Mile 10.9: Harrison Park Fieldhouse has restrooms.
Mile 13.1: Restrooms are available in the Douglas Park Fieldhouse.
Mile 15.9: Garfield Park Conservatory has restrooms.
Mile 18.1: Humboldt Park Fieldhouse has restrooms.

Maps
USGS: Chicago Loop quad, Jackson Park quad, Englewood quad
DeLorme: *Illinois Atlas & Gazetteer*: Page 29

Chicago South Side Loop

This ride reveals a part of Chicago that is vast and persistently interesting. Visit four great Chicago South Side parks, follow the Lake Michigan coastline, and explore Pullman, a nineteenth-century planned neighborhood of Victorian row houses. The route also takes you through areas of heavy industry for which the South Side is known. While exploring the wetlands of the Lake Calumet area, it's hard to believe that you're still in the city of Chicago.

Start: Jackson Park parking area behind the Museum of Science and Industry, east of the Wooded Island

Length: 27.7 miles

Approximate riding time: 3 hours

Best bike: Road bike or hybrid bike

Terrain and trail surface: All the trails on this ride are paved. The landscape is flat throughout.

Traffic and hazards: If riding on a weekday, watch for trucks in the vicinity of Lake Calumet. Most of the roads through this area provide an ample shoulder. While riding in any urban area, keep aware of your surroundings.

Things to see: Calumet Park, Jackson Park, Wolf Lake State Park, Washington Park, Pullman, Calumet Harbor, Lake Calumet wetlands, University of Chicago campus, the Midway Plaisance, the Museum of Science and Industry, and various South Side Chicago neighborhoods.

Getting there: By car: Take South Lake Shore Drive south to the Science Drive exit (just after the 57th Street exit). Stay left as you enter the parking lot, located south of the lagoon at the backside of the Museum of Science and Industry. **By public transportation:** Take the Metra Electric District Main Line to the 59th Street station. On 59th Street, head east (toward the lake) for 0.3 mile, crossing Stony Island Avenue and Cornell Avenue. Cross the bridge behind the Museum of Science and Industry, and start the ride on the far side of the parking lot. GPS coordinates: 41 47.326 N / 87 34.908 W

THE RIDE

This ride starts within Jackson Park, home to one of the most important events in Chicago history: the World's Columbian Exposition of 1893. Some of the features of this world-renowned event still exist within the park. South of the parking area where this ride begins is a lagoon surrounding an island containing a serene Japanese garden. North of the lagoon, the Museum of Science and Industry also serves as a remnant of the event.

In preparation for the enormous fair, a team of the nation's most celebrated architects and sculptors transformed this park on Chicago's South Side into the "White City," as it was called, made largely of plaster buildings designed in a classical style. The city included sculptures, fountains, and some 200 buildings exhibiting art, machinery, animals, plants, food, and many other items. The exposition was a huge success: Over twenty-seven million people turned out to celebrate 400 years of post-Columbus civilization. After the exposition, the city converted the ground's 700 acres back to a park.

As you follow the Lakefront Path south of Jackson Park, there are a few land-marks to admire. The elegant 63rd Street Beach House takes full advantage of the lake with its sprawling open-air balconies and grand porticos. At the beach house, look to the right down Hayes Drive to view the impressive shining statue called *The Republic,* a replica of a much larger statue built for the Columbian Exposition. Leaving Jackson Park, the path threads between the park's outer harbor and inner harbor, by Rabida Children's Hospital, and along a golf course that sits behind the South Shore Cultural Center.

At the corner of 83rd Street and US 41 is the towering spire of St. Michael the Archangel, a Gothic-style church built in 1907 by Polish-American steel-workers from the U.S. Steel South Works. The South Works, located on the lake-front east of the church, closed in 1992. During the mill's heyday in World War II, it employed almost 20,000 people and later produced much of the steel used to build Chicago's skyscrapers, including the Sears Tower and the John Hancock Center. The closing of the South Works has had a devastating effect on the eco-nomic health of its surrounding neighborhood. The city hopes to revitalize the area by transforming the South Works' 650-acre swath of lakefront land into a new residential and retail development.

The drawbridge over the Calumet River offers a bird's-eye view of Calumet Harbor, an intensely industrial port that moves all sorts of cargo, ranging from metals, grains, stone, and ore to food products such as vegetable oil and sugar. Block-long barges motor down the river and then pull alongside the shore so that cranes can offload their freight. There's a boatyard, scrap-metal recycling facility, and vertical lift bridge for trains. Nearby, I-90 follows the Chicago Sky-way Bridge high above the river, bypassing the entire industrial area.

South of the Calumet River you'll enter Calumet Park, a quiet expanse of greenery on the shore of Lake Michigan, fringed by a small neighborhood to the east and heavy industry to the north and south.

The route along the Burnham Greenway Trail from Calumet Park to Wolf Lake follows a noisy stretch of US 41 before entering a quiet neighborhood of bungalows. At Eggers Woods Forest Preserve, the trail passes through a thickly wooded area dotted with wetlands. Wolf Lake is a customary spot to pull up to a picnic table, break out the sandwiches, and watch the waterfowl. Despite the heavy industry and the expressway visible across Wolf Lake, this park on the lakeshore is still a mighty peaceful spot.

The next lake to the west, Lake Calumet, is surrounded by ponds, wetlands, and more heavy industry. The big mounds are, of course, landfills. On top of the mounds you may catch a glimpse of grazing goats. Local industries and municipalities have been dumping trash at Lake Calumet for nearly seventy years. Recently the landfill mounds had to be regraded to prevent what the state calls a "garbalanche" from occurring. After regrading, the state planted prairie grasses to keep the soil in place. The goats have been trained to consume grasses that crowd out the helpful prairie grasses. With cleanup efforts finally under way at Lake Calumet, there are more opportunities to see wildlife such as coyotes, red-tailed hawks, and various waterbirds.

Situated at the western edge of the Lake Calumet area is what's left of a grandiose experiment in town planning and its beautiful old houses and public buildings. In 1881 George M. Pullman, inventor and manufacturer of the Pullman railroad sleeping car, built a town for the employees of his massive manufacturing plant. Rows of simple but elegant row houses extend a few blocks south from 111th Street. At Cottage Grove Avenue stands the Hotel Florence opposite the clock tower and the remains of the factory. One of the most attractive buildings in Pullman is the Greenstone Church (112th Street and St. Lawrence Avenue), with its spire and gabled roof.

> ## Bike Shop
>
> **Blackstone Bicycle Works: Provides educational and recreational opportunities to local boys and girls in addition to standard bike shop offerings; located just south of Midway Plaisance; afternoon hours; 100 South Blackstone Ave., Chicago; (773) 241-5458**

In 1893 George Pullman reduced his employees' wages while maintaining their rents at the same price. The workers went on strike, and rail workers around the country refused to work on trains with Pullman cars. Eventually, troops came to quell the strikers. In 1894 the Illinois Supreme Court determined that Pullman could not lease houses and apartments to his workers, and the structures were sold off to private owners. More than a century later, nearly all of Pullman's 900 residences remain.

On the return trip to the Hyde Park neighborhood, King Drive passes through an assortment of South Side neighborhoods: Roseland, Chatham, Greater Grand Crossing, Woodlawn, and Washington Park. Before heading east through the Midway Plaisance, a mile-long park that runs along the southern edge of the University of Chicago, you'll take a quick tour of Washington Park and pass the 102-foot-long concrete sculpture by Laredo Taft called *The Fountain of Time*.

The heavy industry of Calumet Harbor sits in the shadow of the Chicago Skyway.

Along the Midway Plaisance, architecture fans will enjoy the English Gothic style that characterizes many of the University of Chicago's buildings. During the Columbian Exposition, the Midway Plaisance hosted amusement rides and a collection of re-created villages from around the world; now it's open parkland with statuary and an ice rink that operates in the winter.

At University Avenue, you'll have the opportunity to make a side trip to see the neighborhood where President Barack Obama and his family live when they're not in Washington DC. Head north on University Avenue for 9 blocks, then turn left at 51st Street. The Obamas' handsome redbrick house is near the corner of Greenwood Avenue and 51st Street at 5046 South Greenwood Ave. Don't get your hopes up, though, if you want to snap a picture of it: The Chicago Police and the U.S. Secret Service have erected a security zone several blocks wide around the residence.

Continuing ahead on the Midway Plaisance, you'll see dozens of outdoor statues of religious figures at the Rockefeller Memorial Chapel, and closer to Jackson Park, you'll pass a large round perennial flower garden. Before crossing the bridge to return to the starting spot, you might consider taking the bridge on the right to visit the Wooded Island's small but beautiful Japanese garden.

MILES AND DIRECTIONS

0.0 Start in the parking area behind the Museum of Science and Industry. From the parking lot, head east toward Lake Michigan on the path that runs on the north side of the marina.

0.2 After passing under Lake Shore Drive, go up the ramp and head south onto the Lakeshore Path.

2.3 At the end of the path, follow the bike lane on US 41, heading southeast.

4.0 Turn left onto East 83rd Street.

4.2 Turn right onto Burley Avenue.

4.4 Continue straight ahead and resume following US 41.

5.9 Turn left onto 95th Street, then bear left for a tour of Calumet Park. Stay left on the park road. On the way out of the park, the park road turns into 100th Street, which you'll follow through the underpass.

7.4 Just after the underpass, take the Burnham Greenway Trail left.

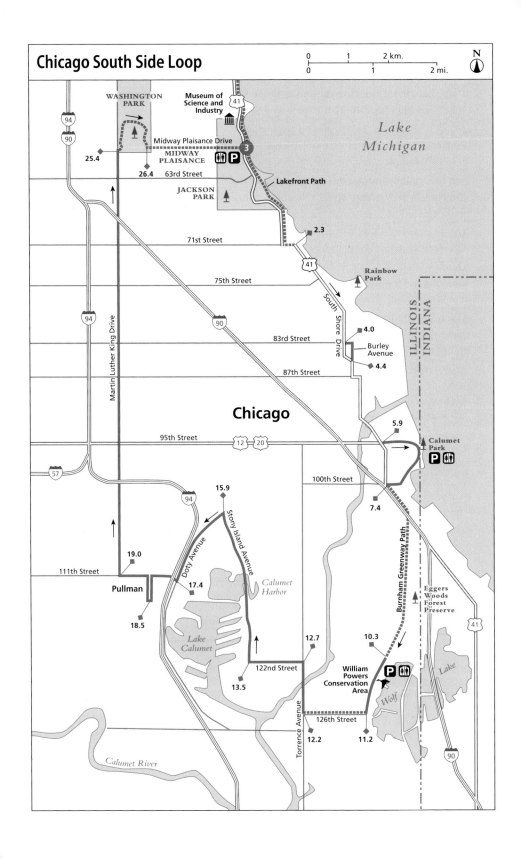

Chicago South Side Loop

0   1   2 km.
0   1   2 mi.

N

WASHINGTON PARK

Museum of Science and Industry

41

Midway Plaisance Drive

25.4

26.4   63rd Street

MIDWAY PLAISANCE

3

Lake Michigan

JACKSON PARK

Lakefront Path

71st Street

2.3

41

75th Street

Rainbow Park

94

90

Martin Luther King Drive

South Shore Drive

83rd Street

4.0

Burley Avenue

4.4

87th Street

ILLINOIS / INDIANA

Chicago

5.9

95th Street

12   20

Calumet Park

P

57

100th Street

7.4

94

15.9

Stony Island Avenue

Doty Avenue

19.0

111th Street

Pullman

17.4

Calumet Harbor

18.5

Lake Calumet

10.3

Burnham Greenway Path

Eggers Woods Forest Preserve

Lake

Wolf

12.7

122nd Street

13.5

William Powers Conservation Area

P

41

90

Torrence Avenue

Calumet River

126th Street

12.2

11.2

10.3 After entering Eggers Woods Forest Preserve, take the first paved trail left. Then take the park road to the right into the William Powers Conservation Area.

11.2 From the William Powers Conservation Area, head west on 126th Street. Follow the bike path along this street.

12.2 Turn right onto Torrence Avenue and cross the Calumet River.

12.7 Turn left onto 122nd Street. If riding on a weekday, watch for big trucks for the next couple of miles. Use the ample shoulder along most of this road.

13.5 Turn right onto Stony Island Avenue.

15.9 Turn left onto Doty Avenue.

17.4 Just after the bridge that carries 111th Street over I-94, take a left on the ramp that goes up to 111th Street.

17.7 Turn left onto 111th Street and cross I-94.

18.2 Turn left onto Champlain Street into Pullman.

18.5 Turn right onto 113th Street, then turn right onto Saint Lawrence Avenue.

18.7 Turn left onto 111th Street.

19.0 Turn right onto Martin Luther King Drive.

25.4 Bear right into Washington Park on Best Drive.

25.5 Take the bike path that circles the lagoon to the right. Go around the Washington Park lagoon clockwise.

26.4 Turn left onto the Midway Plaisance. Returning to Jackson Park, continue straight ahead over the bridge.

27.7 Arrive back at the parking area where the ride started.

RIDE INFORMATION

Local Events/Attractions

DuSable Museum of African American History: Affordable museum with engaging exhibits; located in Hyde Park; 740 East 56th Place, Chicago; (773) 947-0600; www.dusablemuseum.org.

Frank Lloyd Wright's Robie House: Just north of the Midway Plaisance; 5757 South Woodlawn St., Chicago; (773) 834-1847; www.wrightplus.org.

Historic Pullman Foundation Visitor Center: Offers tours and exhibits; a tour held the second weekend in October shows off the house interiors; 112th Street and Cottage Grove Avenue, Chicago; (773) 821-7031; www.pull manil.org.

Museum of Science and Industry: Includes an Omnimax theater and a working coal mine; 57th Street and Lake Shore Drive, Chicago; (773) 684-1414; www.msichicago.org.

Restaurants

Bonjour Bakery and Cafe: Affordable food for breakfast and lunch in Hyde Park; outdoor seating; 1550-52 East 55th St., Chicago; (773) 241-5300.

The Marina Cafe: Mid-priced Creole- and Caribbean-influenced menu; small bar upstairs; located right on the Lakefront Path in Jackson Park; 6401 South Coast Guard Dr., Chicago; (773) 947-0400.

Snail Thai Cuisine: Basic Thai restaurant in Hyde Park; 1649 East 55th St., Chicago; (773) 667-5423; www.snailthai.com.

Restrooms

Start/finish: Restrooms are located at the east side of the parking area. Water fountains appear regularly along the Lakefront Path.

Mile 0.6: Restrooms and water are available at the 63rd Street Beach House.

Mile 2.3: South Shore Cultural Center has restrooms and water (as well as a restaurant).

Mile 6.0: Calumet Park has restrooms in the beach house.

Mile 11.0: The William Powers Conservation Area has restrooms.

Maps

USGS: Jackson Park quad, Lake Calumet quad
DeLorme: *Illinois Atlas & Gazetteer:* Page 29

North Branch and Green Bay Trails Loop

The first part of this ride follows the North Branch Trail, one of the great bike pathways of Chicagoland, as it meanders along the wooded banks of the Chicago River's North Branch, through the Skokie Lagoons, and ending at the Chicago Botanic Garden. The route's second part follows the Green Bay Trail through the tony North Shore towns of Glencoe, Winnetka, Kenilworth, and Wilmette. The route's final leg runs through a small arboretum in Evanston, a 2-mile-long outdoor sculpture park in Skokie, and a handful of Chicago residential neighborhoods.

Start: Bunker Hill Forest Preserve, located on Caldwell Avenue north of Devon Avenue

Length: 32.7 miles

Approximate riding time: 3 hours

Best bike: Road bike or hybrid bike

Terrain and trail surface: All trail segments are pavement or asphalt, except for the first mile of the Green Bay Trail, which is hard-packed gravel. The terrain is flat with some areas that are gently rolling.

Traffic and hazards: Multiple road crossings occur along the North Branch Trail and North Shore Channel Trail. Be alert: Some of these crossings are very busy with car traffic. Fortunately, traffic lights and overpasses simplify the busiest crossings. On summer weekends, the North Branch Trail gets congested. The stretch of the ride along Lake Cook Road is busy with car traffic. While following roads and cutting through parking areas near the many train stations along the Green Bay Trail, watch for parked cars pulling out.

Things to see: Bottomland woods, riverbanks, small bluffs, grassy parkland, the Chicago Botanic Garden, suburban towns, and residential neighborhoods

Getting there: By car: Follow I-94 to Caldwell Avenue (exit 41A) and head north. Enter Bunker Hill Forest Preserve on the left. Park in any of the lots on the left near the entrance. **By public transportation:** From downtown Chicago, take the Milwaukee District North Line Metra train from Union Station to the Edgebrook station. At the Edgebrook station, turn right onto Devon Avenue and catch the beginning of the North Branch Trail less than a block away at the intersection of Devon Avenue and Caldwell Avenue. GPS coordinates: 42 0.191 N / 87 46.947 W

THE RIDE

The lion's share of this route follows two beloved Chicago-area pathways: the North Branch Trail and the Green Bay Trail. Like the river that it runs beside, the North Branch Trail never cuts a straight course for long: The trail continuously curves around little ravines, winds through picnic areas, and snakes along the tops of small river bluffs. The winding, woodsy route of the North Branch Trail offers a stark contrast to the Green Bay Trail, which runs straight-as-an-arrow along train tracks and through a string of small North Shore suburban towns. These two trails and the areas in between offer a scenic and mostly traffic-free sampling of Chicago's northern suburbs.

The Bunker Hill Forest Preserve, where the ride starts, sets the tone for much of the North Branch Trail. The river is not always visible, but it regularly peeks out from behind clusters of trees, through thick stands of bushes, and over the edges of small ravines. During spring and fall, in the absence of leaf cover, more miles of the twisting river will be visible along the path.

North of Touhy Avenue, the path winds along the top of a small river bluff. Trees hang lazily over the river beside the path. After the restored prairie at Miami Woods Forest Preserve, the path cuts through a gently rolling, wooded landscape and over a couple of trickling streams that drain into the river.

Willow Road serves as the gateway to the wooded refuge of the Skokie Lagoons. The Skokie Lagoons have undergone many changes since the area was a marshland that local Potawatomi Indians called Chewab Skokie, meaning "big wet prairie." Like so many other wetlands in the area, the marsh was drained by farmers who arrived in the late 1800s. Their efforts to create farmland fell flat, however; during wet years, the land still flooded, and during dry years, the peat contained in the marsh would actually catch fire, and smoke would drift into the surrounding communities for extended periods.

When Cook County acquired the marshlands in 1933, the Civil-

Bike Shops

Edgebrook Cycle and Sport: 6450 North Central Ave., Chicago; (773) 792-1669

Wilmette Bicycle and Sport Shop: 605 Green Bay Rd., Wilmette; (847) 251-1404

ian Conservation Corps (CCC) started digging a series of connected lakes for flood control and recreation. Using mostly wheelbarrows, picks, and shovels, workers excavated 4 million cubic yards of earth in what became the largest CCC project in the nation. When work finished in 1942, 7 miles of waterway connected seven lagoons. Fed and drained by the Skokie River, three low dams and a main dam at Willow Road were added to control the water level in the lagoons.

As the trail curves left and the traffic noise of I-94 increases, you get farther into the wetlands and bottomland woods that border the lagoons. Along Forest Way, grassy picnic areas provide spots for enjoying expansive views of the lagoon's open water and the thickly wooded islands. Look for waterbirds in the shallows or floating in the open water.

If you love to see carefully selected flowers, trees, and bushes growing in perfectly landscaped environments, the final portion of the North Branch Trail will surely quicken your pulse. Among the Chicago Botanic Garden's 305 acres of artfully landscaped grounds are twenty-three distinct gardens, including Japanese- and English-style gardens, rose and bulb gardens, and fruit and vegetable gardens. Within the gardens are bridges, statues, and fountains situated on nine islands and the surrounding shoreline. Benches along the bike path allow visitors to sit while admiring several of the islands that resemble stunning landscape paintings.

After hopping on the Green Bay Trail about 1 mile east of the botanic garden, you'll soon realize that the trail never strays far from Union Pacific Northwest Metra tracks that run between Chicago and Kenosha, Wisconsin. For the next 8 miles, you'll pass seven Metra stations, many of which are attractive wood, brick, and stone structures set within a small park. Small urban parks tend to crop up frequently on the sides of the Green Bay Trail. In Glencoe, the path passes a bandstand within a grassy lawn in Henry J. Kalk Park, and then, farther south, the trail skirts a couple more small parks with playgrounds.

South of Glencoe, the path and the railroad tracks start to run through a narrow, 30-foot-deep, below-street-level trench created for the railroad. The path ducks under numerous busy roads—out of the wind and away from street sounds. While the route is uninterrupted and peaceful, the scenery is limited within this artificial ravine. After the Winnetka Metra stop, the path and the train tracks emerge from the ditch and slowly rise up above the street level, revealing nearby streets, neighborhoods, and stores.

In Evanston, you'll pass through the Ladd Arboretum, which occupies a thin strip of land between the busy thoroughfare of McCormick Boulevard and North Shore Channel. Many dozens of varieties of trees, shrubs, and prairie grasses grow within the arboretum: Scattered about are gingko, Ohio buckeye, and paper birch trees. Small trailside knolls host five varieties of pine and seven varieties of maple. Left of the trail, the North Shore Channel runs between the North Branch of the Chicago River and Wilmette Harbor.

The end of the arboretum marks the beginning of the Skokie North Shore Sculpture Park, a 2-mile-long series of sixty outdoor sculptures in a park overlooking the North Shore Channel. The pathways weave through artworks created by a mix of regional, national, and international contemporary artists. Large-scale pieces dominate; many are made of metal. The trees on the banks of the channel provide a great background for viewing the work; some pieces tantalizingly appear against the industrial backdrop on the opposite shore of the channel. One sculpture with a strong Midwestern appeal looks like a piece of John Deere farm equipment that was designed by a space alien (*Hero* by artist John Charles Cowles). Another piece uses steel and wood to create an

A quick side trip north on the Green Bay Trail takes you to the historic grounds of the Ravinia Festival.

enormous head that brings to mind the giant sculptures on Easter Island (*Votive Head 2000* by Stacy Latt Savage). Unfortunately, the heavy traffic alongside the park on McCormick Boulevard intrudes upon the enjoyment of the art. (Consider an early morning weekend ride to miss some of the heavy traffic alongside the sculpture park.)

The final 3 miles of the ride take you along Pratt Avenue through residential neighborhoods, by a small cemetery, and past the Bryn Mar Country Club. Before arriving back at the beginning of the ride, you'll enjoy one last wooded mile on the North Branch Trail as it cuts through Bunker Hill Forest Preserve.

MILES AND DIRECTIONS

0.0 Catch the paved trail south of the park road. Bear right at the three-way junction that leads to the Bunker Hill Forest Preserve.

3.9 Dempster Avenue is the trickiest of the road crossings: Cross Dempster Avenue and follow it right to regain the path. Signage marks the way.

8.7 After the pedestrian bridge crossing to the west side of the river, stay right at three-way junction.

11.8 Turn right at a three-way junction before crossing the bridge over the lagoons.

14.0 Skip the first option to cross Highway 68. Turn right at the second three-way junction and cross Highway 68 to enter the Chicago Botanic Garden (look for the sign for the botanic garden across the road).

15.3 Bear right in the botanic garden parking area to reach Lake Cook Road. Turn right onto Lake Cook Road. Ride carefully: Lake Cook Road is busy and the road surface is in poor condition.

15.9 Turn right onto Green Bay Trail.

17.4 For a quick tour of downtown Glencoe, turn right at the Glencoe Metra station.

21.0 Follow the signs for a short on-street section: Turn left onto Ivy Court, then right onto Abbotsford Road, then right again onto Melrose Road.

22.5 When the trail hits Wilmette Avenue, continue straight ahead on Poplar Avenue.

23.0 Follow signs by turning left onto Isabella Street, right onto Woodbine Avenue, then right onto Jenks Street. Return to Poplar Avenue and turn left.

North Branch and Green Bay Trails Loop

0 1 2 km.
0 1 2 mi.

N

41
Lake Cook Road
15.3 **15.9**
Chicago Botanic
Garden
Braeside
Metra Station
94
68
14.0 Dundee Road
Green Bay Trail
Glencoe
Metra Station

Lake Michigan

43
Skokie Lagoons
Glencoe

Hubbard Woods
Metra Station

Winnetka

Green Bay Road

Northfield
Willow Road
Ivy Court
Abbotsford Road
21.0
North Branch Chicago River
Kenilworth
Metra Station
Kenilworth

Lake Avenue
23.0
Wilmette
Isabella Street
Wilmette
Metra Station
Poplar Avenue
Ladd Arboretum
23.9
Waukegan Road
58
Golf Road

41

14
Church Street
Evanston
Linne Woods
58
Dempster Avenue
Skokie North Channel Path
Morton Grove
3.9
North Branch Trail
Miami Woods
North Shore Sculpture Park
2
Oakton Street
Skokie

Milwaukee Avenue
14
Howard Street

McCormick Boulevard

Chicago

Touhy Avenue **31.0**
Bunker Hill Woods
4
Central Avenue
Lincolnwood Town Center
Pratt Avenue
Lincolnwood
28.4
43
31.5
14
90
94
41

23.6 Turn right onto Lincoln Street, pass under the railroad tracks, and then turn left onto Green Bay Road.

23.9 Turn right onto the path that accompanies McCormick Boulevard.

28.4 Turn right onto Pratt Avenue.

31.0 Turn left onto North Central Avenue.

31.5 Turn right onto Devon Avenue.

31.7 Pick up the trail at the corner of Devon Avenue and Caldwell Avenue.

32.7 Arrive back where you began your ride.

RIDE INFORMATION

Local Events/Attractions

Baha'i House of Worship: The most impressive structure on Chicago's North Shore; a huge, intricately carved dome surrounded by rose gardens; 100 North Linden Ave., Wilmette; (847) 853-2300; www.us.bahia.org.

Chicago Botanic Garden: Garden is free; fee for parking; visitor center, cafe, restrooms, gift shop; pick up maps at the visitor center; 1000 Lake Cook Rd., Glencoe; (847) 835-5440; www.chicagobotanic.org.

Chicagoland Canoe Base: Rentals for paddling in the Skokie Lagoons; 4019 North Narragansett Ave., Chicago; (773) 777-1489.

Ravinia Music Festival: Live outdoor concerts all summer long; 418 Sheridan Rd., Highland Park; (847) 266-5000; www.ravinia.org.

Skokie North Shore Sculpture Park: Free public tours offered; P.O. Box 692, Skokie, IL 60076; (847) 679-4265; www.sculpturepark.org.

Restaurants

The Gale Street Inn: Well known for its ribs; moderately priced; 4914 North Milwaukee Ave., Chicago; (773) 725-1300.

The Garden Café: Located at the Chicago Botanic Garden; bakery items and standard lunch fare; 1000 Lake Cook Rd., Glencoe; (847) 835-3040.

Homers Ice Cream & Restaurant: Has been making the creamy good stuff since 1935; allegedly was Al Capone's favorite ice cream parlor; 1237 Green Bay Rd., Wilmette; (847) 251-0477.

Pampanga's Restaurant: Filipino cuisine; 6407 North Caldwell Ave., Chicago; (773) 763-1781.

Superdawg Drive-in: All the menu items you'd expect, most of which have the word "super" in their name; 6363 North Milwaukee Ave., Chicago; (773) 763-0660.

Restrooms

Start/finish: Bunker Hill Forest Preserve has portable restrooms.

Mile 2.6: Miami Woods Forest Preserve has restrooms.

Mile 4.2: Linne Woods Forest Preserve has portable restrooms.

Mile 6.0: Harms Woods Forest Preserve has portable restrooms.

Mile 7.7: Blue Star Memorial Woods Forest Preserve offers restrooms.

Mile 15.1: Chicago Botanic Garden has indoor restrooms and water fountains.

Mile 17.4: The Glencoe Metra station has restrooms and water.

Mile 25.7: Portable restrooms are available at the parking area near Dempster Avenue.

Mile 27.7: Portable restrooms area located between Howard Street and Touhy Avenue.

Maps

USGS: Evanston quad, Highland Park quad, Park Ridge quad

DeLorme: *Illinois Atlas and Gazetteer:* Pages 21 and 29

Salt Creek Trail/Oak Park Loop

After following the Salt Creek Trail through a series of forest preserves strad-dling Cook and DuPage Counties, you'll explore quiet residential neighbor-hoods within a handful of western suburbs that grew up alongside the railroad between Chicago and Aurora. Plan to spend some time gawking at the attractive public buildings and many historic homes in Riverside, a village designed by the great landscape architect Frederick Law Olmstead. Wrap up the ride with a loop through Oak Park and a brief tour of the oldest Jewish cemetery in the region.

Start: Brookfield Woods Forest Preserve on 31st Street in Brookfield

Length: 30.2 miles

Approximate riding time: 3 hours

Best bike: Road bike or hybrid bike

Terrain and trail surface: The western half of this ride—including the Salt Creek Trail—includes many areas that are gently rolling. The rest is flat. About 7 miles of the route follow the paved Salt Creek Trail. A short section of the ride follows a crushed gravel trail through Fullersburg Woods Forest Preserve.

Traffic and hazards: Most of these streets have little traffic. There are a few short sections on busier roads, such as Des Plaines Avenue, 31st Street, and Cermak Road.

Things to see: Salt Creek, various county forest preserves (Brookfield Woods, Bemis Woods, Possum Hollow Woods, and Fullersburg Woods), the Graue Mill, Riverside, Oak Park, and Waldheim Jewish Cemeteries

Getting there: By car: Take I-290 to SR 171 (First Avenue). Head south on SR 171, then turn right onto 31st Street. Look for Brookfield Woods Forest Preserve on the right. Park at the back of the lot where the Salt Creek Trail starts. **By public transportation:** Take the BNSF Metra line to the Brookfield station. From the station, follow Prairie Avenue north for about 1 mile to 31st Street. At 31st Street, turn right, cross Salt Creek, and pick up the path at the far back parking area of Brookfield Woods. GPS coordinates: 41 50.174 N / 87 50.469 W

For most of its 50-mile-long route, Salt Creek winds through a series of densely populated western Chicago suburbs. The section of the creek that accompanies the first 10 miles of this ride, however, runs through a handful of county-operated forest preserves that feature gently rolling topography and lush bottomland woods.

Starting at the east end of the Salt Creek Trail in Brookfield Woods, the path takes you on a curving route through a small savanna before arriving at the creek. While tracing the route of the creek, you'll see that this 40-foot-wide waterway occupies a shallow ravine that is wide in some places, narrow in others. After the first road crossing (Maple Avenue, not to be confused with Maple Street), one of Salt Creek's few major tributaries, Addison Creek, merges with Salt Creek from the north.

Now on the south side of Salt Creek, the trail wiggles back and forth between the creek bank and the nearby floodplain tangled with shrubs, deadfall, and small trees. Of course, better views of the creek and the surrounding landscape are granted when the trees are bare. After crossing 31st Street, the terrain acquires a gently rolling character. This is where the trail mounts a few small bluffs overlooking bends in the creek. If you look closely when the trees are bare, you'll notice a couple of sharp bends in the process of getting cut off from the rest of the creek.

Before entering Fullersburg Woods Forest Preserve, stop at the Graue Mill and

Salt Creek runs through the leafy refuge at Fullersburg Woods Forest Preserve.

Museum. Check out the grinding demonstrations on the first floor, then head down to the basement to learn about the mill's history with the Underground Railroad. The mill also contains a collection of doodads and antiques from the late 1800s, such as room settings, farm implements, and a re-created general store.

Within Fullersburg Woods Forest Preserve, you'll again follow Salt Creek as it meanders beneath small bluffs, around a couple of islands, and under footbridges. Saying good-bye to the forest preserve, you'll ascend a modest-size hill and then pass a string of large, lavish homes along Spring Road and Madison Street. One of the more adventurously designed houses is a triangular-shaped dwelling with slanted sides.

As you make your way along the quiet residential streets in Hinsdale, Western Springs, La Grange, and Brookfield, you'll see parks, schools, churches, and plenty of well-kept yards. This series of quiet, leafy suburban communities grew up along the Chicago, Burlington & Quincy Railroad line (now a Metra line) that ran between Chicago and Aurora.

Crossing the Des Plaines River, you'll arrive at one of the more well-known communities situated alongside this train line: the historic suburb of Riverside. Designed by Frederick Law Olmstead, who designed New York's Central Park and the grounds of the Chicago Columbian Exposition, Riverside was one of the first planned communities in the nation. Chosen for its pleasant location along the Des Plaines River and rail access, the village claims an impressive collection of historic homes. Also eye-catching are the public buildings in the downtown area, such as the water tower, the library, and the village hall topped with a clock tower. Even the schools were elegantly designed: The redbrick Central School at 61 Woodside Rd. may be the only school in the Chicago area with gargoyles on its facade. Behind the village hall is a pedestrian suspension bridge over the Des Plaines River that leads into one of the many swaths of local parkland.

Longcommon Road features an assortment of historic homes built in a variety of styles. Many of them are large, rambling, wood-frame Victorian homes; some are clearly inspired by the Prairie style; and interestingly enough, others are rather modest brick ranch houses. After the elegant Prairie-style structure at 135 Longcommon Rd., which houses a church, look for 225 Longcommon Rd., a huge three-story Victorian home built for John F. Palmer, inventor of the pneumatic tube first used in bicycle tires and then used in car tires.

In Berwyn, the 2.5-mile ride on East Avenue starts off with several blocks of 1920s bungalows—all uniform except for minor variations in color and ornamentation. As you enter Oak Park, the monolithic Ascension Catholic Church appears on the left. Built of limestone in a Romanesque style, the church is topped with a tiled roof and a dome. Large Victorian homes decorate the sides of East Avenue as you get closer to Oak Park's downtown. After brushing against the south edge of downtown Oak Park, you'll roll into Forest Park.

In Forest Park, you will encounter Waldheim Jewish Cemeteries, the largest Jewish graveyard in the Chicago area, containing about 240 smaller, separate cemeteries and totaling over 175,000 individual plots. The smaller cemeteries—some of which still have their own gates of stone or brick, sometimes with iron doors facing in various directions—are composed of individuals from family groups, synagogues, and various Jewish organizations. Heading south on Hannah Avenue, the cemeteries on the left contain newer grave sites, many of them established after the 1940s. Turning on Greenberg Road takes you alongside older plots, many bordered by small roads named for biblical figures such as Abraham, Isaac, Jacob, Sarah, and Rebecca.

Bike Shops

Oak Park Cyclery: Rentals available; 1113 Chicago Ave., Oak Park; (888) 371-2453; www.oakparkcyclery.com

Westchester Wheels: Rentals available; located right next to the trail; 10411 Cermak Rd., Westchester; (708) 562-0330

The 200-acre Waldheim Jewish Cemeteries is just one of the several large cemeteries that together occupy the majority of the land in Forest Park. After encountering another cemetery and a massive mausoleum on Des Plaines Avenue, you'll pass five different forest preserves on the banks of the Des Plaines River. Once the Brookfield Zoo comes into view on 31st Street, you'll know you've arrived back at the starting point.

MILES AND DIRECTIONS

0.0 Shortly after picking up the trail in Brookfield Woods, follow the signs pointing left on McCormick Avenue for a short on-street section. After the on-street section, you'll reconnect with the Salt Creek Trail and follow it for the next 7 miles.

7.0 After passing under I-294, follow the path to the right through a small nature sanctuary to Canterberry Lane. Turn left onto Canterberry Lane.

7.5 Turn left onto York Road and follow the bike path on the left side of the road.

8.1 Turn right onto the crushed gravel path into Fullersburg Woods Forest Preserve before crossing Salt Creek. But first, consider a stop at the Graue Mill on the other side of the creek at York Road.

9.5 In Fullersburg Woods Forest Preserve, cross Salt Creek on the second bridge on the left. Stay to the left to reach the visitor center. Follow the park driveway out to Spring Road.

10.5 Turn right onto Spring Road.

10.8 Turn left onto Madison Street.

12.1 Turn left onto Hickory Street.

13.0 Turn left onto Oak Street.

13.3 Turn right onto Minneola Street.

13.6 Take the pedestrian bridge over I-294. Continue straight ahead on Maple Street.

14.4 At Wolf Road, take a slight jog to the left and continue east on 41st Street.

15.2 Turn left onto Edgewood Avenue.

16.0 Edgewood Avenue curves right and turns into Harding Avenue.

17.1 Harding Avenue becomes Washington Avenue. At the roundabout, continue straight ahead on Washington Avenue.

18.6 In Brookfield, Washington Avenue turns into Ridgewood Road and then turns into Forest Avenue.

19.3 Turn left onto Longcommon Road. Longcommon is a diagonal road with lots of streets merging with it at various angles—let the street signs guide the way. First, though, take a tour of Riverside's handsome downtown area.

20.5 Longcommon Road turns into Riverside Drive.

21.4 Turn right onto Cermak Road. Watch for traffic; this is a busy road.

21.6 Turn left onto East Avenue.

24.1 Turn left onto South Boulevard.

24.9 At Harlem Avenue, take a slight jog to the left and then continue ahead on Circle Avenue.

Salt Creek Trail/Oak Park Loop

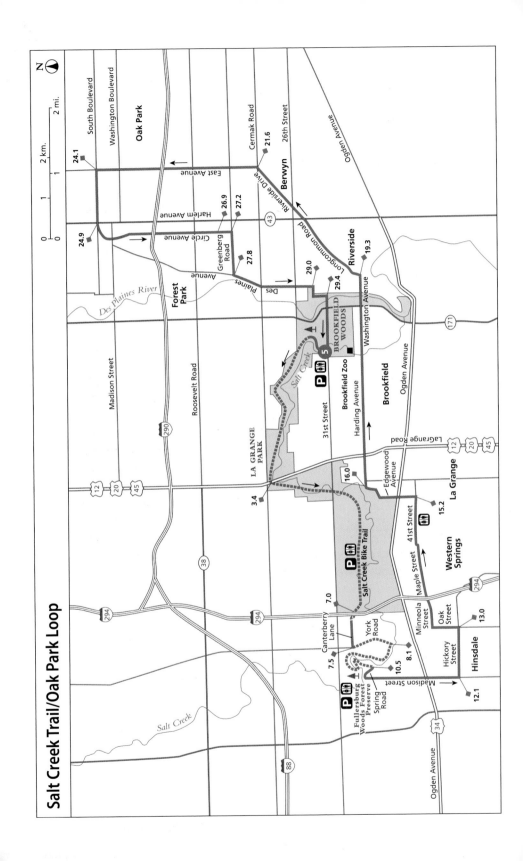

26.9 Turn right onto 15th Street and then immediately turn left at the dead end, which is Hannah Avenue but has no street sign.

27.2 Turn right where Hannah Avenue ends at Greenberg Road; no street sign is posted at this intersection.

27.8 Turn left onto Des Plaines Avenue. This street can be busy, but it is wide.

29.0 Turn right at the sign for National Grove Forest Preserve. The street is 29th Street, but there is no street sign. Follow 29th Street as it curves left.

29.4 Turn right onto 31st Street. Proceed with care; this street can be busy.

30.1 Turn right to enter Brookfield Woods Forest Preserve.

30.2 Return to the parking area.

RIDE INFORMATION

Local Events/Attractions

Brookfield Zoo: One of the largest zoos in the world with more than 2,500 animals, including frolicking dolphins and big apes; First Avenue and 31st Street, Brookfield; (708) 485-2200; www.brookfieldzoo.org.

Fullersburg Woods Forest Preserve Visitor Center: Displays a 13,000-year-old wooly mammoth skeleton uncovered locally in 1977; in April or May, ask for the wildflower guide; 3609 Spring Rd., Oak Brook; (630) 850-8110; www.dupageforest.com.

Graue Mill and Museum: A National Historic Landmark, now a living-history museum; 3800 York Rd., Oak Brook; (630) 655-2090; www.grauemill.org.

Riverside Historic District: Enjoy the gaslit street lamps, winding streets, and attractive historic neighborhoods; start your visit at the Riverside Historical Museum, 10 Pine Ave., Riverside; (708) 447-2574.

Restaurants

Benjarong Thai Restaurant: Well-regarded Thai restaurant located yards from the Salt Creek Trail near the LaGrange Road crossing; 2138 Mannheim Rd., Westchester; (708) 409-0339; http://benjarong.us.

Grumpy's Coffee and Ice Cream: A comfortable atmosphere to pursue your fix; 1 Riverside Rd., Riverside; (708) 443-5603.

Khyber Pass: This Indian restaurant is a local favorite; delicious lunch buffet; 1031 Lake St., Oak Park; (708) 445-9032; www.khyberpassrestaurant.com.

Little Bohemian Restaurant: Hearty fare of pierogies, Cornish hen, and potato pancakes; 25 East Burlington St., Riverside; (708) 442-1251.

York Tavern: Reliable spot for burgers and beer; next to Fullersburg Woods Forest Preserve; 3702 York Rd., Oak Brook; (630) 323-5090.

Restrooms

Start/finish: A portable restroom is available in Brookfield Woods.

Mile 3.0: Brezina Woods has restrooms.

Mile 6.2: Bemis Woods North has restrooms.

Mile 10.0: Water and restrooms are available at the Fullersburg Woods visitor center.

Mile 14.9: Gilbert Park has restrooms and water.

Maps

USGS: Berwyn quad, Hinsdale quad, River Forest quad

DeLorme: *Illinois Atlas & Gazetteer*: Page 29

South Chicagoland, Indiana, and Michigan

This part of Chicagoland encompasses a huge and varied area that includes sizable cities and the largest concentration of heavy industry in the nation. This is where steel is made, oil is refined, and limestone is quarried. This is also where you'll see farmland and pastures splayed out for many miles in every direction. This region contains places like Midewin National Tallgrass Prairie, Cedar Lake, the Kankakee River, and the Indiana Dunes National Lakeshore.

While many of the towns in this region serve as Chicago bedroom communities, the larger cities of Joliet, Gary, and Michigan City operate largely as independent population centers firmly rooted within their own histories. In the nineteenth century, Joliet was known as the City of Steel and Stone. The stone was quarried from the nearby banks of the Des Plaines River while the steel was produced at its own mills. As these major industries dried up, the railroads that carried the goods in and out of the city were abandoned. Thanks to the far-

In La Salle, visitors can board an authentic canal boat for a short trip on the I&M Canal. See Ride 8.

The town of Frankfort is a popular stop for c
using the Old Plank Road Trail. See Ride 13.

sighted efforts of individuals in the area, these abandoned rail lines—and abandoned canals—have been transformed into a great collection of bike trails. Not far from downtown Joliet, you can catch four different trails that spin off for more than 20 miles in each direction.

Each of the four trails possesses a unique character: The Wauponsee Glacial Trail tours farmland to the south and brushes against the Midewin National Tallgrass Prairie, the Old Plank Road Trail guides you through attractive leafy suburbs east of the city, and the Centennial/I&M Canal Trails trace the route of the Des Plaines River and the I&M Canal north of Joliet. The longest and most scenic of these trails is the main section of the I&M Canal Trail, which runs west from Joliet along an old transportation canal that helped link Chicago with the Mississippi River. The trail takes you through a handful of historic towns that grew up alongside the canal; you'll see the mighty Illinois River, as well as numerous parks, wetlands, remote wooded areas, and rural agricultural land.

Heading east into Indiana offers an assortment of road rides where you can visit pleasant towns, become enveloped in attractive countryside, and explore the stunning shoreline at the Indiana Dunes National Lakeshore. Expect to see plenty of rolling farmland patchworked with woods and wetlands. Expect to see deer and birds on the side of the road. Those looking for a longer cycling trip far off the beaten path will find the Southwest Michigan ride well worth the journey: woods, vineyards, a hilly landscape, and some of the loveliest roads you'll find in the area.

Looking to escape the bustle of Chicagoland without going too far? This region could keep you busy for many days exploring scenic trails, quiet farm roads, parks, and pleasant towns.

6

Cedar Lake Loop

This ride takes you through a scenic setting that straddles the Illinois-Indiana state line just 40 miles south of downtown Chicago. The landscape features gently undulating farmland broken up regularly by swaths of woodland, occasional small hills and ravines, and streams that braid the landscape. At the ride's halfway point, you'll explore the Indiana community of Cedar Lake, a former resort town on the shore of a gleaming natural lake.

Start: Goodenow Grove Forest Preserve in eastern Will County south of Crete

Length: 44.7 miles

Approximate riding time: 3.5–4 hours

Best bike: Road bike

Terrain and trail surface: Gently rolling terrain, wooded areas, and a small town on a lake

Traffic and hazards: For riders sporting spaghetti-thin tires, approach with caution the occasional sections of pavement with potholes and patches of loose gravel.

Things to see: Farms, cropland, Cedar Lake (the town and the lake), patches of wetlands, wooded areas, small streams, and Goodenow Grove Forest Preserve

Getting there: From Chicago, take I-94 south to I-80. At this junction, continue straight ahead on SR 394. Turn left onto Goodenow Road and then left again onto Dutton Road. Park at the Plum Creek Nature Center. GPS coordinates: 41 24.083 N / 87 36.374 W

THE RIDE

It's easy to see why people once flocked to Cedar Lake for their vacations: Bluffs decorate the northern shore of the lake and sprawling wetlands—said to be among the largest in Indiana—border the south shore. The lake is large enough to instill a feeling of grandeur, but small enough to lend it intimacy. Known for its wooded shoreline, the 787-acre lake was originally named Lake of the Red Cedars.

Around the turn of the century, Cedar Lake claimed dozens of hotels, several steamboat tour lines, and numerous upscale lakeside cottages. Trains brought visitors in from Chicago and other population centers. Luminaries such as the retailer John G. Shedd (benefactor of the Shedd Aquarium), the Armour brothers (of meatpacking fame), and the famous foot doctor William Scholl owned vacation property on Cedar Lake, while nationally known bands played in ballrooms and pavilions on the lakefront. As automobiles allowed people to vacation in more out-of-the way destinations, Cedar Lake's status as a resort community dissolved. Except for some newer developments, the homes now tend to be modest, and there is little to indicate the community's former life as a popular vacation spot.

Before getting to Cedar Lake, you'll spend the first 10 miles of this ride exploring vast expanses of farmland, occasionally sprinkled with farmhouses and barns set back from the road. Watch the roadside for small streams twisting through the cornfields and under the road; look overhead for red-tailed hawks and American kestrels perched on the power lines and poles, waiting for a rodent snack.

On State Line Road, cropland gives way to a series of small wooded ravines; little streams multiply, and wetlands flood the low spots. The approach to Cedar Lake reveals a landscape where the new world meets the old: New housing developments are surrounded by farmland, and the curving streets of subdivisions meet up with the straight old farm roads.

Bike Shop

Trek Bicycle Store: 651 East Lincoln Hwy., Schererville, Indiana; (219) 322-2453; http://trekbikestore.com

Along the shore of Cedar Lake, Lauerman Street squeezes between a marina on the left and the vast wetland on the right. This outsize marshland was part of the lake at one time, before its southern shore was drained and built up. After taking in the full lake views at the boat launch on Lake Shore Drive, the road follows a thin strip of land between the 60-foot-high bluff and the modest lake houses. When the road mounts the bluff on the lake's northern tip, whip out your camera for shots of the water from the roadside viewing platform.

After contending with the hustle-bustle along 133rd Avenue and crossing US 41, you'll return to farmland and encounter several scenic pieces of roadway. White Oak Avenue is particularly pleasing for its accompanying wooded ridge on the right. The gently rolling topography of Bemes Road is interrupted by an enormous horse care and training facility. Stony Island Avenue takes you through woodland that gradually slopes down before cutting left and dipping down to cross the sublime Plum Creek. Many creeks on the route have been straightened to prevent flooding, but the wriggling form of Plum Creek certainly has not. The 41st mile of the ride introduces you to the dense, tangled bottomland woods that occupy the northern section of Goodenow Grove Forest Preserve. As you climb out the ravine created by Plum Creek, a wooded slope drops down steeply on the left.

Wrapping up the ride at Goodenow Grove Forest Preserve, you might consider exploring the park's hills, grasslands, ravines, and more of Plum Creek along several miles of trails. At the very least, take a walk up the sledding hill for a view of the surrounding area and then stroll the 0.25-mile-long Trail of Thoughts, which starts adjacent to the nature center in the Nodding Oaks picnic area.

MILES AND DIRECTIONS

0.0 Leave Goodenow Grove Forest Preserve via Dutton Road, the same way you entered. At Goodenow Road, jog to the left and continue heading south on Park Avenue.

2.4 Turn left onto Eagle Lake Road.

3.9 Turn right onto Stony Island Avenue.

8.9 Turn left onto CR 1200 North. No street sign is posted, but it is easy enough to navigate because it's where Stony Island Avenue ends.

11.2 Turn right onto State Line Road/CR 1800 North.

12.3 Turn left onto 185th Avenue.

13.6 Turn left onto Hadders Road.

14.1 Turn right onto 181st Avenue.

14.6 Turn left onto White Oak Avenue.

17.6 Turn right onto 157th Avenue. Be careful while crossing US 41.

19.6 Turn left onto Parrish Avenue.

21.4 Turn right onto 142nd Place.

21.9 Turn right onto Lauerman Street, which turns into 147th Avenue as it curves.

22.8 Turn left onto Cline Avenue, which becomes Lake Shore Drive.

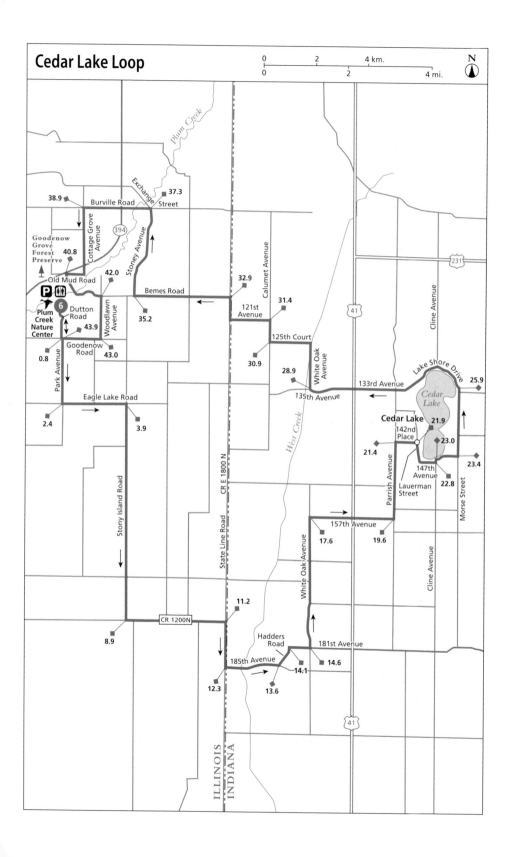

Cedar Lake Loop

0   2   4 km.
0   2   4 mi.

N

Plum Creek

Exchange Street

37.3

38.9   Burville Road

Goodenow Grove Forest Preserve

394

Cottage Grove Avenue

Stoney Avenue

40.8

42.0   Old Mud Road

P

6   Dutton Road

Plum Creek Nature Center

43.9

0.8   Goodenow Road   43.0

Woodlawn Avenue

35.2

Bemes Road

121st Avenue

32.9

31.4

Calumet Avenue

125th Court

30.9

28.9   White Oak Avenue

133rd Avenue

135th Avenue

41

231

Cline Avenue

Lake Shore Drive

25.9

Cedar Lake   21.9

Cedar Lake   23.0

142nd Place

21.4   147th Avenue

23.4

22.8   Morse Street

Lauerman Street

Parrish Avenue

Cline Avenue

2.4   Eagle Lake Road

3.9

Stony Island Road

Park Avenue

CR E 1800 N

West Creek

157th Avenue

17.6   19.6

White Oak Avenue

State Line Road

11.2

CR 1200N

8.9

Hadders Road   181st Avenue

14.6

185th Avenue   14.1

12.3   13.6

41

ILLINOIS   INDIANA

23.0 Turn right onto 145th Avenue.

23.4 Turn left onto Morse Street.

25.9 Turn left onto Lake Shore Drive. On the west side of Cedar Lake, Lake Shore Drive turns into 133rd Avenue, and then farther out it becomes 135th Avenue. Use care on 133rd Avenue: Traffic can be busy, and there are many commercial driveways along the way.

28.9 Turn right onto White Oak Avenue, which becomes 125th Court as the road turns left.

30.9 Turn right onto Calumet Avenue.

31.4 Turn left onto 121st Avenue.

32.3 Turn right onto State Line Road.

32.9 Turn left onto Bemes Road.

35.2 Turn right onto Stony Island Avenue.

37.3 Stony Island Avenue becomes Burville Road as it curves left.

38.9 Turn left onto Cottage Grove Avenue. As Cottage Grove Avenue curves right, it becomes Old Mud Road.

40.8 Turn left onto Bemes Road.

42.0 Turn right onto Woodlawn Avenue.

43.0 Turn right onto Goodenow Road.

43.9 Turn right onto Dutton Road.

44.7 Return to Plum Creek Nature Center at Goodenow Grove Forest Preserve.

RIDE INFORMATION

Local Events/Attractions

Barn and Field Flea Market: Antiques and collectibles, right on the route; open weekends; 9600 West 151st St., Cedar Lake, IN; (219) 696-7368.

Cedar Lake Summerfest: Four-day event over July 4 includes activities such as a cardboard boat race, checkers tournament, live music, boat and land parade, and talent show; Morse Street and Constitution Avenue, Cedar Lake, IN; (219) 374-4444; www.cedarlakesummerfest.com.

Lake of the Red Cedars Museum: Housed in a former hotel; exhibits focus on the history of Cedar Lake; open early May to Labor Day, limited hours of operation; 7308 West 138th Pl., Cedar Lake, IN; (219) 374-7000.

Lemon Lake County Park: 400-acre park with 5 miles of hiking trails and an impressive 27-hole disc golf course; located less than 1 mile east of Cedar Lake; 6322 West 133rd Ave., Crown Point, IN; (219) 945-0543 or (219) 755-3685; www.lakecountyparks.com/lemonlake.html.

Restaurants

Bolda's Dawg House: Yes, Chicago-style hot dogs are available in Indiana; 9720 West 133rd Ave., Cedar Lake, IN; (219) 374-3466.

Carlo's Restaurant and Pizzeria: 13231 Wicker Ave. (US 41), Cedar Lake, IN; (219) 374-5500.

Cedar Lake Kitchen: Basic diner fare; 9525 West 133rd Ave., Cedar Lake, IN; (219) 374-8888.

Princess Cafe: Upscale dining with a menu focusing on steak and seafood; 502 South Dixie Hwy., Beecher, IL; (708) 946-3141; www.theprincesscafe.com.

Restrooms

Start/finish: Goodenow Grove Forest Preserve has restrooms and water.

Mile 27.5: A gas station/convenience store on 133rd Avenue in Cedar Lake offers a restroom and refreshments.

Maps

USGS: Dyer IL quad, Beecher East IL/IN quad, Lowell IN quad, S. John IN quad

DeLorme: *Illinois Atlas & Gazetteer*: Page 37

DeLorme: *Indiana Atlas & Gazetteer*: Page 18

7

I&M Canal/Centennial Trails

This route is jammed with scenic vistas and fascinating local history. While tracing the route of the Des Plaines River, the Chicago Sanitary and Ship Canal, and the I&M Canal, you'll pass two museums, several parks, and a couple of historic sites. Much of the northern half of the route offers a surprisingly remote feel as it cuts through many acres of wetlands and bottomland woods.

Start: Columbia Woods Forest Preserve, located along the Des Plaines River in Cook County

Length: 20.1 miles one way

Approximate riding time: 2 hours

Best bike: Mountain bike, hybrid bike, or a road bike with wider tires

Terrain and trail surface: The trail is paved for the first 9.2 miles in Cook County; the trail surface is crushed gravel for the remaining 10.9 miles in Will County. The terrain is flat throughout.

Traffic and hazards: Watch for trucks while traveling along the on-street section of the route.

Things to see: Des Plaines River, Chicago Sanitary and Ship Canal, bottomland woods, prairie, Isle a la Cache Museum, the I&M Canal, the I&M Canal Museum and Visitor Center, and the Joliet Ironworks

Wheelchair access: The trail is wheelchair accessible, but the 3.0-mile section upon entering Will County has a gravel surface that is rough in places.

Getting there: By car: From I-55 head south on US 12/20. Turn right onto IL 171 (Archer Avenue). Turn right again onto Willow Springs Road. Turn left into Columbia Woods Forest Preserve after crossing the Chicago Ship and Sanitary Canal and the Des Plaines River. In the forest preserve, stay left to reach the trailhead. GPS coordinates: 41 44.226 N / 87 53.077 W

To reach the parking area on Kingery Highway (IL 83), head south on Kingery Highway from I-55. After crossing the Des Plaines River, park in the small lot on the right.

To park at the Schneiders Passage parking area on 135th Street, head south on Weber Road from I-55. Turn left onto 135th Street. Look for the parking area on the left after crossing the Des Plaines River.

To park in Lockport, head south on Weber Road from I-55. Turn left onto Renwick Road. In Lockport turn left onto State Street and then left again onto Eighth Street. Park in the lot on the right next to the Gaylord Building.

By public transportation: The trail can be accessed by taking Metra trains to Willow Springs, Lemont, Lockport, and Joliet. In Lockport the Heritage Corridor Metra train stops mere yards from the trail.

THE RIDE

Heading south from Columbia Woods, the first section of this trail follows a thin sliver of land between the Des Plaines River and the Chicago Sanitary and Ship Canal. As the trail traces the top of a small bluff, the Des Plaines River appears on the right, fringed by moisture-loving trees such as box elder, maple, and cottonwood. Amid the dense bottomland woods along the trail, you'll see piles of limestone excavated from the digging of the canal. Finished in 1900, the Sanitary and Ship Canal reversed the flow of the Chicago River in order to flush waste away from Chicago toward the Mississippi.

Soon the Des Plaines River meanders away from the trail and is replaced by a remarkably quiet stretch of open grassland. A bit farther south, the first bridge you pass under, IL 83 (Kingery Road), offers an opportunity for an extended side trip. A trail over the bridge leads to a section of the I&M Canal Trail on the opposite side of the Sanitary and Ship Canal. The path is 8.6 miles long and contains two connected loops that run beside the former shipping canal.

After the bridge, a small lighthouse-looking structure marks the confluence of the Sanitary and Ship Canal and the Calumet Sag Canal. Barges and tugboats chug along the Cal-Sag Canal on their way to and from Calumet Harbor, the largest industrial port on Lake Michigan.

The next stretch of trail runs through wetland, bottomland woods, and patches of savanna before meeting up with a heavily industrial area crowded with barge offloading facilities. Near the town of Lemont, the Centennial Trail shares its route with Canal Bank Road. (Despite all the industrial facilities and piers along this route, the road is fairly quiet.) One offloading area contains mountains of salt; another is piled high with landscaping mulch.

As you pass under I-355 and enter Will County, the pavement ends and the trail surface becomes a slightly rough combination of dirt and gravel. Bicyclists shouldn't have a problem on this section of trail unless riding on the skinni-

Once the administrative offices for the I&M Canal, the Gaylord Building now houses a museum devoted to the history of the canal.

est of tires. The next 3.0 miles follow a raised embankment through wet bottomland woods at the edge of the Des Plaines River. The Centennial Trail ends with a crossing of a 300-foot-long historic swing bridge that once spanned the Sanitary and Ship Canal, nearby on 135th Street. The bridge, still with its pilothouse up top for controlling the bridge's movement, was transferred to this spot in 1990. (Note that in future years the Cook County Forest Preserve District expects to extend the Centennial Trail several miles north to Lyons.)

At the end of the Centennial Trail, you may enjoy a quick trip to the Isle a la Cache Museum, which focuses on local Native American culture and early European explorers and trappers in the area. The museum contains a birch bark canoe, an example of American Indian lodging used in the area, and items that were commonly traded between the Europeans and Indians. A handful of pleasant picnicking spots overlooking islands within the Des Plaines River backwater sit behind the museum. To reach the museum from the parking area at the end of the Centennial Trail, go several hundred yards to the right on 135th Street.

Best Bike Rides Chicago

As you make your way alongside the I&M Canal Trail from the 135th Street Bridge for a few miles south to Lockport, you'll pass an enormous coal-fired power plant and then cut through an open area that once was the site of a massive oil refinery. This trail is one of three different segments of the I&M Canal Trail in the Chicago region. Earlier when you passed IL 83 on the Centennial Trail, you had the option to take a side trip to visit the northernmost section of the I&M Canal Trail. Southwest of Joliet is a segment of the I&M Canal Trail that runs for 61.9 miles to La Salle. The trail you're on now is a 7.6-mile segment of the I&M Canal Trail that runs between 135th Street and Joliet.

Once you arrive in Lockport, be sure to check out some of the historic attractions that are remnants from the days when the town hosted the headquarters for the I&M Canal. One of these is

Bike Shop

The Wheel Thing: 15 South La Grange Rd., La Grange; (708) 352-3822

the Gaylord Building, which served as a warehouse for materials used in building the canal. The building now contains a museum focusing on the history of the canal, a visitor center, and an upscale restaurant.

In the museum you'll learn that the canal was built to provide the final shipping link between the East Coast of the United States and the Gulf of Mexico. From Chicago the canal angled southwest, running halfway across the state, first beside the Des Plaines River and then beside the Illinois River to where the Illinois was deep enough for boat traffic. After it was finished in 1848, the 96-mile-long canal catapulted Chicago into its position as the largest and most efficient grain market in the world.

Another historic structure alongside the path in Lockport is the Norton Building, which was used for grain storage and as a grocery store. Today the Norton Building houses a state-run art gallery that focuses on past and present Illinois artists. South of Lockport you'll find the first of many locks canal boats would encounter after leaving Chicago.

Getting closer to Joliet, a spur trail heads left into Dellwood Park, followed by a section of trail that zigzags back and forth across the canal as it passes a jumble of bridges, railroad tracks, and another lock. This is also where you'll see the castle-like guard tower for the Joliet Prison, built with locally quarried limestone in 1858 and codesigned by the same architect who designed Chicago's famous Water Tower. During its heyday, the prison was the largest and most state-of-the-art facility in the nation. Numerous films, including *The Blues Brothers*, have used the prison as a movie set. Since it's the most famous attraction in

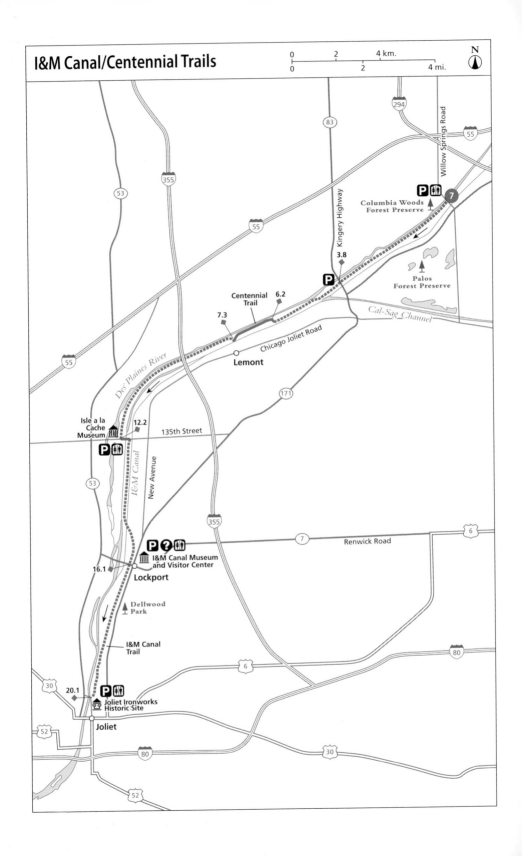

I&M Canal/Centennial Trails

N

0   2   4 km.
0   2   4 mi.

294

Willow Springs Road

83

55

P [WC] 7

Columbia Woods
Forest Preserve

Kingery Highway

3.8

P

Centennial
Trail   6.2

7.3

Palos
Forest Preserve

Cal-Sag Channel

Chicago Joliet Road

Des Plaines River

Lemont

171

355

53

55

Isle a la
Cache
Museum

12.2

135th Street

New Avenue

I&M Canal

P [WC]

53

355

7   Renwick Road   6

P ? [WC]

I&M Canal Museum
and Visitor Center

16.1

Lockport

Dellwood
Park

I&M Canal
Trail

80

6

30

80

20.1

P [WC]

Joliet Ironworks
Historic Site

Joliet

52

30

52

Joliet, the city recently built a small park outside the prison and is considering opening up the building for visitors.

The final stretch of the trail takes you through the Joliet Ironworks Historic Site, which provides a snapshot of how a large-scale iron-making operation worked more than one hundred years ago. In the nineteenth century, Joliet was known as the City of Steel and Stone. The stone was quarried from the nearby banks of the Des Plaines River, while the steel was produced here at the ironworks. Through interpretive signs posted among the crumbling ruins, you can trace the practice of iron making from raw materials to the casting bed. Constructed in the 1870s, the Joliet Ironworks employed some 2,000 workers when production reached its peak at the turn of the twentieth century. Much of the steel made in Joliet was used in the production of barbed wire and train rail.

MILES AND DIRECTIONS

0.0 Start by heading southwest from Columbia Woods Forest Preserve on the Centennial Trail.

3.8 Pass underneath IL 83/Kingery Highway.

6.2 Keep straight to begin a 1.1-mile-long on-street section of the route that follows Canal Bank Road.

7.3 Pick up the trail again on the right.

12.2 Take the path left over the bridge alongside Romeo Road/135th Street. Follow signs for the I&M Canal Trail to the left.

16.1 Pass the I&M Canal Visitor Center in Lockport.

20.1 End the ride in the parking lot for the Joliet Ironworks Historic Site.

RIDE INFORMATION

Local Events/Attractions

Joliet Area Historical Museum: Offers a thorough introduction to the history of the Joliet area; 204 North Ottawa St., Joliet; (815) 723-5201; www .jolietmuseum.org.

Joliet-area rail trails: Three other long rail trails can be accessed in Joliet; read route advice for on-street connections at the website; www.oprt.org/ maps/westcon.html#iandm.

Lockport Gallery: Located in a historic building alongside the trail, features Illinois artists; 201 West 10th St., Lockport; (815) 838-7400; www.museum .state.il.us/ismsites/lockport.

I&M Canal Visitor Center and Museum: Located alongside the trail in the historic Gaylord Building, a National Trust Historic Site; 200 West Eighth St., Lockport; (815) 838-9400; www.canalcor.org.

Restaurants
Merichka's: Serving up American food since 1933; try the poor boy sandwich; 604 Theodore St., Crest Hill; (815) 723-9371; www.merichkas.com.
Public Landing Restaurant: Fish, seafood, and steak; sandwiches served at lunch; located next door to the Gaylord Building; 200 West Eighth St., Lockport; (815) 838-6500; www.publiclandingrestaurant.com.

Restrooms
Start: There are public restrooms and water at Columbia Woods Forest Preserve.
Mile 12.2: The Isle a la Cache Museum (0.3 mile off the trail) has facilities.
Mile 16.1: The I&M Canal Museum and Visitor Center in Lockport has facilities.

Maps
USGS Joliet, Romeoville, and Sag Bridge
DeLorme: Illinois Atlas and Gazetteer: Pages 28 and 29

I&M Canal Trail

In 1848 the Illinois and Michigan Canal provided the final shipping link between the East Coast of the United States and the Gulf of Mexico. From Chicago the canal angled southwest, running beside the Des Plaines and Illinois Rivers halfway across the state. Thanks to the 96-mile-long canal, Chicago quickly became the largest and most efficient grain market in the world. The canal towpath, originally used by mules for pulling boats through the canal, has been transformed into a 61.9-mile crushed gravel path running from the outskirts of Joliet to the town of La Salle. From end to end, the route wanders through a variety of landscapes: dense woods, marshes, prairies, riverbank, agricultural land, and small towns.

Start: Southwest of Joliet at the Brandon Road trail parking area

Length: 61.9 miles one way

Approximate riding time: 6 hours

Best bike: Road bike with wider tires. Hybrid and mountain bikes will work, too, if you aren't planning on tackling too many miles.

Terrain and trail surface: The trail surface is crushed gravel; the terrain is flat.

Traffic and hazards: The length of this trail may present a challenge even for well-prepared athletes. While amenities exist along the way, some sections are very remote. The trail crosses a handful of busy roads. Use caution while crossing these. Small sections of the trail are occasionally closed due to erosion.

Things to see: I&M Canal, aqueducts, locktenders' houses, woodland, wetlands, the Illinois River, the Des Plaines River, Morris, Seneca, Marseilles, Utica, La Salle, and Buffalo Rock State Park, Channahon State Park, Gebhard Woods State Park

Wheelchair access: The trail is wheelchair accessible.

Getting there: By car: From I-55 head east on I-88. Go south on Raynor Road (exit 131). Continue ahead as Raynor Road swings to the right and turns into Meadow Avenue. Turn left onto Brandon Road. The parking area is on the right. GPS coordinates: 41 30.244 N / 88 6.368 W

To park at Rock Run Forest Preserve, head south on Empress Road from I-80. The forest preserve is on the right.

To park at Channahon State Park, exit west on US 6 from I-55. In Channahon turn left onto Canal Street. The entrance to the park is on the right.

To reach the Aux Sable Aqueduct parking area, take I-55 south to exit 248 and head southwest on US 6. Turn left onto Tabler Road and then right onto Cemetery Road.

To park at Gebhard Woods State Park, head south from I-80 into Morris on IL 47. Turn right onto Jefferson Street, which soon becomes Freemont Street. Turn left onto Ottawa Street; the entrance to the park is on the left.

To park in Seneca, head south on US 6 from I-80. Turn left onto IL 170. Look for the trailhead on the right.

To park in Marseilles, head south from I-80 on 24th Road. Look for on-street parking as you cross over the trail while following Main Street.

To access the trail in Ottawa, head south on IL 23/71 from I-80. Turn left onto Superior Street. Before reaching the Fox River, park in the lot on the left.

To access the trail from the Buffalo Rock parking area, head south from I-80 on IL 23. Turn right onto US 6 and then left onto Boyce Memorial Drive. Veer left onto Ottawa Avenue, which soon becomes Dee Bennett Road.

To park in Utica, head south on IL 178 from I-80. In Utica keep straight ahead on Division Street as IL 178 turns left. Park in the lot straight ahead, and catch the trail on the other side of the pedestrian bridge.

To park at the west end of the trail in La Salle, exit south onto St. Vincents Avenue from I-80. Keep straight ahead as St. Vincents Avenue becomes Joliet Street. Look for the entrance to the parking area on the right.

By public transportation: The Heritage Corridor and the Rock Island District Metra train lines both end in Joliet. The trailhead is several miles from the train station.

THE RIDE

Joliet to Seneca

Heading west from the Brandon Road parking area, wetlands rule much of the landscape. There are algae-covered ponds littered with deadfall, huge expanses of cattails, and swaying stands of 15-foot-tall sedge grasses. Water-loving birds such as red-winged blackbirds, green night herons, and kingfishers seem unfazed by the sounds of heavy industry nearby on US 6.

Before reaching Channahon, short spur trails head left into Rock Run Forest Preserve and Channahon Community Park. Both parks are less than 0.25 mile off the I&M Canal Trail, and each has a picnic areas, restrooms, and water. At Rock Run a short hiking trail leads to the shore of Rock Run Creek. After passing under I-55, the path runs through attractive bottomland terrain alongside the canal's open water.

The diminutive Channahon State Park contains a tenting campground, a picnic area, a former canal lock, and one of only two locktender's houses remaining along the canal. Locktenders had to be available day or night to keep the boat traffic moving. They opened the gate for the canal boat to enter the 12- by 100-foot lock, closed the gate, and then filled or drained the lock to raise or lower the boat. Fifteen locks were needed along the canal for 141 feet of elevation change between Chicago and the Illinois River.

After the path crosses the DuPage River and passes two more locks, you'll embark on one of the best stretches on the eastern side of the I&M Canal Trail. For most of the next 5.5 miles, the trail occupies a 15-foot-wide strip of land between two bodies of water: The 20- to 30-foot-wide canal is on the right; the broad and mighty Des Plaines River is on the left. The surrounding landscape is wooded and hilly with bluffs and patches of farmland. With good weather, expect to see plenty of pleasure boats on the Des Plaines. Barges may come lumbering by, too, some as long as 2 city blocks. At McKinley Woods a pedestrian bridge over the canal leads to a picnic area, a small campground, and the hiking trails that lead through the park's rugged terrain.

The bluffs continue beyond McKinley Woods all the way to the Dresden Lock and Dam. Near the dam is the only mule barn left standing along the canal. (Mule barns once were situated every 10 to 15 miles so that the mules and horses could eat and rest before their next haul.) Another locktender's house appears along the path at Aux Sable Creek. This is also where you'll find a small camping area and an aqueduct where the canal is directed over the 40-foot-wide creek. (The I&M Canal Museum and Visitor Center in Lockport contains a scale model of the Aux Sable Aqueduct and locktender's house as it looked when the canal was in use.)

Before passing downtown Morris you'll likely see some anglers and boaters in a riverside park. Morris's surprisingly vibrant main strip runs straight north from a pedestrian bridge that spans the canal. Across the street from the bridge sits the Grundy County Historical Society.

After the aqueduct over Nettle Creek at Gebhard Woods State Park, the canal dries up and bottomland woods and sedge grasses take over. You'll see

Seneca hosts the only grain elevator still standing along the I&M Canal.

I&M CANAL STATE TRAIL
SENECA ACCESS

a small stream that trickles under the trail toward the Illinois River. Beyond the stream you'll duck under the curving wooden supports of a new bridge for Old Stage Road. Dense stands of bottomland woods occasionally open up to reveal big sprawling wetlands sprinkled with downed trees and muskrat lodges.

Seneca contains the only grain elevator that still stands along the I&M Canal. Built in 1861 and placed on the National Register of Historic Places in 1997, the 80-foot structure is a reminder of what weighed down most canal boats as they were hauled up and down the canal.

Seneca to La Salle

Leaving Seneca, the path follows a dirt road for a mile or so through farm fields. Once you've regained the trail, you'll catch glimpses of the Illinois River beyond the field on the left. In a residential area within the town of Marseilles, the trail passes a former lock beside the trail.

A dramatic crossing of the Fox River marks your arrival in Ottawa. Alongside the pedestrian bridge that takes you over the river is an enormous aqueduct that shuttled canal boats 50 feet above the Fox River. The riverside park on the west bank of the Fox River serves as a perfect picnicking spot. If you're in the mood for exploring, a few blocks south of the trail in Ottawa (on IL 71) is Washington Square, which hosted the first of the series of U.S. Senate debates between Abraham Lincoln and Stephen Douglas.

The remaining 15 miles of trail from Ottawa to La Salle feature a number of scenic stretches of river bluffs, wetlands, and open water. Exposed sandstone appears now and then on the 80-foot-high bluffs to the right. In some places the exposed rock

Bike Rentals

Mix's Trading Post: 602 Clark St., Utica; (815) 667-4120

is the result of dynamite used to clear the route for a railroad line that runs at the foot of the bluff.

For those with the time and inclination to explore the area, Buffalo Rock State Park is well worth a brief detour. At the Buffalo Rock parking area, you can cross Dee Bennett Road to visit this park perched on a bluff above the Illinois River. Buffalo Rock State Park is a reclaimed strip mine that contains five enormous earthen mounds depicting creatures commonly found near the river.

Entering Utica, the trail shares the route with a quiet country road.

At the parking area near the end of the trail in La Salle, you'll come upon a full-size replica of a canal boat that traveled the canal more than 150 years ago. The wooden boat is long and narrow, with an open-air deck on the second level. During an hour-long boat ride, tour guides dressed from the era provide narra-

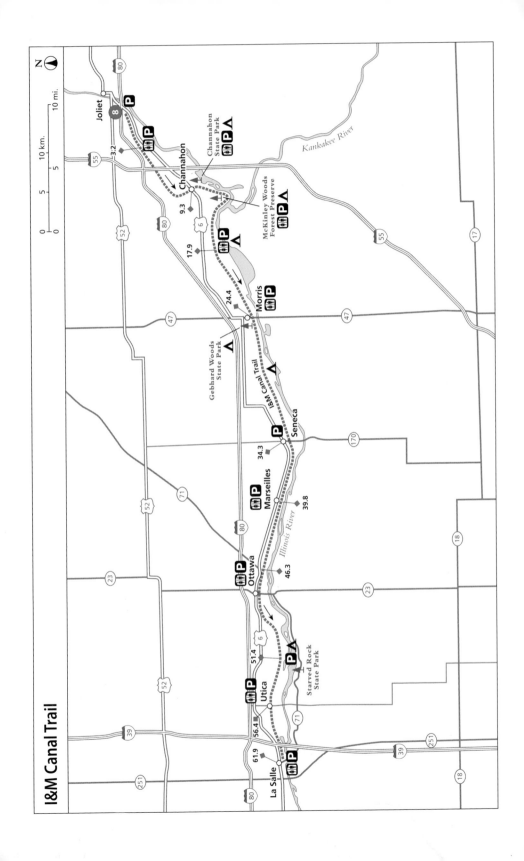

I&M Canal Trail

tion. At the end of the trail, about 1 mile beyond the parking area in La Salle, you can see the canal's confluence with the Illinois River off to the left.

MILES AND DIRECTIONS

0.0 Start from the Brandon Road Trailhead.

3.2 Pass the Rock Run Forest Preserve on the left.

9.3 Pass through Channahon State Park.

12.5 Pass McKinley Woods Forest Preserve on the right.

17.9 Pass Aux Sable Creek Aqueduct.

24.4 Look for Gebhard Woods State Park on the right, after passing through Morris.

29.0 Pass under Old Stage Road.

34.3 Cross IL 170 in Seneca.

39.8 Cross CR 15 in Marseilles.

46.3 Cross the Fox River before entering Ottawa.

51.4 Pass the Buffalo Rock parking area.

56.4 Cross IL 178 in Utica.

60.9 Pass the La Salle parking area on IL 351.

61.9 Arrive at the end of the trail.

RIDE INFORMATION

Local Events/Attractions

Hegeler Carus Mansion: Huge mansion from 1874 occupies an entire city block; tours provided; 1307 Seventh St., La Salle; (815) 224-6543; www .hegelercarus.org.

Joliet Area Historical Museum: Offers a thorough introduction to local history; 204 North Ottawa St., Joliet; (815) 723-5201; www.jolietmuseum.org.

Joliet-area rail trails: Three other long rail trails can be accessed in Joliet; get route advice and on-street connections on the website; www.oprt.org/maps/ westcon.html#iandm.

Illinois Waterway Visitors Center: Observation decks allow you to watch the boats using the locks; Route 1, Dee Bennett Road, Ottawa; (815) 667-4054.

Lock 16 Visitor Center: Located several blocks from the trail, with exhibits, a cafe, and a gift shop; buy tickets for La Salle Canal Boat rides; 754 First St., La Salle; (866) 610-7678; www.lasalleboat.org.

Starved Rock State Park: Visit the canyons, bluffs, and campgrounds at one of the state's best (and most popular) state parks; at Highways 178 and 71, Utica; (815) 667-4726; www.dnr.illinois.gov.

Pitch a tent along the way!

If you like riding on trails and you like camping, the I&M Canal Trail is one of the best options in the area because it offers an assortment of camping possibilities. You can pitch your tent in remote trailside campsites or find a more social camping atmosphere in state and county parks along the way. From the east, tent camping is offered at Channahon State Park, McKinley Woods Forest Preserve, the Aux Sable Aqueduct, and three hike-in sites along the trail between the Aux Sable Aqueduct and Seneca. There's also camping at Gebhard Woods State Park and three hike-in sites on the trail west of the Buffalo Rock parking area. For remoteness and beauty, the hike-in sites west of Buffalo Rock are the best choices. These sites can serve as home bases for exploring Buffalo Rock and Starved Rock State Parks, the town of Utica, and the Illinois Waterway Visitor Center, where you can see a functioning lock and exhibits on the history of Illinois waterways.

Restaurants

Tracy's Row House: A nice atmosphere and good food in downtown Ottawa; 728 Columbus St., Ottawa; (815) 434-3171; http://tracysrowhouse.net.

Triple J Ice Cream: Located on the trail; 110 East Canal Ave., Ottawa; (815) 434-8888.

Starved Rock Lodge and Conference Center: Guest rooms and cabins at the state park, located at IL 178 and IL 71; P.O. Box 570, Utica, IL 61373; (800) 868-7625; www.starvedrocklodge.com.

Restrooms

Mile 3.3: Rock Run Forest Preserve has restrooms and water.

Mile 9.0: Channahon State Park has restrooms and water.

Mile 12.6: McKinley Woods Forest Preserve has restrooms and water.

Mile 18.0: The Aux Sable Aqueduct has restrooms.

Mile 24.8: Gebhard Woods State Park has restrooms and water.

Mile 34.5: Restrooms available in the gas station next to the trail in Seneca.

Mile 39.5: Marseilles offers a portable toilet next to the trail.

Mile 47.0: The riverside park in Ottawa contains restrooms.

Mile 56.4: Utica offers restrooms; water is also available (take pedestrian bridge on right after crossing IL 178).

Mile 60.9: The La Salle parking area offers restrooms and water.

Maps

USGS Channahon, Elwood, La Salle, Marseilles, Minooka, Morris, Ottawa, Seneca, Starved Rock

DeLorme: Illinois Atlas and Gazetteer: Pages 34–36

Illinois Bicycle Map, Region 3, Illinois Department of Transportation, www.dot.state.il.us/bikemap/state.html

Indiana Dunes/Porter County Loop

The 3 miles of beachfront on this ride offer one of the most delightful stretches of bike-able lakeshore in the region, the sort of road that makes you want to pull off every half-mile just to gaze at the striking scenery. Along this stretch, you'll come upon some curious houses transplanted in the 1930s from Chicago's World's Fair. Before arriving at the shoreline, the ride takes you through about 15 miles of quiet, gently rolling rural roads located south of the park.

Start: Start the ride at the Ly-co-ki-we Trailhead parking area, operated by the Indiana Dunes National Lakeshore, at the corner of US 20 at CR 275 North

Length: 22.4 miles

Approximate riding time: 1.5 hours

Best bike: Road bike or hybrid bike

Terrain: Other than a few small dune ridges, nearly all of the ride is flat or gently rolling.

Traffic and hazards: If you're riding on a summer weekend, the park may be busy. Fortunately, cars must travel very slowly throughout the park. If you choose to hike up dunes along the way or lounge on the beach, be sure to lock up your bicycle.

Things to see: Dunes, beach, wetlands, woods, historic homes, and farmland.

Getting there: Take I-90/94 south until reaching the Chicago Skyway (I-90), exit 59A. After traveling southeast for nearly 30 miles on the Skyway and the toll road, take exit 21 to return to I-94. Follow I-94 to Highway 49. Go north on Highway 49 until reaching US 20. Turn right onto US 20 and then look for the Li-co-ki-we Trail parking lot on the left several miles up the road. GPS coordinates: 41 38.918 N / 87 0.905 W

THE RIDE

The parks of the Indiana Dunes are chock-full of scenic vistas and appealing places to explore. Far and away, though, most people come to the dunes for the beaches. Perfect for swimming, picnicking, tossing a Frisbee, and working on a sunburn, the wind-scoured beaches sit beside monster sand dunes. The smaller, exposed sand dunes closer to the water are topped off with hearty dune grasses; moving farther inland, the dunes are blanketed with dense forests of oak.

First-time visitors to the dunes may find the beaches take some getting used to. This is because there's typically a smokestack or two rising in the background, reminding you that this national park—and the smaller state park—are situated on an unlikely piece of real estate smack-dab in the middle of the

Lakefront Drive offers a perfect stretch of roadway for biking on the Lake Michigan shoreline.

highest concentration of heavy industry in the nation. For some, the nearby smokestacks disturb and distract; for most people, though, the industrial backdrop soon becomes barely noticeable and makes this improbable location for a park all the more significant.

After setting out from the Ly-co-ki-we Trail parking area, the landscape is flat and largely agricultural, with patches of wetlands and plots of woodland rising up now and then, particularly after crossing I-94. Other than the occasional house, cropland mostly dominates the views as you head west along CR 1200 North. On LaPorte Road, you'll pedal in a straight line north for 5 miles past a handful of houses and through inviting swaths of woodland, grassland, and savanna. Before and after turning onto CR 1675 East, dense, lush woods and wetlands appear on the left. By now, you'll have noticed a proliferation of wet areas on this ride. Indeed, the entire dunes area is known for its wetlands—all these ponds, marshes, bogs, wet prairies, and damp hollows help support a huge array of local plant species.

Getting closer to the lakeshore, a small dune ridge requires a short climb just before passing a retail business called the Junk Shop, featuring a fenced-in yard of castaway appliances, old mechanical equipment, and derelict vehicles. From the Junk Shop it's a short trip through a small residential strip on Central Avenue into the Indiana Dunes National Lakeshore. After passing through the old limestone pillars north of US 12, tangled woods and wetlands suddenly swallow up the terrain. This low-lying damp forest, which runs along nearly the entire length of the dunes shoreline about 0.5 mile south of the water, was likely one of the previous shorelines many thousands of years ago when the lake sat at a higher level. Crossing this stretch of roadway is the Calumet Trail, a 9.1-mile-long crushed gravel path that runs parallel to US 12 along a power line right-of-way.

At the intersection of Central Avenue and Beverly Drive, you have options for two beach-bound side trips. Continuing straight brings you to Central Beach where cars must park 0.25 mile from the beach, but cyclists can get much closer to the water (ha-ha!) by following the service road straight ahead. Turning right onto Beverly Drive takes you on a 1-mile trip east to visit Mount Baldy. A 0.5-mile hike to the top of this 130-foot dune grants stunning views of the shoreline and the lake.

Staying on the main route is a good choice, too. Pedaling east along Beverly Drive takes you through a landscape of cattails, reed grasses, and large expanses of low, shrubby wetland. A steady chorus of birdsong accompanies you through this moist terrain. Montana Avenue guides you over a few small wooded dunes and along one of the many winding streets within Beverly Shores, a town developed in the 1920s and '30s, and now completely surrounded by the national park.

The veil is lifted as Lake Front Drive launches you on a perfect ramble alongside our great inland sea. The lake is constantly visible on the right as the road shoots straight ahead, just above the shoreline. Patches of marram grass huddle at the tops of the small dunes that swell up from the beach. The wooded dunes on the left contain well-tended houses set on twisting roads through what looks like a fairy tale village.

Initially, this little community of Beverly Shores was slated to be less of a lakeside idyll and more of a glitzy spectacle. Robert Bartlett, the developer of Beverly Shores, hoped to create another Atlantic City. He built roads, a school, a golf course, a botanical garden, a riding academy, and a hotel, and he bought structures from Chicago's 1933–34 Century of Progress World's

Bike Shops

Chesterton Bicycle Station: Rentals offered; 116 South Fourth St., Chesterton, Indiana; (219) 926-1112

My Bike of Michigan City: 1801 Franklin St., Michigan City, Indiana; (219) 879-0899

Fair and moved them to Lake Front Drive (four of these homes were actually barged across Lake Michigan). He moved a colonial village that was featured at the fair to Beverly Shores as well.

The World's Fair homes were specially built to demonstrate modern architectural design, experimental materials, and new technologies such as central air-conditioning and dishwashers. Among the four houses near the west end of Lake Front Drive, the House of Tomorrow, which looks something like a layered cake, features the most striking design (it's located across the road from the unmistakable Florida House). The first floor of the House of Tomorrow originally contained the garage and an airplane hangar (every family would soon own an airplane, the architect surmised). The second and third floors contained the main living spaces and a solarium. The original all-glass walls reduced the heating bills during the winter; during summer, however, the home's cutting-edge air-conditioning couldn't handle the job of cooling off the house. Now the house stands with typical wood-framed exterior walls and functioning windows.

After leaving the beachfront, you'll wrap up the ride with a quick jaunt through more of the park's attractive woodland, and another crossing of the Calumet Trail. Before arriving back in the parking area where you started, consider dropping in at the Schoolhouse Shop and Antiques on Furnessville Road for a selection of local food and crafts mixed in with the antiques.

Indiana Dunes/Porter County Loop

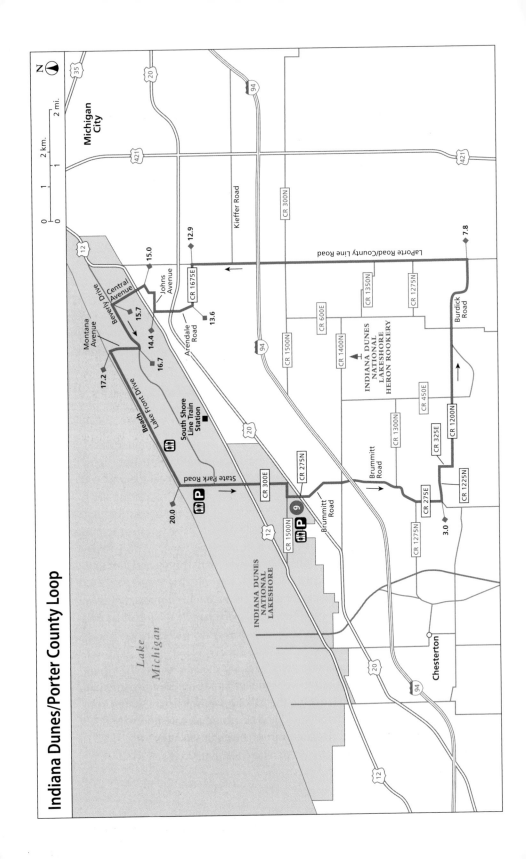

MILES AND DIRECTIONS

0.0 From the Ly-co-ki-we Trailhead on CR 275 North (Schoolhouse Road), head south across US 20. On the south side of US 20, CR 275 North becomes Brummitt Road. It's also called CR North 300 East.

3.0 Turn left onto CR 1225 North. After the first curve, this road becomes CR 325 East. After the second curve, it becomes CR East 1200 North.

7.8 Turn left onto County Line Road (LaPorte Road).

12.9 Turn left onto CR 1675 North.

13.6 Turn right onto North 625 East (Ardendale Road).

14.4 Turn right onto Johns Avenue. Continue ahead as Johns Avenue curves left to become Second Place. Pass the big fenced-in junk store on the right.

15.0 Turn left onto Central Avenue. There's no road sign to identify Central Avenue. It should be easy to identify, however: it's the next street after Delaware Street and it runs north from the junk store.

15.7 Turn left onto Beverly Drive. **Side trips:** Turn right onto Beverly Drive for a 2-mile round-trip to Mount Baldy or continue straight ahead on Central Avenue for a 1-mile round-trip to Central Beach.

16.7 Turn right onto Montana Avenue.

17.2 Turn left onto Lake Front Drive.

20.0 Turn left onto State Park Road.

22.0 Turn right onto CR 1500 North.

22.3 Turn left onto CR 275 East.

22.4 Return to the Ly-co-ki-we Trail parking area on the right.

RIDE INFORMATION

Local Events/Attractions

The Depot of Beverly Shores: Museum and art gallery is a former train depot from 1929; open Saturday and Sunday; 525 Broadway, Beverly Shores, Indiana; (219) 871-0832.

Indiana Dunes National Lakeshore's Dorothy Buell Memorial Visitor Center: 1420 Munson Rd. (Highway 49 between I-94 and US 20), Indiana; (219) 926-7561, ext. 3; www.nps.gov/indu.

Indiana Dunes State Park: Highway 49 north of US 12, Chesterton, Indiana; (219) 926-1952; www.dnr.in.gov/.

Restaurants

Popolano's Restaurant: Italian food priced reasonably; 225 South Calumet Rd., Chesterton, Indiana; (219) 926-5552; www.popolanosrestaurant.com.

Restrooms

Start/finish: Restrooms, water, and a small picnic shelter are available at trailhead.

Mile 20.0: Restrooms and water are available at Kemil Beach near the junction of Lake Front Drive and State Park Road.

Maps

DeLorme: Indiana Atlas and Gazetteer: Page 19

Northwest Indiana Bike Map, Northwest Indiana Regional Planning Commission; (219) 763-6060; www.nirpc.org

USGS 7.5" Dune Acres IN quad, USGS 7.5" Westville IN quad, USGS Michigan City IN 7.5" quad

Joliet Area Trails Loop

As you circle the far western edge of Joliet on this ride, you'll get an inkling of the city's industrial heritage, as well as its residential life, its parks, and its commercial districts. The first half of the ride guides you through the wooded campus of Joliet Junior College and the Rock Run Greenway, which comprises several connected parks and forest preserves. The second half of the ride features a series of neigh-borhoods, a swath of heavy industry, and the I&M Canal Trail.

Start: Begin the ride at the Rock Run Preserve on Empress Road southwest of Joliet

Length: 15.9 miles

Approximate riding time: 1.5 hours

Best bike: Road, hybrid, or mountain bike

Terrain and trail surface: The trails on the route are all asphalt except for the final 2 miles on the I&M Canal Trail, which is crushed gravel.

Traffic and hazards: The Rock Run Greenway section of the ride has many turnoffs and spurs that can lead you temporarily astray. Fortunately, the trail is well marked.

Things to see: Ponds, wetlands, streams, woods, residential neighborhoods, and a taste of local commercial and industrial areas.

Getting there: From Chicago, take I-55 south to I-80. Go east on I-80 and then exit immediately on Empress Drive heading south. The entrance to Rock Run Preserve is on the right 0.5 mile south of I-80. GPS coordinates: 41 29.188 N / 88 9.789 W

To park at the Rock Run Preserve Black Road parking area, take I-55 south from Chicago, exit on Jefferson Street, and head east. Turn left immediately onto Frontage Road, and then turn right onto Black Road. The parking area appears immediately on the left.

The Rock Run Preserve is a popular cycling destination in Joliet.

THE RIDE

Joliet's history is strongly rooted in the industries of steelmaking, quarrying, and railroading. Much of the limestone was quarried from the banks of the Des Plaines River and then shipped to places within the state like Rock Island for building its arsenal and Springfield for building the state house and Lincoln Memorial. The steel industry, attracted to the soft coal in the vicinity, flourished in Joliet until Chicago took over the mantle as the region's steel producer. Situated just 35 miles south of Chicago, Joliet's industrial heritage lends it an atmosphere that appears separate from Chicago, different from many other suburban cities in the region.

It's Joliet's industrial heritage that gave birth to the collection of enviable local biking trails. Half of this ride follows an abandoned railroad and another segment follows the banks of the Illinois and Michigan Canal, once the main shipping artery for the region.

Less than 1 mile after starting the ride at Rock Run Preserve, you'll arrive at the campus of Joliet Junior College. The college sits just north of I-80 and next to an array of fast-food joints and hotels that sprout up along any busy interstate. Some visitors may want to explore the campus's eleven-acre arboretum featuring many dozens of tree species arranged by family and evolutionary history. Also on campus is a hiking trail that passes an old one-room schoolhouse, a 200-year-old oak tree, and part of an old wall likely built by Confederate Civil War prisoners (the foot trail starts where the bike trail brushes against the small lake). While passing the lake on the bike trail, watch for the spot where the campus building spans the width of the narrow lake.

North of campus, an oak-hickory woodland dominates for a spell, and then eventually opens into grassland dotted with shrubs and small trees. As the trail curves left, a bench overlooks a gently rolling savanna. At McDonough Street, the trail again accompanies Houbolt Avenue and passes the runways at Joliet Regional Airport. After Jefferson Street, the grassland returns: Look for plants such as milkweed, goldenrod, and thistle in between the wetlands and patches of open water. One stretch of trail is squeezed between a wide stretch of Rock Run Creek on the right and big suburban homes surrounded by what looks like a moat—minus the drawbridges.

The wet, grassy landscape continues to unfurl as you enter another section of the Rock Run Preserve at Black Road. Anglers cast into the small ponds as waterbirds drift by stands of cattails. Despite the nearby bustle, Rock Run Creek, located off to the right, provides a home to beaver and muskrat. The next couple miles of trail take you through a patchwork of prairies, savannas, and wetlands that have been spared from the steady march of the surrounding development. After crossing Theodore Street and Rock Run Creek for the third time, a grove of towering cottonwood trees offers a sharp contrast to the grassy landscape around you.

Crossing over Theodore Street again launches you on the Joliet Junction Trail, which cuts a narrow path between dozens of backyards—some big and open, others small and cluttered. The trail, a former rail route, runs straight as a yardstick and smooth as a baby's bottom. At Jefferson Street, a shopping district with several restaurants appears next to the trail. Leaving the commercial strip behind,

Bike Shop

Sumbaum Cycle: 114 North Larkin Ave., Joliet; (815) 744-5333

you'll pass under I-80 and then cruise by a large wetland area on the left. As you head back toward the Des Plaines River, the route takes a gentle downward slope as it cuts through a shallow ravine.

The sound of crushed rock signals a nearby gravel mining operation. There's a waste transfer facility and a coal-fired power plant in the distance. As the heavy industries proliferate, the trail ends, and 0.25 mile later, you're in the

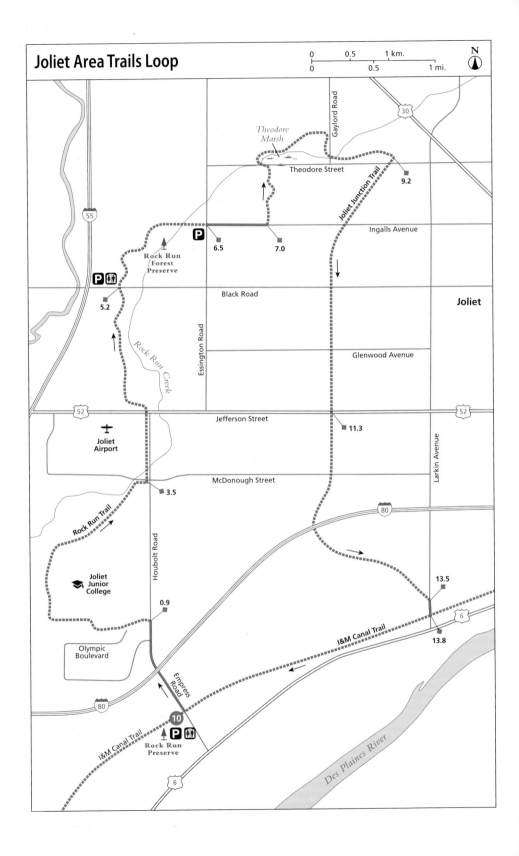

Joliet Area Trails Loop

0   0.5   1 km.

0   0.5   1 mi.

N

Theodore Marsh

Gaylord Road

30

Theodore Street

9.2

Joliet Junction Trail

Ingalls Avenue

Joliet

P

6.5   7.0

Rock Run
Forest
Preserve

55

P

5.2

Black Road

Essington Road

Rock Run Creek

Glenwood Avenue

52   Jefferson Street   52

11.3

Joliet
Airport

Larkin Avenue

McDonough Street

3.5

80

Rock Run Trail

Houbolt Road

Joliet
Junior
College

13.5

0.9

I&M Canal Trail

6

13.8

Olympic
Boulevard

80

Empress Road

10   P

I&M Canal Trail

Rock Run
Preserve

6

Des Plaines River

cozy embrace of the greenery along the I&M Canal Trail. Just before getting on the trail, watch for a sign on the right along Larkin Avenue that marks the former location of Joliet Mound, a natural landmark that was used as a navigation aid on the Des Plaines River between Chicago and the Mississippi River. The mound, made mostly of clay, was carted away in the nineteenth century for making drain tiles.

The final 2 miles of the ride take you along the eastern end of the I&M Canal Trail (the entire trail runs for 60 miles between Joliet and La Salle; see Ride 8, I&M Canal Trail, for more about riding the trail). The canal was shut down long ago; now this section of the canal is merely a gulley containing small algae-covered ponds, reedy grasses, and water-loving birds like red-winged blackbirds and kingfishers.

Returning to Rock Run Preserve, you may want to linger a bit in the shade of the picnic pavilion while admiring the surrounding prairie. Perhaps your picnic basket needs some attention. Or you may want to take a short walk to the nearby banks of Rock Run Creek to look for green herons, ducks, and turtles.

MILES AND DIRECTIONS

0.0 Head north alongside Empress Road from the Rock Run Preserve.

0.9 Follow the trail as it runs left onto the campus of Joliet Junior College.

6.5 Leaving Rock Run Preserve, continue straight ahead on Ingalls Avenue for 0.5 mile. Traffic is minimal on Ingalls Avenue.

7.0 Return to the bike trail on the left, just after passing Pleasant Knoll Road.

13.5 The path ends at the corner of Mound Road and Larkin Avenue. Turn right onto Larkin Avenue and ride on the wide shoulder.

13.8 Just after crossing the I&M Canal and before reaching US 6, catch the trail on the right.

15.9 Return to the Rock Run Preserve parking area.

RIDE INFORMATION

Local Events/Attractions

Joliet Area Historical Museum: Offers a thorough introduction to the history of the Joliet area; 204 North Ottawa St., Joliet; (815) 723-5201; www.joliet museum.org.

Joliet-area rail trails: Three long rail trails can be accessed in Joliet; www
.reconnectwithnature.org.

Restaurants
Merichka's: Serving up American food since 1933; try the poor boy sandwich;
604 Theodore St., Crest Hill; (815) 723-9371.
A slew of fast-food joints pepper Houbolt Road on the short stretch between
I-80 and Joliet Junior College.

Restrooms
Start/finish: Restrooms and water are available at Rock Run Preserve on
Empress Drive.
Mile 5.2: Restrooms and water are available at Rock Run Preserve at Black
Road.

Maps
USGS 7.5" Plainfield quad
DeLorme: Illinois Atlas and Gazetteer: Pages 28 and 36

LaPorte Loop

Enjoy plenty of ups and downs along this route as you follow a series of nearly perfect cycling roads outside of LaPorte, Indiana. Take a break from the rolling—sometimes hilly—terrain as you follow the shoreline of a couple of lakes north of town. At Stone Lake, you may want to take a dip in the lake and then unpack the pannier for a picnic.

Start: Begin at Red Mill County Park, located 8 miles south of Michigan City in northwestern LaPorte County, Indiana

Length: 32.3 miles

Approximate riding time: 2.5 hours

Best bike: Road bike

Terrain: Small rolling hills dominate with occasional larger climbs mixed in. Some sections are fairly flat.

Traffic and hazards: Most of these roads are quiet; the busier roads, such as Johnson Road, tend to have a good-size shoulder for riding.

Things to see: Farms, quiet roads, parks, beaches, and small lakes

Getting there: From Chicago, head into Indiana on I-90 (the Skyway). Continue east on I-90 as it merges with I-80. Exit I-80/90 at US 421. Turn left (north) onto US 421, and then turn right 0.3 mile ahead onto Snyder Road. Nearly 1 mile ahead, turn left onto Holmesville Road. Enter Red Mill County Park immediately on the right. GPS coordinates: 41 36.238 N / 86 52.74 W

THE RIDE

Sometimes called "The City of Lakes," LaPorte, Indiana, is unusual for the many natural bodies of water clustered tightly together on the north side of the town. In addition to the scenic lakes and plenty of local parkland, LaPorte hosts a collection of large Victorian homes, an extensive local history museum, and a well-appointed courthouse in the center of town. Sound idyllic? Well, not always. On the north edge of LaPorte, you'll pass near a place where morbid events interrupted life in this peaceful town during the early years of the twentieth century.

Saddle up at Red Mill County Park and head into a rolling landscape that contains a smattering of lakes, ponds, and wetlands. Patches of woods come and go. The first Europeans settlers in the area named the area "LaPorte"—meaning "the door" in French—because it marked the transition from forest on the east to prairie on the west. The flat, former prairie takes over as you approach CR 500 West; getting closer to the city of LaPorte, the farmland gives way to lightly wooded residential neighborhoods.

Bike Shop

My Bike of Michigan City: 1801 Franklin St., Michigan City, Indiana; (219) 879-0899

As you enter the environs of Soldiers Memorial Park, branches of mature oak, hickory, and maple reach out overhead. Passing the boat ramp on the left, you'll ride mere yards from the shore as the road traces the south edge of Stone Lake. This mile or so stretch offers stellar views of the entire sparkling lake and the small wooded bluffs rising from the opposite shore.

The 550-acre park continues as the road snakes between Stone Lake on the left and the lily-pad-laden Soldiers Memorial Park Lake on the right. Hot weather may call for a pit stop at the pleasant beach and picnic area on the shore of Stone Lake. While enjoying the lake, keep an eye out for the rich variety of birds seen on the local waters. Loons often appear in April and May. Spring also brings ring-necked ducks, northern shovelers, and blue-winged teal. Throughout the summer, woodpeckers, kingfishers, and hawks (including the occasional osprey) loiter along the wooded shores.

On Waverly Road, you'll pull alongside Pine Lake, the largest and most residential of LaPorte's lakes. Pass a scattering of wetlands and plenty of homes as you take a trip up a small bluff for a big view of this lake.

Just on the other side of the next lake you'll encounter—Fishtrap Lake—was a farm where a gruesome story unfolded in the early twentieth century. No one knows the actual body count, but it's been pretty well established that over a period of several decades Belle Gunness killed her two husbands, a half-dozen or so children (some her own), and an estimated forty men who responded to her newspaper ads seeking well-heeled suitors. Gunness, a Norwegian immigrant, apparently killed her family members for insurance money. Her motivation for killing the suitors, however, was to steal their life savings. Typically, the suitors were poisoned or bludgeoned, and then buried on the McClung Road farm. In many cases, the bodies were dismembered and fed to her hogs. After apparently faking her own death, she disappeared and was never caught.

Once you leave the stomping grounds for this local serial killer behind, the bustle of LaPorte is quickly replaced by a rural landscape containing no shortage of scenic beauty. CR 100 West offers some gradual climbs, an equal number of downhills, and plenty of gently rolling terrain. Wooded areas appear frequently among the expanses of cropland.

After ducking under the Indiana Toll Road, the wavy profile of CR 450 North leads you through intermittent stretches of tree-sheltered passageways. Just after arriving on Schultz Road, the pavement begins a gradual slope downward for about 2 miles. While descending about 200 feet, you'll pass a steady progression of modest homes adorned with cheery yards. CR 850 West slowly takes you back to higher ground. The winding and rolling contours of Shebel Road present you with more miles of gratifying riding. The same goes for Holmesville Road, where you'll take a couple of brief dips down into wetlands before arriving back at Red Mill County Park where the ride began.

LaPorte possesses a handful of attractive lakes.

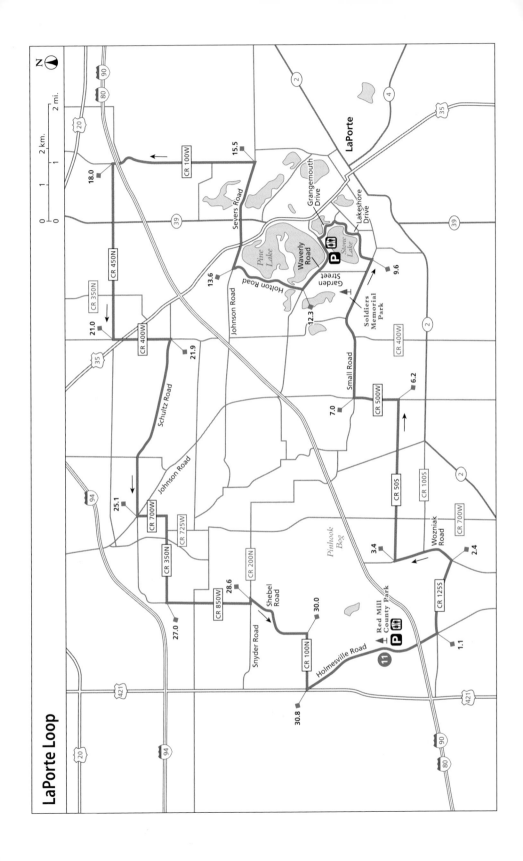

LaPorte Loop

MILES AND DIRECTIONS

0.0 From Red Mill County Park, turn left onto Holmesville Road.

1.1 Turn left onto CR West 125 South.

2.4 Turn left onto Wozniak Road.

3.4 Turn right onto CR 50 South.

6.2 Turn left onto CR South 500 West.

7.0 Turn right onto Small Road.

9.6 Turn left onto Lakeshore Drive and enter Soldiers Memorial Park.

10.8 Turn left onto Grangemouth Drive and cross the canal connecting two lakes.

11.3 Turn left onto Waverly Road.

12.3 Turn right onto Holton Road.

13.6 Turn right onto Johnson Road, which soon becomes Severs Road. This road is busier than the others but has a generous shoulder.

15.5 Turn left onto CR 100 West.

18.0 Turn left onto CR 450 North.

21.0 Turn left onto CR 400 West.

21.9 Turn right onto Schultz Road.

25.1 Use the traffic light to take a sharp left onto Johnson Road, and then immediately turn right onto CR 700 West. (This intersection was recently reconfigured—some local maps don't show the new configuration.) As CR 700 West curves to the right, it becomes CR 350 North.

27.0 Turn left onto CR 850 West.

28.6 Jog left onto CR 200 North, and then immediately turn right onto Shebel Road.

30.0 Turn right onto CR 100 North.

30.8 Take a sharp left onto Holmesville Road.

32.3 Turn left at the entrance to Red Mill County Park and arrive back where you began.

RIDE INFORMATION

Local Events/Attractions

LaPorte County Bikeway System: LaPorte, Indiana; (219) 325-8315; www .laportecountyparks.org/biking.html.

La Porte County Historical Society Museum: Extensive county museum; includes some items related to Belle Gunness; 2405 Indiana Ave., Suite 1, LaPorte, Indiana; (219) 324-6767; www.laportecountyhistory.org.

Restaurants

East Shore Of Pine Lake: Steak house with Italian food; 1110 Lakeside St., LaPorte, Indiana; (219) 362-5077; www.pleastshore.com.

Shoreline Brewery and Restaurant: 208 Wabash St., Michigan City, Indiana; (219) 879-4677; www.shorelinebrewery.com.

Restrooms

Start/finish: Red Mill County Park contains restrooms, water, and picnic shelters.
Mile 11.2: Soldiers Memorial Park contains restrooms and water fountains.

Maps

DeLorme: Indiana Atlas and Gazetteer: Pages 19 and 20
Northwest Indiana Bike Map, Northwest Indiana Regional Planning Commission; (219) 763-6060; www.nirpc.org
USGS 7.5" LaPorte West quad, USGS Michigan City East 7.5" quad, USGS 7.5" Springville quad

Oak Savannah/Prairie Duneland Trails

It's surprising that the Oak Savannah Trail and the Prairie Duneland Trail aren't better known in the region. Given the abundance of scenic spots that grab your attention and the generally quiet ambience along these trails, one would expect more cyclists saddling up here to enjoy the wetlands, parks, and plenty of wild and wooded terrain mixed in with patches of suburbia. At mile 7, you'll leave the trail and follow a 2.5-mile-long circuitous route along the quiet streets of Hobart.

Start: Start at the west end of the Oak Savannah Trail at Oak Ridge Prairie County Park on the border of Merrillville and Griffith, Indiana

Length: 19.7 miles one way

Approximate riding time: 2 hours

Best bike: Road or hybrid bike

Terrain and trail surface: The terrain is flat and wooded with patches of wetlands.

Traffic and hazards: At nearly all the road crossings, be prepared to navigate around heavy metal gates that block vehicle access to the trail. The trail either runs underneath or over nearly every major road along the way.

Things to see: Oak Ridge Prairie County Park, woods, prairie, wetland, suburban neighborhoods, Lake George, Hobart, and Chesterton

Getting there: Take I-90/94 south to the Chicago Skyway (I-90), exit 59A. At exit 10, take Gary Road to Highway 912 (Cline Avenue) and go south. Proceed along Cline Avenue to Ridge Road. Turn left onto Ridge Road and drive 1 mile to Colfax Street, where you'll turn right. The entrance to the park is 2.2 miles ahead on the left. Whenever the Oak Ridge Prairie County Park gatekeeper is on duty, a small parking fee is charged for vehicles. Call (219) 769-7275 for more information. The Oak Savannah Trail begins between the restrooms and the fishing pond. GPS coordinates: 41 31.009 N / 87 23.617 W

To park at John Robinson Park, take I-65 south to Ridge Road (US 6). Head east on US 6 and then turn right onto Liverpool Road. The park is on the right as the trail crosses the road. To reach the parking area on the east side of Hobart, head south on Highway 51 from I-80/94. Look for the parking area on the left just before Cleveland Avenue. To park at the McCool Road parking area, head south on Highway 149 from US 20. Turn right onto Lenburg Road and then left onto McCool Road. The parking area is on the right. To park at the east end of the Prairie Duneland Trail, head south on Highway 49 from I-94. Turn right onto Boundary Road and then bear left onto Calumet Road. Turn right onto Broadway Avenue. Turn left onto Jackson Boulevard and look for the parking area on the left.

THE RIDE

As you follow the first half of this ride along the Oak Savannah Trail, you'll encounter wetlands, woods, and fetching views of Lake George outside of Hobart. In Hobart, the route guides you along 2.5 miles of quiet streets and through the downtown area before catching up with the rest of the trail. (In future years, Lake County expects to connect the trail gap in Hobart with a new section of trail.) The Porter County line marks the beginning of the 9-mile-long Prairie Duneland Trail that shoots straight toward Chesterton.

The 700-acre Oak Ridge Prairie County Park, where this ride begins, contains a mix of woodland, marshes, and prairie. But the park's main attraction is the fishing pond. You'll likely pass a few anglers casting their lines and waiting on the shore of the pond as a squiggly trail leads you through a picturesque oak woodland. Keep your head low as the trail comes remarkably close to the east end of the 4,900-foot runway at the Griffith-Merrillville Airport. During the warmer months, this single-runway airport is used by small, banner-toting planes that fly up and down Chicago's lakefront.

During the first couple of miles, the trail passes a large gravel mining operation and then dips into a wooded area dotted with marshes and small ponds. After soaring 50 feet over Highway 55 on an arched trail bridge, the trail loses some luster due to the amount of trash strewn about.

As the trail tidies up, you'll pass a lengthy string of backyards attached to modest suburban homes. Yard gawkers will enjoy the excellent vantage point from

Bike Shop

Trek Bicycle Store: Located a few miles south of Oak Ridge Prairie Park, 651 East US 30, Schererville, Indiana; (219) 322-2453; www.trekbikestore.com

A steel bridge allows cyclists to bypass a busy highway on the Oak Savannah Trail.

the raised railroad embankment. After emerging from the dimly lit tunnel under I-65, you'll pedal past the postage-stamp-size John Robinson Park and Robinson Lake.

Two miles before Hobart, the landscape suddenly starts to dip and rise every which way. These wooded ravines seem far removed from the nearby suburban sprawl. After crossing a small, winding creek, the trail mounts an embankment separating two arms of Lake George. From the 40-foot-high embankment above the water, you'll enjoy expansive views of this lake created by the damming of the Deep River. To the south, cattails and lily pads fringe the open water; to the north, gentle wooded bluffs border a large swath of open water.

As you start on the intricate route through Hobart's quiet city streets, keep an eye peeled for Lake George as it plays peek-a-boo: The 2-mile-long lake sprawls through much of Hobart. On the way through town, Lakeview Park offers an inviting rest stop, as does the waterfront park in downtown Hobart.

After picking up the trail on east side of Hobart, you'll encounter a pleasant mix of cropland, residential areas, patches of woodland, and small marshes. A small creek winds along the south side of the trail after crossing County Line Road (County Line Road marks the beginning of the Prairie Duneland Trail).

East of US 6, you'll arrive at Countryside Park, containing a small museum and a historic farmstead. The museum focuses on the history of Portage, Indiana, with items such as a spiffy fire truck from the 1920s, a miniature replica of the historic village, and local Native American artifacts. On one side of the museum is a sledding hill; a fishing pond sits on the other.

Residential developments come and go for the next few miles following Countryside Park. Not long after passing under I-80, the trail awkwardly crosses a railroad line and then mounts an arched trail bridge over Highway 149. Following Highway 149, the Iron Horse Heritage Trail spurs to the north, offering quick access to the 256-acre Imagination Glen Park.

Dense woodland lines the trail for the final few miles to its endpoint next to a new skate park at the outskirts of Chesterton. Since you've come this far, don't pass up a visit to downtown Chesterton. The 0.5-mile trip will take you past local attractions such as the Red Cup Café and Deli, the Butler Winery, and the Chesterton Art Center. After browsing the shops on the main strip, a small downtown park offers a perfect spot to take a break before returning to your starting point at Oak Ridge Prairie County Park.

MILES AND DIRECTIONS

0.0 Catch the Oak Savannah Trail from the northeast corner of the parking area at Oak Ridge Prairie County Park.

6.9 Where the Oak Savannah Trail ends, turn left at Wisconsin Street.

7.0 Turn right onto Eighth Street.

7.8 Turn left onto Water Street. Follow the curve right as Water Street becomes Sixth Street. Then follow the curve left as Sixth Street becomes Center Street.

8.5 Turn right on Third Street. (Check out Hobart's downtown strip and its lakefront park by turning left onto Third Street and continuing ahead for 2 blocks.)

8.8 Take a soft left turn onto Illinois Street.

9.0 Get ready for a short obstacle course: After crossing the train tracks, turn right onto Lillian Street, immediately turn left onto Indiana Street, and then turn right again onto Devonshire Street.

9.2 At the end of Devonshire Street, turn left onto Liberty Place.

9.3 Turn right onto Cleveland Avenue. Use caution: Cleveland Avenue will be busy.

9.4 Catch the next segment of the Oak Savannah Trail at the northeast corner of Cleveland Avenue and Highway 130 (Hobart Road).

19.7 Arrive at the end of the trail. **Option:** You may want to a take trip to downtown Chesterton by turning left onto Jackson Boulevard and then turning right onto Broadway Street. The downtown area is about 0.5 mile ahead.

RIDE INFORMATION

Local Events/Attractions

Butler Winery Chesterton: Tasting room and wine for sale from locally grown grapes; 401 Broadway, Chesterton, Indiana; (219) 929-1400; www.butlerwinery .com/chesterton.html.

Chesterton Art Center: Has regular gallery exhibits; 115 South Fourth St., Chesterton, Indiana; (219) 926-4711; www.chestertonart.com.

Oak Savannah/Prairie Duneland Trails

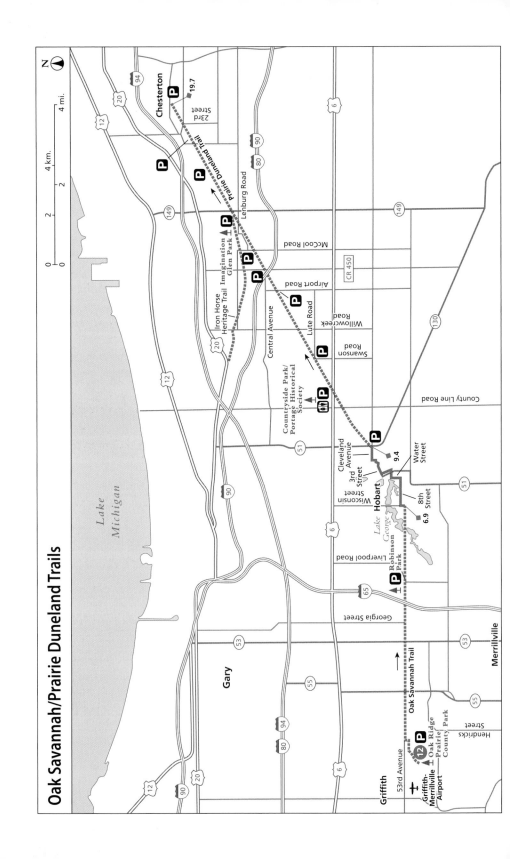

Portage Historical Society: Operates a small museum at Countryside Park; open April to mid-November, Wednesday, Friday, and Saturday, 11:00 a.m. to 3:00 p.m.; 5250 US 6, Portage, Indiana; (219) 762-8349 or (219) 762-1675.

Restaurants

Red Cup Café and Deli: Nice selection of homemade pies and deli sandwiches; located between the east end of the Prairie Duneland Trail and downtown Chesterton; 520 Broadway, Chesterton, Indiana; (219) 929-1804.

Tate's Place: Diner food; outdoor patio overlooking the trail; 3051 Willowcreek Rd., Portage, Indiana; (219) 764-8283.

Restrooms

Start: Water and restrooms are available at Oak Ridge Prairie County Park.

Mile 5.0: Restrooms are available at John Robinson Park.

Mile 11.2: Restrooms are available at Countryside Park near the historic homestead.

Maps

DeLorme: Indiana Atlas and Gazetteer: Pages 18 and 19

Northwest Indiana Bike Map, Northwest Indiana Regional Planning Commission; (219) 763-6060; www.nirpc.org

USGS 7.5" Chesterton quad, USGS 7.5" Gary quad, USGS Portage 7.5" quad

Old Plank Road Trail

This long suburban trail offers a surprising array of scenic spots. You'll see cattail-fringed ponds, patches of prairie, numerous parks, and small suburban towns with quiet, wooded neighborhoods. At about the halfway point you'll take a side trail through Hickory Creek Forest Preserve, where the route bounds over wooded hills and makes a couple of crossings of Hickory Creek. In the town of Frankfort, check out the historic architecture and the interesting shops before investigating several good dining options.

Start: At Logan Park in Park Forest at the corner of Orchard Drive and North Street

Length: 26.5 miles one way

Approximate riding time: 2.5 hours

Best bike: Road or hybrid bike

Terrain and trail surface: The trail is flat and paved.

Traffic and hazards: Watch for traffic at the numerous road crossings.

Things to see: Frankfort's historic downtown, woods, grassy parks, and wetland

Wheelchair access: The trail is wheelchair accessible; some parking areas are surfaced with gravel.

Hazards: A handful of the road crossings have heavy traffic.

Getting there: By car: Heading south of Chicago on I-57, get off at exit 340A and head east on US 30 (Lincoln Highway). After passing US 54, turn right onto Orchard Drive and then right onto North Street. Park at Logan Park on the right. GPS coordinates: 41 29.91 N / 87 41.067 W

To reach the parking area in Matteson, head east on US 30 from I-57. Turn right onto Main Street and right again onto 215th Street. The parking area is on the right.

Parking is available in the northeast corner of the Target store parking lot on Cicero Avenue. From I-57 drive east on US 30 and turn right onto Cicero Avenue.

To park in Frankfort, head west from I-57 on US 30. Turn left onto La Grange Road (US 45) and left again onto White Street. Turn right onto Kansas Street and park in the lot on the right.

To park at Hickory Creek Junction, drive east on US 30 from I-80. The parking area is on the left.

To reach the Lions Den Park parking area, take I-80 to US 30. Head east on US 30 and turn right onto Cedar Road. Continue south after making a slight jog to the left. Lions Den Park is on the left.

By public transportation: The Matteson station on Metra's Electric District Line is located right on the trail, not far from the eastern terminus. The Rock Island District Metra stops about 6 blocks north of the trail in New Lenox.

THE RIDE

The Old Plank Road Trail was never actually a plank road. A plank road is a dirt road covered with a series of planks, similar to wooden sidewalks seen in Western films. During the first half of the nineteenth century, when plank roads were wildly popular in the Northeast and Midwest, a plank road was slated to be built along this stretch of landscape between Joliet and the Indiana border. But railroads began to boom, so train tracks were laid down instead. Finished in 1855, the rail line was called the Joliet Cutoff because it allowed trains to avoid going through Chicago. The Joliet Cutoff served as one of the first rail connections between Illinois and East Coast cities like Boston and New York.

During the early years of the twentieth century, the railroad right-of-way also was home to an interurban trolley line. While on the trail, look for Michigan Central Railroad concrete mile markers still in place. Etched with the letters EG, the markers likely refer to East Gary, the dividing point on this section of the railroad.

Heading west on the Old Plank Road Trail from the starting point at Logan Park, the first section of the trail runs through the downtown area of Matteson, by a couple of parks, and through some scenic wetlands that sit behind a sprawling shopping mall. In Matteson the Metra station on the left and the red caboose permanently parked alongside the trail both point to the town's rich rail history. After passing Governors Trail Park, you'll see the first trail that branches off from Old Plank Road Trail. This is Preservation Trail, which heads north for 1.5 miles to Oakwood Park on the north side of Matteson. Continuing ahead on the Old Plank Road Trail, you'll squeeze between the backside of the huge Lincoln Mall on one side and a series of wild-looking ponds and wetlands on the other. You'll see more of these startling juxtapositions between the wild and the urbanized before the route is done.

Across Cicero Avenue, patches of prairie show up on the edges of the trail. One motivating factor for establishing this trail was the variety of prairie plants growing in the vicinity. Only a couple decades after the first settlers arrived in Will and Cook Counties, agencies began buying property for this right-of-way. As a result, plows never touched much of the land alongside the trail. Of the 200 types of prairie plants identified along the trail, you'll find not only such common species as goldenrod, compass plant, shooting star, and butterfly weed but also rarer specimens like scurfy pea, prairie lily, savanna blazing star, and silky aster. Pockets of prairie appear scattered along the trail between Cicero Avenue west all the way to New Lennox. Most, however, are located on the mile-long stretch between Cicero and Central Avenues, even under I-57.

Bike Rentals

The Wheel Thing: 15 South La Grange Rd., La Grange; (708) 352-3822

Like other spots along this trail, the twelve-acre Dewey Helmick Nature Preserve offers a surprising patch of wildness within a thoroughly built-up landscape. West of Central Avenue the trail traverses a thin strip of land that cuts through the middle of a big pond. On the left, watch for great blue herons standing like statues on the shore of a small wooded island; on the right, a cattail-fringed pond contains a graveyard of still-standing dead trees. Refocusing your eyes beyond the edges of this small wetland reveals dense housing subdivisions blanketing the surrounding landscape.

After crossing Harlem Avenue, the trail gradually descends through a leafy landscape thick with elm, hickory, and maple—it's one of several stretches of trail that deserve a visit during fall color displays. Before entering Frankfort you'll pass a couple of small parks, including Prairie Park, which is primarily a wetland that the town uses to clean and recycle its stormwater runoff. In Frankfort, the first landmarks that come into view are the grain elevator, a trailside park, and a handsome iron sign for Old Plank Road Trail above the trail. Frankfort requires some exploration: A number of well-kept old buildings with interesting shops sit within the compact downtown area. Just south of the trail on White Street, stop in at the trolley barn, a building that once housed the trolleys that operated on the trail. Now it contains an ice-cream shop, a deli, a comic book store, and a coffee shop, as well as displays about the interurban trains and trolleys that ran through Frankfort at the beginning of the twentieth century.

During summer, a farmers' market sets up shop along the Old Plank Road Trail in Frankfort.

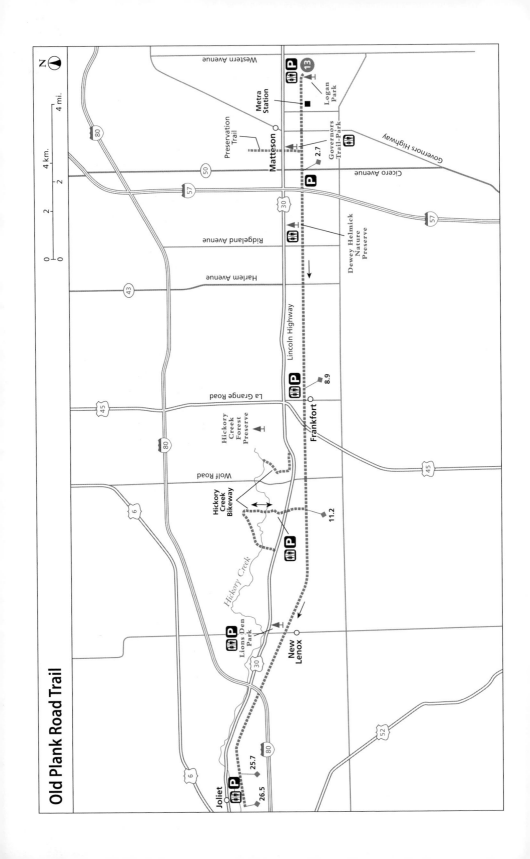

Old Plank Road Trail

West of Frankfort the trail mounts the appropriately named Arrowhead Bridge over La Grange Road. The bridge boasts an unusual design, with a pair of legs that straddle the highway and suspend the walkway with a series of four cables coming from the center of the joined struts. The struts come together at the top like the point of an arrowhead. Before the bridge, the trail passes plantings of ash trees, witch hazel, and pine; just after the bridge, Elsner Road provides access north to the Hickory Creek Bikeway East Branch.

Nearly 2 miles ahead, don't miss the turnoff for Hickory Creek Junction. After crossing the pedestrian bridge, the path leads you through a picnic area at Hickory Creek Forest Preserve and through its groves of hickory and oak. While following the West Branch of the Hickory Bikeway, you'll cross Hickory Creek twice on the 3.3-mile trip to the trail's endpoint. Once you've reached the one-room schoolhouse museum at the end of the trail, turn around and retrace your path back to the Old Plank Road Trail.

Much of the final 7.5 miles of trail runs through the community of New Lenox. After crossing Spencer Road, the Old Plank Road Trail intersects a 1-mile-long paved trail leading to the local high school. Farther ahead on the Old Plank Road Trail are the New Lenox Village Hall, library, and police department. Residential areas come and go. Many of the home owners' backyards mingle with the path—no fences or shrubbery separate people's backyards from the path. Shortly after brushing against the backside of the sports stadium at Providence High School, you'll arrive at the end of the trail at Washington Street.

MILES AND DIRECTIONS

0.0 Start at Logan Park by heading west on the trail.

2.7 Cross Cicero Avenue/IL 50.

8.9 Pass through Frankfort.

11.2 Turn right for an out-and-back side trip through Hickory Creek Forest Preserve. Once you've reached the end of the trail within Hickory Creek, retrace your path back to the Old Plank Road Trail.

18.2 Back at the Old Plank Road Trail, turn right to continue on the path.

26.5 Arrive at the end of the trail at Washington Street in Joliet.

RIDE INFORMATION

Local Events/Attractions
Frankfort Country Market: Sunday farmers' market operates along the trail; www.frankfortcountrymarket.org.

Joliet Area Historical Museum: Provides a thorough introduction to the Joliet area; 204 North Ottawa St., Joliet; (815) 723-5201; www.jolietmuseum .org.

Joliet-area rail trails: Three other long rail trails can be accessed in Joliet; get route advice for on-street connections at www.oprt.org/maps/westcon.html.

Restaurants
Francesca's Fortunato: Northern Italian fine dining; part of the popular chain of Francesca restaurants that began with the original Mia Francesca in Chicago's Lakeview neighborhood; 40 Kansas St., Frankfort; (815) 464-1890; www .miafrancesca.com/restaurants/fortunato.

Frankfort Deli and Meats: Offers sandwiches and homemade soups; located in the trolley barn just south of the trail; 11 South White St., Frankfort; (815) 469-1145.

Restrooms
Start: There are public restrooms and water at the Logan Park trailhead.

Mile 2.3: Governors Trail Park has water and restrooms.

Mile 4.8: You'll find a portable toilet next to the trail at Ridgeland Avenue.

Mile 9.1: Public restrooms and water are available in Frankfort.

Mile 11.5: Hickory Creek Forest Preserve has restrooms and water.

Mile 26.7: The trail's western terminus at Washington Street has restrooms and water.

Maps
USGS Steger, Frankfort, Manhattan, Mokena, and Joliet
DeLorme: Illinois Atlas and Gazetteer: Pages 28, 36, and 37
Old Plank Road Trail Management Commission online map, www.oprt.org

Southwest Michigan Loop

It's easy to understand why the Apple Cider Century attracts some 7,000 bicyclists every year: Quiet roads, vineyards, rolling terrain, the primo beaches, and the pleasant little towns offer some of the most scenic and enjoyable riding in the region. This ride follows much of this classic Midwestern riding route through the lovely landscape of far southwestern Michigan.

Start: Start in the small town of Three Oaks at the corner of Oak Street and Pulaski Highway (US 12)

Length: 67.7 miles

Approximate riding time: 4–5 hours

Best bike: Road bike

Terrain: Mostly rolling and occasionally hilly with plenty of flat sections

Traffic and hazards: Nearly all these roads are very quiet. You'll encounter traffic in New Buffalo, but it's slow moving. At mile 46.5, you'll encounter 0.25 mile of roadway with gravel surface.

Things to see: Small lakes, wetland, lush woods, farmland, streams, small towns, beach, the lakeshore, and vineyards

Getting there: From Chicago, take I-94 into Michigan. A few miles north of the Indiana/Michigan border, exit on US 12 and head east. In the town of Three Oaks, turn left onto Oak Street. Park in one of the spots on the left in front of the small park. GPS coordinates: 41 47.959 N / 86 36.572 W

THE RIDE

Every September since the early 1970s, cyclists throughout the region have descended on Three Oaks, Michigan, for one of the largest single-day rides in the Midwest. The Apple Cider Century is known for its pastoral environs and rolling terrain. There are orchards, vineyards, and plenty of woodland. You'll see Lake Michigan shoreline and two vibrant little towns. The ride described here shadows much of the Apple Cider Century as it heads north from Three

Oaks, angles toward Lake Michigan, and then passes through New Buffalo before dipping down into Indiana on the return trip.

Three Oaks, where the ride begins, is a small rural town unusual for its downtown strip peppered with art galleries, good restaurants, and interesting shops. There's a movie theater, an ice-cream parlor, and a bakery. A local man put the town on the map in the 1880s when he established a technique for using turkey feather quills as stiffeners in women's garments such as corsets. This replacement for whalebone material was welcomed by the garment industry of the late nineteenth century, and, as a result, the Warren Featherbone Company soared, eventually expanding to other products in the fashion and sewing industries.

After leaving Three Oaks, the first 10 miles of the ride send you through flat farmland where long, wide views of cultivated terrain are occasionally interrupted by patches of woods. In September and October along Warren Woods Road, you'll pass Dinges' Fall Harvest—part farm stand and part kiddie theme park. Farther out on Warren Woods Road, the landscape transforms from flat to rolling to hilly. Climb an 80-foot hill and then whiz downward. As the landscape dips and rises through groves of walnut trees, you may catch glimpses of a couple small lakes near the road.

Soon the route starts heading north on a series of utterly perfect cycling roads—quiet and winding and scenic. Within this heavily textured landscape, watch for a stately brick farmhouse or two, an abandoned wooden church, and sprawling wetlands alongside Madron Lake Road. Continuing north, the vineyards multiply. At 19.4 miles, Round Barn Winery offers an opportunity to treat your palette to a selection of reds and whites, fruit and dessert wines, and beer brewed on-site (thankfully, food is also available in the tasting room to help soak up the alcohol).

On Snow Road the landscape flattens again, permitting long views of the surrounding agricultural fields. Rural homes are sprinkled within the cropland, vineyards, and patches of woods. By now you'll have noticed that the county has established a series of color-coded bike routes along many of these roads. Posted signs remind drivers they have cyclists in their midst.

Just before turning off from Browntown Road, you'll have an opportunity to visit one of the best beaches on the south shore of Lake Michigan. If time permits, Warren Dunes State Park shouldn't be missed: Its lovely beach and monster sand dunes make it a popular summer destination. Tower Hill, located next to the parking area, is a favorite dune to climb. Once at the top, the only reasonable choice is to run, roll, or tumble back down. Standing 240 feet above the surface of the lake, Tower Hill is also a popular spot for sand boarding (check YouTube). While the park does get busy, quiet spots are easily found along the park's 2.5-mile-long beach.

Expect plenty of big trees and lush greenery while pedaling the Southwest Michigan Loop.

Continuing south on Flynn Road, you'll zoom downward toward a swath of wetlands and cross the winding route of the Galien River. On Warren Woods Road, cross the Galien River again as it flows into the lush woodland at Warren Woods State Park, home to the last mature beech-maple forest in southern Michigan. The towering maple and hickory trees on the side of the road lead the way to another attractive park, Chikaming Township Park and Preserve, which appears on the left before crossing I-94. The terrain mellows the closer you get to Lake Michigan.

After crossing I-94, the larger houses and landscaped lawns signal that the big lake is near. On Lakeshore Road, you'll smell the wet air carried by a light breeze as flashes of the big blue yonder peek out between the houses and rental cottages. After turning onto Marquette Drive, you'll enter the old resort community of Sturgeon Beach. These lakeside homes offer a mix of both the gaudy and the elegant; several stone houses will likely catch your eye.

Bike Shop

Outpost Sports: Bike supplies and rentals; 105 West Buffalo St., New Buffalo, Michigan; (269) 469-4210; www.outpostsports.com

Marquette Drive drops you off at the entrance to New Buffalo Beach—another fine spot for local lollygagging. If taking a break on the sandy beach seems like a bother, there's a picnic shelter in the small park across the road from the beach. On the way into downtown New Buffalo, you'll pass acres of boats moored in the marinas on each side of the road. This is also where you'll make your third crossing of the Galien River—this time at its final destination just before it empties into Lake Michigan.

Consider hopping off the saddle for leg stretching in the compact downtown area of New Buffalo. If you can't be enticed by the ice-cream parlor, the chocolate shop, the hot dog stand, or the full complement of watering holes, I'm afraid you're out of luck.

Indiana arrives during a straight and flat journey for 5 miles on CR West 1000 North. Small farms and patches of woodland occasionally rise up from a landscape largely covered with crops. Just before turning onto CR North 125 East, you'll pass the Hesston Steam Museum, a local attraction since the 1950s. On the grounds is a steam locomotive that travels on 2.5 miles of tracks, a couple of kiddie trains, and other steam-powered machinery, such as a sawmill and a crane.

The route becomes more varied and scenic as you trace the 10-mile-long lobe that dips into Indiana. You'll cross a couple of creeks, cruise through dense stands of woods, and brush up against ponds and wetlands. On CR 700 North, a big climb is followed by a long, gradual descent underneath gnarled arms of oak trees reaching over the road. In some spots along this part of the ride, the road dips, rises, and rolls as it shifts every which way. Variations of this theme continue as you head back toward Three Oaks on Fail Road and CR East 1000 North. A couple more climbs will ensure that you're thoroughly exhausted before returning to the residential streets of Three Oaks.

MILES AND DIRECTIONS

0.0 From the corner of Pulaski Highway (US 12) and Oak Street in Three Oaks, head north on Oak Street and follow it as it curves left.

0.1 At Elm Street, turn right and proceed through Three Oaks' downtown strip.

1.0 Turn right onto Kruger Road.

3.4 Turn left onto Mill Road.

5.5 Turn right onto Warren Woods Road.

12.3 Turn left onto Clear Lake Road.

12.8 Turn right onto Wagner Road. Take note of the abandoned wooden church on the left.

13.7 Turn left onto Madron Lake Road. Stay on Madron Lake Road as it curves around.

17.4 Turn left onto Glendora Road.

17.8 Turn right onto Hills Road.

20.8 Turn left onto Snow Road. Follow Snow Road as it curves to the left near I-94.

28.2 Turn right onto Browntown Road. **Side trip:** To visit Warren Dunes State Park, keep straight ahead on Browntown Road instead of turning left onto Flynn Road. When you reach the Red Arrow Highway, turn right (be careful of traffic during the brief stretch on the Red Arrow). The

Southwest Michigan Loop

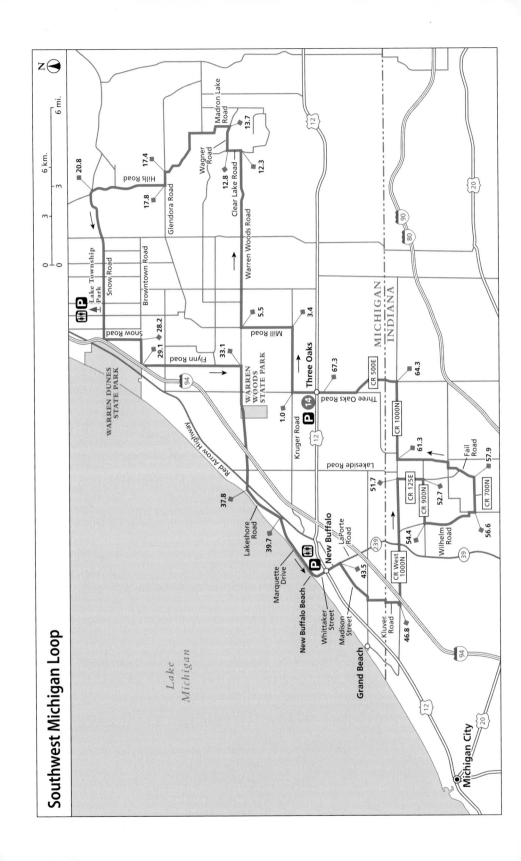

entrance to the park is just ahead on the left. The total distance is less than 1 mile to the park.

29.1 Turn left onto Flynn Road just before crossing over I-94. No road sign at the junction with Flynn Road, but it should be clear.

33.1 Turn right onto Warren Woods Road.

37.8 At the Red Arrow Highway, take a slight jog left and then continue ahead on Warren Woods Road. At the first junction, turn left onto Lakeshore Road. (The junction is not identified with signs.)

39.2 To visit a quiet beach located just a few hundred yards off the route, turn right onto Townline Road.

39.7 Turn right onto Marquette Drive. Ignore the signs indicating that the road has no outlet and that it is a private drive. Stay on Marquette Drive as it curves left and becomes Whittaker Street before hitting downtown New Buffalo.

43.5 Turn right onto Madison Street. Keep straight ahead as Madison turns into Stromer Road.

45.3 Turn right onto Wilson Road.

45.4 Turn left onto Kluver Road. Continue ahead as Kluver Road becomes CR 350 West. Expect to encounter a short stretch of gravel road.

46.8 Turn left onto CR West 1000 North.

51.7 Turn right onto CR North 125 East.

52.7 Turn right onto CR 900 North.

54.4 Turn left onto Wilhelm Road.

56.3 When Wilhelm Road forks, go left. Right away at the junction with Range Road, turn right.

56.6 Turn left onto CR 700 North.

57.9 Turn left onto Fail Road.

61.3 Turn right onto CR East 1000 North.

64.3 Turn left onto CR North 500 East. As you return to Michigan, this road becomes Three Oaks Road. Stay on Three Oaks Road as it curves to the left.

67.3 Turn right onto Michigan Street East and then take an immediate left onto Oak Street.

67.7 Return to the starting point at Oak Street and Pulaski Highway.

RIDE INFORMATION

Local Events/Attractions

Backroads Bikeway: Fourteen routes on paved area roads, with lengths from 5 to 60 miles; www.applecidercentury.com/trails/backroad.htm.

Lake Michigan Shore Wine Trail: Eight wineries and tasting rooms are in the vicinity of this route; www.miwinetrail.com.

Apple Cider Century: At the end of September; starts and ends in Three Oaks; seven different mileage options ranging from 15 to 100 miles; (888) 877-2068; www.applecidercentury.com.

Dinges' Fall Harvest: September and October; pumpkins, gourds, and grapes; games and rides for kids; 15219 Mill Rd., Three Oaks, Michigan; (269) 426-4034.

Hesston Steam Museum: An impressive collection of railroad steam engines, 1201 East 1000 North, LaPorte, Indiana; (219)-872-5055; www.hesston.org.

The Round Barn Winery, Distillery, and Brewery: Nice selection of wines and several beers; 10983 Hills Rd., Baroda, Michigan; (800) 716-9463; www.roundbarnwinery.com.

Warren Dunes State Park: Offers more than 200 campsites; 12032 Red Arrow Hwy., Sawyer, Michigan; (269) 426-4013; www.michigandnr.com/Parks andTrails.

Restaurants

Elm Street Bistro: Great local dining spot right on route; 8 South Elm St., Three Oaks, Michigan; (269) 756-9274; www.elmstreetbistro.com.

Froehlich's: Baked goods as well as jams and other canned items; 26 North Elm St., Three Oaks, Michigan; (269) 756-6002; www.shopfroehlichs.com.

Restrooms

Start/finish: Restrooms and water can be found within a gas station and several restaurants in Three Oaks.

Mile 25.4: Lake Township Park has restrooms, water fountains, and picnicking facilities. It's on the corner of Snow and Gast Roads.

Mile 36.4: Chikaming Township Park and Preserve has restrooms and a picnic shelter.

Mile 42.5: Restrooms, water, and concessions are available at the New Buffalo Beach. Bicyclists and pedestrians can enter the park for free.

Maps

DeLorme: Michigan Atlas and Gazetteer: Pages 18 and 19

Southwestern Michigan Bicycle Map, Michigan Department of Transportation; (517) 373-2090; www.michigan.gov/mdot

USGS 7.5" Galien, Michigan quad; USGS New Buffalo East, Michigan 7.5" quad; USGS New Buffalo West, Michigan 7.5" quad; USGS Springville, Indiana 7.5" quad; USGS Three Oaks, Michigan 7.5" quad

Valparaiso Loop

Barns. Cow pastures. Gently rolling farmland. Streams. Patches of woods. Shake the accumulated stress of daily life as you work the pedals along these quiet rural roads south of Valparaiso, Indiana. Along the way, you'll get an introduction to a couple subtle—but significant—local landforms.

Start: Boone Grove Elementary/Middle School, located about 20 miles southeast of Gary, Indiana

Length: 26.6 miles

Approximate riding time: 2.5 hours

Best bike: Road or hybrid bike

Terrain: A mix of gently rolling and flat roads. A few small hills appear on the northern side of the route.

Traffic and hazards: These roads are very quiet. A bit more traffic appears along Division Road.

Things to see: Barns, open farmland, quiet farm roads, streams, and patches of woodland

Getting there: Take I-90 southwest to I-65. Go south on I-65 to US 231 (Highway 53). In Hebron, turn left onto Highway 8 (Sigler Street). Several miles ahead, turn left onto CR South 400 West. Proceed another few miles and then turn right onto CR West 550 South. Park at one of the roadside parking spaces alongside Boone Grove Elementary/Middle School (CR 550 South). GPS coordinates: 41 21 303 N / 87 7.644 W

THE RIDE

Like most of the Midwestern landscape, the terrain of the Chicago area was shaped by glaciers on the move. Besides Lake Michigan, the most significant glacial legacy in the Chicago area is the Valparaiso Moraine, a huge band of rolling and hilly terrain containing a mix of sand, dirt, small rocks, and occasional larger rocks. This glacial till, as it's called, was picked up and dropped off as the glacier advanced and then retreated about 16,000 years ago. Fanning out along the whole southern shore of Lake Michigan, the moraine sometimes reaches a height of 300 feet and a width of 20 miles. The moraine was named after Valparaiso, Indiana, because the city marks the highest and narrowest point of the moraine.

Setting out on this ride from the microscopic village of Boone Grove, the landscape starts flat but soon develops some gentle rolls as you get closer to Valparaiso Moraine territory. Pass a little nature preserve and then curve right on CR 250 West as it passes through a wooded grove and then crosses a stream called the Ludington Ditch. Getting farther into the moraine on CR 200 West, long views open up and the terrain starts to roll gently. The waves in the landscape become more distinct after passing the next creek up the road. Near the turn onto Division Road, a few small subdivisions offer the reminder that civilization is not far away.

The quiet farm roads south of Valparaiso offer a peaceful atmosphere.

After attending to a few minor hills on Division Road, the route turns onto a scenic stretch of South Sager Road, where wetlands appear on each side of you and stately walnut trees hang overhead. CR 150 East takes you on a straight, gently rolling trajectory into an agricultural checkerboard that spreads out in every direction. Streams and patches of woods come and go. When the landscape looks like a tabletop, you'll know that you've left the Valparaiso Moraine behind and have entered the former basin of the Grand Kankakee Marsh.

Bike Shop

Buck's Bike Shop: 610 Silhavy Road, Valparaiso, Indiana; (219) 462-3411 or (800) 863-6593; www.bucksbikeshop.com

At one time, the Kankakee River made 2,000 bends as it traveled west from its source near South Bend, Indiana, to the Illinois state line. The slow-moving river meandered through what was once the largest freshwater wetland in the nation, encompassing some 500,000 acres. Known as the Grand Kankakee Marsh, it was roughly 75 miles long and 30 miles wide, and famous throughout the Midwest for its abundance of wildlife. As population grew in the area, efforts to convert the massive marsh into farmland prevailed.

The Kankakee River was straightened and the enormous marshland was drained through an elaborate system of ditches. The newly claimed farmland proved to be extremely fertile. Now, only small patches of the marsh remain. While pedaling along CR East 900 South, you'll cross over a couple of the ditches that helped drain the wetlands into the Kankakee River, located 1 mile south.

Because the landscape is so flat, the big red barn adorned with the lettered advertisement is visible from some distance while pedaling on CR 750 South. The sign, which reads SEE 7 STATES FROM ROCK CITY, harkens back to an early twentieth-century advertising campaign to promote Rock City Gardens, a tourist attraction of rock formations near Chattanooga, Tennessee. After the attraction opened in 1932, the owners hired a sign painter to hit the road and offer to paint farmers' barns in exchange for including a Rock City ad on the barn. Over the next thirty years, the painter brushed lettering on some 900 roadside barns as far away as Michigan, Florida, and Texas.

With no major roads close to this barn, it seems an odd place to promote a tourist trap some 550 miles away. Well, this barn wasn't one of the original barns to display a Rock City ad, but was painted in 2007 at the request of its owner, who grew up near Rock City and liked the idea of this reminder of his childhood years (visit www.seerockcity.com for photos of dozens of original "See Rock City" barns). As you're passing by the Rock City barn, notice the Hoosier Homestead Farm sign in front of the farmhouse, commemorating the fact that this farm has been in the same family since 1840—eight generations, they say.

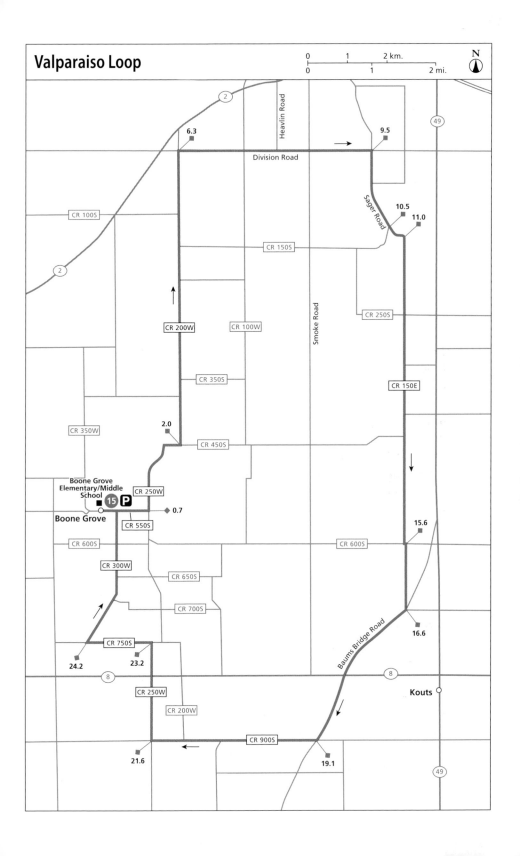

Valparaiso Loop

0 1 2 km.
0 1 2 mi.

N

2

Heavlin Road

6.3

9.5

49

Division Road

CR 100S

Sager Road

10.5

11.0

2

CR 150S

Smoke Road

CR 250S

CR 200W

CR 100W

CR 150E

CR 350S

CR 350W

2.0

CR 450S

Boone Grove
Elementary/Middle
School

CR 250W

15 P

0.7

Boone Grove

CR 550S

15.6

CR 600S

CR 600S

CR 300W

CR 650S

CR 700S

Baums Bridge Road

16.6

CR 750S

24.2

23.2

8

8

Kouts

CR 250W

CR 200W

CR 900S

21.6

19.1

49

A few miles of enjoyable riding through lightly rolling terrain bring you back to Boone Grove, where the ride began.

MILES AND DIRECTIONS

0.0 From the Boone Grove Elementary/Middle School, head to the left on CR 550 South.

0.7 Turn left onto CR 250 West. As this road curves to the right, it becomes CR West 450 South.

2.0 Turn left onto CR 200 West.

6.3 Turn right onto Division Road.

9.5 Turn right onto Sager Road.

10.5 Turn left onto CR East 125 South.

11.0 Turn right onto CR 150 East.

15.6 Jog left onto CR 600 South, and then immediately turn right to resume your southbound course on CR 150 East.

16.6 Turn right onto Baums Bridge Road.

19.1 Turn right onto CR 900 South.

21.6 Turn right onto CR 250 West.

23.2 Turn left onto CR 750 South.

24.2 Turn right onto CR 300 West.

26.3 Turn left onto CR 550 South.

26.6 Return to the Boone Grove Elementary/Middle School, where the ride began.

RIDE INFORMATION

Local Events/Attractions

Indiana Dunes National Lakeshore's Dorothy Buell Memorial Visitor Center: 1420 Munson Rd. (Highway 49 between I-94 and US 20); (219) 926-7561, ext. 3; www.nps.gov/indu.

Indiana Dunes State Park: Highway 49 north of US 12, Chesterton, Indiana; (219) 926-1952; www.dnr.in.gov.

Taltree Arboretum and Gardens: 71 North 500 West, Valparaiso, Indiana; (219) 462-0025; www.taltree.org.

Restaurants
Broadway Café and Ice Cream Parlor: Typical diner fare; good prices; 1805 Morthland Dr., Valparaiso, Indiana; (219) 464-0112.
Pestos: Moderately priced Italian food; good variety of pizzas; 3123 Calumet Ave., Valparaiso, Indiana; (219) 462-0993; www.pestos.net.

Restrooms
Mile 6.3: Take a short side trip at the junction of CR 200 West and Division Road. At this junction, turn left onto Division Road and proceed for 0.25 mile to the junction with Highway 2. The gas station on this corner has restrooms.

Maps
DeLorme: Indiana Atlas and Gazetteer: Page 19
Northwest Indiana Bike Map, Northwest Indiana Regional Planning Commission; (219) 763-6060; www.nirpc.org
USGS 7.5" Kouts quad, USGS 7.5" Valparaiso quad

Wauponsee Glacial Trail

One of the newest rail trails in the state, the Wauponsee Glacial Trail runs from Joliet to the Kankakee River, mostly through wide-open farmland. After passing the town of Manhattan, the trail skirts the eastern edge of the sprawling Midewin National Tallgrass Prairie, formerly the largest ammunition-production plant in the world. The trail ends at the Kankakee River, where you'll enjoy long views from a former railroad bridge.

Start: On the south side of Joliet on Rowell Avenue

Length: 22.3 miles one way

Approximate riding time: 2 hours

Best bike: A hybrid, mountain, or road bike with wider tires

Terrain and trail surface: The trail has paved surface for first several miles and crushed gravel for the remainder. The landscape is flat.

Traffic and hazards: Beware, once you get away from Joliet, there's a lack of trail amenities like water and restrooms. Bring plenty of water; there is no drinking water available on the trail south of Manhattan. Sections of this trail offer little shelter from the wind and sun.

Things to see: Open farmland, streams, woods, Manhattan, Midewin National Tallgrass Prairie, and the Kankakee River

Wheelchair access: The trail is wheelchair accessible.

Getting there: By car: From I-80 go south on Briggs Street (exit 134). Immediately, turn right onto New Lenox Road and right again onto Rowell Avenue. Look for the beginning of the trail on the left. There is no parking lot at the trailhead—you must park on the road's ample shoulder. (The closest access spot with off-street parking is the Sugar Creek Forest Preserve—see below.) GPS coordinates: 41 30.757 N / 88 3.747 W

To catch the trail at Sugar Creek Forest Preserve, take Briggs Street (exit 134) south from I-80. Continue ahead as Briggs Street merges with US 52. Turn right onto Laraway Road; the entrance to the forest preserve is on the right.

To park at the Manhattan Road parking area in Manhattan, continue south on US 52 and then right onto Manhattan Road. The trail parking area is on the left.

To reach the parking area in Symerton, head south on I-55. Exit east on River Road (exit 241). Turn right onto IL 53 and then left onto Peotone Road. Turn left onto Symerton Road and right onto Commercial Street. Look for the trail parking area 2 blocks ahead.

To park at the south end of the trail, take IL 53 south to IL 102. Turn left onto IL 102 in Wilmington. Turn right onto Rivals Road. Park on the side of the road near the trail crossing.

By public transportation: Metra's Southwest Service goes to Manhattan, but service is very limited. The Rock Island District and Heritage Corridor Metra lines serve Joliet. Both train lines are accessible a few miles north of the trailhead.

THE RIDE

This trail is named for a glacial lake that covered much of the local terrain some 16,000 years ago. Lake Wauponsee reached a depth of 100 feet but lasted for a relatively short period of time before draining away into the Illinois River Valley. The glacial lake takes its name from Chief Waubonsee, an influential Potawatomi chief who lived near Aurora in the early 1800s.

Leafy residential neighborhoods and a dash of light industry show up on the first few miles of the trail. At Mill Street you'll pass the manufacturing facility and retail store for the Mancuso Cheese Company, local purveyors of mozzarella and ricotta since 1907. After crossing Sugar Creek, the trail briefly accompanies the creek through adjoining bottomland woods.

The Will County Forest Preserve administration building sits alongside the trail at Sugar Creek Forest Preserve. This environmentally friendly structure was built using recycled materials and has solar energy panels mounted on the roof. The building sits within an attractive prairie and is angled to maximize natural light inside. Southwest of the Sugar Creek Preserve, the 75,000-seat Chicagoland Speedway rises from the cropland. Across the road from the speedway is another smaller car racing venue, the Route 66 Raceway, with seating for around 30,000.

With a few exceptions, farmland dominates the landscape for the remainder of the trail. Farmhouses, silos, and barns often appear in the distance. Patches of trees sometimes offer shade, and small creeks regularly meander across the trail, flowing from one field to another. New housing developments spring up as you enter the town of Manhattan. The trail starts angling south-

Watch out for equine gifts left behind on the Wauponsee Glacial Trail.

west as you leave Manhattan and pass the local commuter train station and a cluster of oil storage tanks.

South of Hoff Road, the Wauponsee Trail intersects the Bailey Bridge Trail at the edge of the Midewin National Tallgrass Prairie. Once the site of the largest ammunition-production plant in the world, Midewin is now the biggest—and perhaps the most tranquil—piece of protected land in northeastern Illinois. The park contains woodland, savanna, prairie, and many remnants of the former arsenal, but mostly it's composed of farmland that is slowly being converted back to prairie and woodland. Today Midewin encompasses more than 15,000 acres. After the U.S. Army finishes its cleanup efforts, the park will add another 4,000 acres and eventually some 40 miles of trails. About 7,200 acres containing nearly 15 miles of trails are now open to the public. (A 5.2-mile hike at Midewin is described in my book *60 Hikes within 60 Miles: Chicago*.)

Bike Rentals

The Wheel Thing: 15 South La Grange Rd., La Grange; (708) 352-3822

At its peak, the Joliet Arsenal employed some 14,000 people and produced 5.5 million tons of TNT a week. The arsenal—in operation from World War II through the Korean and Vietnam Wars—was shut down in 1975, leaving some 1,300 structures, including 392 concrete bunkers that were used to store the TNT.

If you take a quick side trip on the Bailey Bridge Trail, you'll immediately pass a small pioneer cemetery established in 1877 by a local homesteader from Pennsylvania. Just after the cemetery you'll enter a swath of land containing many dozens of the earth-covered bunkers designed to withstand explosive blasts and conceal the location of the TNT in case of an enemy attack.

Before and after the village of Symerton, shade trees thin out along the trail and a carpet of cropland unrolls for miles in every direction. Before reaching Ballou Road, the path crosses a small stream and passes through a patch of woodland that offers a needed break from the yawning open space. More woodland develops as the trail hops over Forked Creek and crosses IL 102. Just before reaching the Kankakee River, you'll brush against a sizable wetland on the right. As you cross the Kankakee River on a rehabbed railroad bridge, breathtaking views of the wide river and its wooded banks open up on each side. The trail ends on the south bank of the Kankakee River.

MILES AND DIRECTIONS

0.0 Start at the Rowell Avenue access location.

2.8 Pass Sugar Creek Forest Preserve on the left.

7.0 Pass through Manhattan.

9.9 Cross Hoff Road.

15.2 Pass through Symerton.

17.8 Cross Kahler Road.

22.3 Cross the Kankakee River before arriving at the end of the trail.

RIDE INFORMATION

Local Events/Attractions

Joliet Area Historical Museum: Offers a thorough introduction to the history of the Joliet area; 204 North Ottawa St., Joliet; (815) 723-5201; www.joliet museum.org.

Joliet-area rail trails: Three other long rail trails can be accessed in Joliet; check the website for route advice and on-street connections; www.oprt.org /maps/westcon.html#iandm.

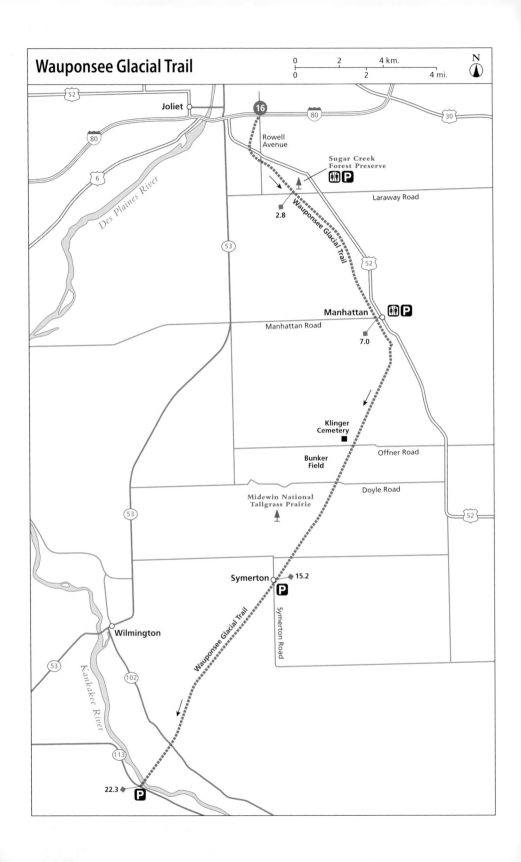

Kankakee River State Park: Hiking trails, horse rentals, and 10.5 miles of crushed gravel bike trails; 5314 IL 102, Bourbonnais; (815) 933-1383; http://dnr.state.il.us/lands/landmgt/parks/r2/kankakee.htm.

Midewin National Tallgrass Prairie: The visitor center has exhibits and maps of the park; 30239 IL 53, Wilmington; (815) 423-6370; www.fs.fed.us/mntp.

Restrooms

Mile 2.8: There are public restrooms and water at Sugar Creek Forest Preserve.

Mile 7.0: There are restrooms and water available in the trail parking area in Manhattan.

Maps

USGS Bonfield, Elwood, Joliet, and Symerton

DeLorme: Illinois Atlas and Gazetteer: Pages 28 and 36

West Chicagoland: To the Fox River and Beyond

The western region of Chicagoland—largely made up of DuPage and Kane Counties—offers an excellent system of bike trails and forest preserves that allow cyclists multiple opportunities to escape into the greenery. The abundance of old train lines through the area made it possible to create one of the best collections of rail trails in the Midwest. Nearly all the trails in this region are connected to one another, allowing you to pedal for many miles without having to use on-street routes. This is especially appealing for adults who have children along or those who simply prefer their cycling traffic-free.

Some of these trails, such as the Illinois Prairie Path, have been around for decades. As one of the first rail trails in the nation, the Prairie Path has become an indelible part of the communities it connects, including Elmhurst, Glen Ellyn, Wheaton, Aurora, and South Elgin, among others. The trail makes ample use of

The western segment of Great Western Trail runs between Sycamore and St. Charles. See Ride 19.

The Fox River Trail is a popular destination for families. See Ride 17.

the local forest preserves, some of them offering a thoroughly wild and remote feel.

After the Illinois Prairie Path, the other main trail in the area is the Fox River Trail, which runs through more than a dozen community parks and forest preserves along the Fox River between Aurora and Algonquin. In Elgin, the Fox River Trolley Museum sits alongside the trail, and in Geneva, the 300-acre Fabyan Forest Preserve features a restored Dutch windmill that dates back to the 1850s. On the trail, you're never far from one of the nearby towns featuring a selection of restaurants, ice-cream parlors, and watering holes.

Other trails you'll encounter include the Virgil Gilman Trail and two sections of the Great Western Trail. The Virgil Gilman Trail offers a perfect introduction to the attractive landscape between the city of Aurora and Waubonsee Community College campus to the west. The stretch of the Great Western Trail that runs through Kane and DeKalb Counties takes you to the far western edge of the region through expansive farmland and a few small communities. The east section of the Great Western Trail offers opportunities to visit a handful of top-notch DuPage County forest preserves, including Timber Ridge, Churchill Woods, and the Kline Creek Farm.

Cyclists with a yen for rail trails will be enthralled with this region. As you bounce from park to park on this outstanding network of long trails, you'll get a close-up view of some thoroughly scenic spots—without having to lace up your hiking boots.

Fox River Trail

Located only 30 miles west of downtown Chicago, the Fox River Trail has plenty of great things going for it. As this pathway hugs the Fox River between Aurora and Algonquin, it passes numerous community parks and forest preserves. In Elgin the Fox River Trolley Museum sits alongside the trail. In Geneva the 300-acre Fabyan Forest Preserve contains a restored Dutch windmill. Also alongside the trail at Fabyan are a pristine Japanese garden and the Villa Museum, designed by Frank Lloyd Wright. Some of the towns the trail passes through—such as Elgin, Geneva, and Batavia—contain attractive urban riverfront areas with flower and sculpture gardens, pedestrian bridges, and scenic walkways.

Start: In Algonquin, which is located in southeast McHenry County

Length: 32.8 miles one way

Approximate riding time: 3 hours

Best bike: Road or hybrid bike

Terrain and trail surface: Nearly the entire trail is paved; a couple brief sections have a smooth, crushed gravel surface. The trail is flat and shaded for most of the route. Difficulty level increases in a few spots where you must climb river bluffs.

Traffic and hazards: Watch carefully for signs while following the brief on-street section in St. Charles. Watch for traffic in the handful of places where the trail crosses busy streets. Sections of this trail are closed periodically for construction. Signs usually direct trail users along detours. Check with the Kane County Forest Preserve District for the latest construction news.

Things to see: Fox River, islands, woods, a slew of riverside parks and forest preserves, Fox River Trolley Museum, East Dundee, Geneva, Batavia, St. Charles, Elgin, and Aurora

Wheelchair access: The trail is wheelchair accessible.

Getting there: By car: From I-90 west of the Fox River, head north on IL 31 toward Algonquin. In Algonquin turn left onto Algonquin Road. Turn right onto Meyer Drive and then left into the Algonquin Road Trail Access parking area. GPS coordinates: 42 10.358 N / 88 18.039 W

To park at Fox River Shores Forest Preserve, head north on IL 25 from East Dundee. Turn left onto Lake Marian Road and then right onto Williams Road.

To park in South Elgin, head south on IL 31 from Elgin. Turn left onto State Street and then right onto Water Street. Park and catch the trail as it runs through the riverside park.

To park at the Fabyan Forest Preserve, head south on IL 25 from Geneva. The parking area is just after the windmill on the right.

To park near the south end of the trail at River Street Park in Aurora, head south on IL 31 from I-88. At Park Avenue turn left, and then turn right onto River Street. The park and the trail are on the left.

By public transportation: Metra trains bring you close to the trail in Elgin, Geneva, and Aurora. In Elgin the Milwaukee District West Metra line stops across the river from the trail. In Geneva the Union Pacific West Metra line stops about 0.5 mile from the trail. From the station, go north on Third Street and then turn right onto State Street. The BNSF Railway Metra line stops in Aurora across IL 25 from the trail.

THE RIDE

The Fox River Trail promises an enjoyable excursion for people who like to explore. There are towns of varying size; many scenic natural areas; and a host of parks, museums, and options for dining and shopping. The many towns along the way contain an assortment of restaurants, ice-cream parlors, coffee shops, and watering holes. If you're keen on a longer trip, the trail allows you to hook up with a handful of other Chicagoland recreation trails. Heading north, for example, connects you with the Prairie Trail, which runs all the way to the Wisconsin border. The gamblers among us will be happy to know that the Fox River Trail might be the only long recreation path in the nation with two riverboat casinos located steps from the trail.

On the first mile of the trail, you'll make a dramatic crossing of the Fox River on a pedestrian bridge before entering a residential area, where you'll pass many dozens of wooded backyards. Before reaching Fox River Shores Forest Preserve (where you'll find a collection of perfect picnicking spots on the shore of the river), the trail meets up with a wide spot in the river where kingfishers and great blue herons loiter on the deadfall in the river.

It may be difficult to get through East Dundee without stopping at one of the coffee shops along the trail, a bakery that makes pies and cookies, or the Dairy Queen that's several feet from the edge of the trail. You'll also pass a for-

In the Fabyan Forest Preserve, the trail passes underneath this Dutch windmill.

mer train depot with picnic tables at which you can sit to admire the handsome historic architecture on the surrounding streets.

On the way into Elgin, the trail runs through a long wooded stretch parallel to Elgin Avenue. Along the way is a remarkable brick house built to resemble a small tower. You'll also encounter Trout Park, which contains a rich display of spring wildflowers and a pedestrian bridge that crosses the Fox River.

Elgin's river walk is an enjoyable stretch. Amid the plantings of flowers and trees, bridges reach out to islands in the Fox River. If you have kids along, they'll be thrilled with the imaginative sculptures and playground equipment at Festival Park, located just upstream from Elgin's riverboat casino.

After passing the Elgin Spur of the Prairie Path, the trail runs through the arched opening of a stone train bridge. From there you'll take a roller-coaster ride up and down a series of river bluffs. After crossing the river in South Elgin, the trail runs through a couple of riverside parks and then sweeps past a collection of old trolley cars on display at the Fox River Trolley Museum.

Just before making the biggest climb on the route at Tekakwitha Woods, the trail mounts a pedestrian bridge that meets a couple of islands as it crosses over the Fox River. More wooded islands are visible as you look downstream. After the long steep climb up the river bluff, you'll leave the shore of the river and share the route for 1 mile along Weber Drive. (Weber Drive has some traffic, but it moves slowly.) Returning to the shore of the river,

Bike Rentals

The Bicycle Garage: 11 Jackson St., East Dundee; (847) 428-2600; located across the street from the trail

the quiet savanna and woodland at Norris Woods Nature Preserve offers refuge at the foot of a small river bluff. As you pass through St. Charles, you'll embark on another 1-mile-long stretch of on-street travel.

A host of scenic spots crop up south of Geneva. The trail traverses Island Park before arriving at the Dutch windmill, built in 1914. After the windmill, cross the river to visit a serene Japanese garden—carefully landscaped with ponds, walkways, and a small arched bridge—in the Fabyan Forest Preserve. The park also contains the Frank Lloyd Wright–designed Villa Museum, which showcases the history of the park and the family that once owned it.

In Batavia the trail runs by an old train depot that now serves as a local history museum. A collection of outdoor sculpture appears within Batavia's pleasant downtown riverside area. The final section of the path between Batavia

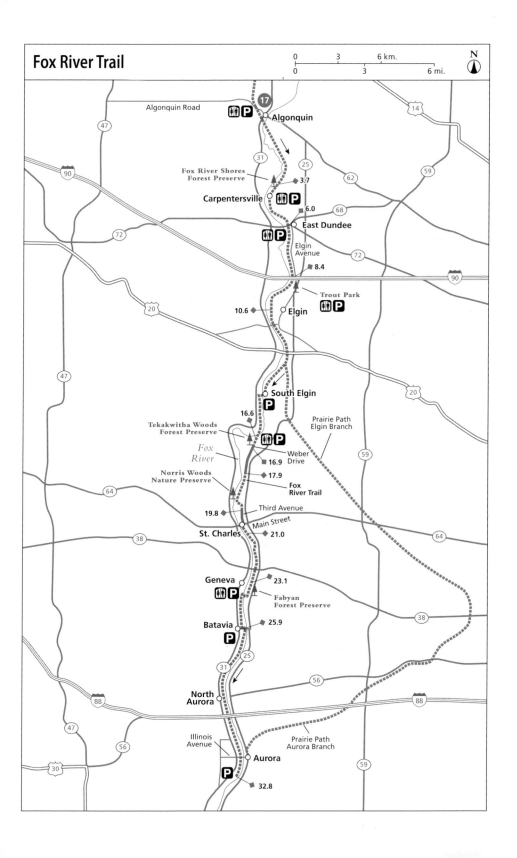

Fox River Trail

0   3   6 km.

0   3   6 mi.

N

Algonquin Road

17

Algonquin

47

31

25

62

14

90

59

Fox River Shores
Forest Preserve

3.7

Carpentersville

6.0

68

East Dundee

72

Elgin
Avenue

90

72

8.4

Trout Park

20

10.6

Elgin

South Elgin

20

59

16.6

Tekakwitha Woods
Forest Preserve

*Fox
River*

Weber
Drive

16.9

Prairie Path
Elgin Branch

Norris Woods
Nature Preserve

17.9

Fox
River Trail

64

19.8

Third Avenue

Main Street

St. Charles

21.0

64

38

Geneva

23.1

Fabyan
Forest Preserve

Batavia

25.9

38

59

25

31

56

North
Aurora

88

47

56

88

Illinois
Avenue

Prairie Path
Aurora Branch

Aurora

30

32.8

59

and Aurora cuts through a wooded riparian terrain sprinkled with homes set back from the trail and the river. Brilliant views come and go as the path traces the top edge of a small bluff above the river. Aurora welcomes you with open grassy areas and a riverside park. After passing a fish ladder within the river, the trail ends at the back door of the Hollywood Casino.

MILES AND DIRECTIONS

0.0 Start at the Algonquin Road access parking area.

3.7 Pass the Fox River Shores Forest Preserve on the right.

6.0 Pass through East Dundee.

8.4 Pass Trout Park on the right.

10.6 Cross Kimball Street in Elgin.

16.6 Pass Tekakwitha Forest Preserve on the right.

16.9 Begin a brief on-street section following Weber Drive.

17.9 Resume riding on the trail.

19.8 Turn right onto Third Avenue to begin a 1.2-mile-long on-street section of the route in St. Charles.

20.3 Turn right onto North Avenue.

20.4 Turn left onto Second Avenue.

20.7 Turn right onto State Avenue.

20.8 Turn left onto First Avenue and cross IL 64.

21.0 Return to the Fox River Trail.

23.1 Pass through Island Park in Geneva.

25.9 Pass through Batavia.

32.8 Arrive at the end of the trail in Aurora.

RIDE INFORMATION

Local Events/Attractions
The Depot Museum: Sits alongside the trail; chronicles the local history of Batavia.; 155 Houston St., Batavia; (630) 406-5274; www.bataviahistorical society.org.

Fox River Trolley Museum: Old trolleys on display; operates a trolley along a 4-mile section of track that parallels the Fox River Trail; 361 South LaFox St., South Elgin; (847) 697-4676; www.foxtrolley.org.

Restaurants

Batavia Creamery: Great selection of premium ice creams; located on the trail; 4 North Island Ave., Batavia; (630) 482-3729; www.bataviacreamery.com.
The Mill Race Inn: Outdoor seating at a great riverside setting; 4 East State St., Geneva; (630) 232-2030; www.themillraceinn.com.

Fabyan Forest Preserve

Alongside the Fox River in Geneva, you'll find Fabyan Forest Preserve—one of the more interesting county parks in Chicago's western suburbs. The park contains a five-story Dutch windmill erected in 1914 by George Fabyan, an eccentric millionaire whose estate once sprawled along the riverbank. (The windmill was first constructed in the 1850s in Holland but was then dismantled, transported, and resurrected by Fabyan on the shore of the Fox River.) In addition to the windmill, Fabyan's estate included a private zoo and a laboratory that performed research on acoustics, code cracking, and—believe it or not—human levitation. Fabyan's Japanese garden remains, as does his farmhouse remodeled by Frank Lloyd Wright, now containing a museum. Many different research activities occurred at his laboratory, including decoding and deciphering enemy messages during World War I, deciphering alleged secret messages in the works of William Shakespeare, research in the field of architectural acoustics, research and development of tuning forks, and studies of human fitness and anatomy. The list is varied and fascinating.

Restrooms

Start: The Algonquin Road trail access has water and restrooms.
Mile 3.7: Fox River Shores Forest Preserve offers water and restrooms.
Mile 6.0: East Dundee Depot has water and restrooms.
Mile 8.4: Trout Park has restrooms.

Mile 16.6: Tekakwitha Woods Forest Preserve has restrooms.
Mile 23.1: Island Park in Geneva has water and restrooms.

Maps

USGS Aurora North, Crystal Lake, Elgin, and Geneva
DeLorme: Illinois Atlas and Gazetteer: Pages 20 and 28
Kane & Northern Kendall Counties Bicycle Map; Kane County Division of
Transportation; www.co.kane.il.us/dot/com/publications

Great Western Trail: DuPage County

As the Great Western Trail makes a straight shot west from Villa Park, it cuts through residential areas and brushes against community parks and forest preserves. On the second half of the route, woods, prairie, and wetlands become more abundant as houses and trail users grow sparse. Consider short side trips to Churchill Woods Forest Preserve at the halfway point and Kline Creek Farm near the end of the trail.

Start: The Villa Park Museum in Villa Park, located about 20 miles west of downtown Chicago

Length: 11.7 miles one way, with options for short side trips

Approximate riding time: 1 hour

Best bike: A mountain bike, hybrid bike, or road bike with wider tires

Terrain and trail surface: The terrain is flat; the trail surface is crushed gravel.

Traffic and hazards: Some sections of the trail leave you fully exposed to the elements. Use caution while crossing a few busy roads along the way.

Things to see: Woods, prairie, wetlands, residential neighborhoods, municipal parks, forest preserves, Churchill Woods Forest Preserve, and the Kline Creek Farm

Wheelchair access: The trail is wheelchair accessible.

Getting there: By car: To reach the Villa Park Museum, head west on St. Charles Road from I-290. In Villa Park turn left onto Villa Avenue. Park in the lot at the museum on the right. The museum is located on the main stem of the Illinois Prairie Path. Catch the Great Western Trail by heading west on the Prairie Path and then following signs north 1 block via Myrtle Avenue. GPS coordinates: 41 53.086 N / 87 58.1 W

The best place to start the trail from the west end is the Timber Ridge Forest Preserve parking area on Prince Crossing Road. From I-355 head west on IL 64 and turn left onto Prince Crossing Road. The parking area is on the left; the trail is 20 yards south of the parking area.

THE RIDE

Many people use this section of the Great Western Trail (GWT) as an alternative to the Illinois Prairie Path, which runs parallel to the GWT for its full distance. While the two trails hit some similar terrain, they also possess important differences. The GWT tends to go through fewer residential areas and as a result is less used than the Prairie Path. In this case, fewer trail users also mean fewer trailside amenities such as restrooms, drinking fountains, and benches. The GWT intersects the Prairie Path's main stem at the beginning of this route and intersects the Prairie Path's Elgin Branch at the end of the route.

Look for prairie flowers and songbirds in the restored tallgrass prairie along the trail.

There are two sections of the Great Western Trail. This eastern section of the trail, which runs across the northern section of DuPage County, does not directly connect with the western section of the Great Western Trail (GWT), which starts in Kane County near St. Charles and runs west to Sycamore.

As you start the trail westward, the first few miles pass a couple of parks that are mixed in with residential backyards. In Lombard a trail leading into Westmore Woods Park branches right. This paved path hugs the shore of a small pond while taking a short trip to a grassy community park. Also in Lombard is a sprawling park called Lombard Commons, which contains more open grassy areas, a public pool, and multiple sports fields. (At the park, watch carefully for signs as they direct you across the railroad tracks and across St. Charles Road and back to the trail's right-of-way.) Heading west from Lombard, more residential backyards appear as the path traces the top of a 10- to 15-foot railroad embankment.

After crossing I-355 take the crushed gravel trail that branches left alongside Swift Road for a side trip to Churchill Woods Forest Preserve. On the left, a hiking trail winds through the second largest prairie in DuPage County. Prairie flowers such as asters, bottle gentian,

Bike Rentals

Prairie Path Cycles: 27 West 181 Geneva Rd., Winfield; (630) 690-9749; http://prairiepathcycles.com; located fairly close to the trail

and prairie sundrops decorate this grassland during spring and fall. Continue ahead on the main trail for a winding wooded route through Churchill Woods. At St. Charles Road go left and head through the underpass. On the other side of St. Charles Road, continue ahead on the trail to a scenic picnic area alongside a series of islands within the East Branch of the DuPage River.

Back on the GWT, the path begins to do that magical thing that rail trails tend to do. The landscape surrounding the trail dips and rises, but thanks to surface grading for the railroad right-of-way, the trail remains extremely level.

Not far ahead, just after the path cuts straight through the middle of a gravel and concrete operation, you'll see a tiny old cemetery on the right. If the chain-link fence didn't prevent access, you would see that the gravestones date back to the 1850s, many with German names on them.

At County Farm Road you'll have the opportunity to visit a local landmark—the Kline Creek Farm. Kline Creek Farm is a county-operated living-history farm that demonstrates local farm life in the 1890s. Along with chickens, cows, sheep, and horses, there are several barns, an icehouse, a windmill water pump, and a

Great Western Trail: DuPage County

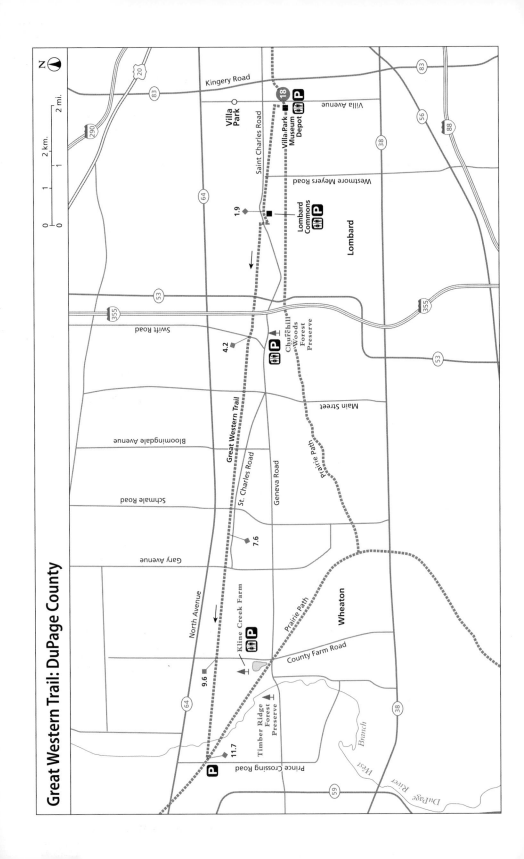

farmhouse containing decor and furnishings of a DuPage County Victorian-era farm.

The final section of the GWT takes you on a very gentle downhill through rolling savanna and prairie in the Timber Ridge Forest Preserve. Wetlands with patches of open water and sedge grasses show up near the crossing of the West Branch of the DuPage River. The trail ends as it intersects with the Elgin Branch of the Prairie Path.

MILES AND DIRECTIONS

0.0 Start at the Villa Park Museum.

1.9 Pass Lombard Commons Park.

4.2 Cross Swift Road and the access trail for Churchill Woods Forest Preserve.

7.6 Pass St. Stephens Cemetery on the right.

9.6 Cross County Farm Road and the access trail for Kline Creek Farm.

11.7 Arrive at the end of the trail as it meets up with the Elgin Branch of the Illinois Prairie Path.

RIDE INFORMATION

Local Events/Attractions

Kline Creek Farm: Living-history farm with education programs and a visitor center; 1 mile south of North Avenue (IL 64); (630) 876-5900; www.dupage forest.com/page.aspx?id=228.

Villa Park Museum: Contains exhibits relating to the town and the railroad line; serves as the starting point for this route; 220 South Villa Ave., Villa Park; (630) 941-0223; www.vphistoricalsociety.com.

Restaurants

Augustinos Rock and Roll Deli: Burgers, pasta, pizza, and submarine sandwiches in a 1950s-style diner with outdoor seating; located right on the path; 246 South Schmale Rd., Carol Stream; (630) 665-5585; www.augustinos.com.

Pad Thai Etc. Restaurant: Basic Thai offerings; 563 West Liberty Dr., Wheaton; (630) 653-5337.

Restrooms

Start: There are public restrooms and water at the Villa Park Museum.

Mile 1.9: Lombard Commons Park has restrooms and water.

Mile 4.2: Churchill Woods Forest Preserve has restrooms (about 0.5 mile off the GWT).

Mile 9.6: Kline Creek Farm has restrooms and water (about 0.25 mile off the GWT).

Maps

USGS Elmhurst, Lombard, and West Chicago
DeLorme: Illinois Atlas and Gazetteer: Page 28

Great Western Trail: Kane and DeKalb Counties

Setting out toward Sycamore from St. Charles, the first half of the path presents you with attractive woodland intermingled with acres of bright and shiny housing developments. A rural landscape takes over on the second half of the path as it slices through wide-open agricultural land alongside IL 64.

Start: LeRoy Oaks Forest Preserve northwest of St. Charles

Length: 17.1 miles one way

Approximate riding time: 2 hours

Best bike: Road or hybrid bike

Terrain and trail surface: The landscape is flat; the trail features crushed gravel with a short stretch of asphalt.

Traffic and hazards: The length of the trail and its lack of amenities may offer a challenge to some trail users. Use caution while crossing a few busy streets.

Things to see: Woodland, farmland, wetland, and streams

Wheelchair access: The trail is wheelchair accessible.

Getting there: By car: From I-355 go west toward St. Charles on IL 64. After passing through St. Charles, turn right onto Randall Road and then left onto Dean Street. The Great Western Trail parking area is on the left, across the road from the main entrance to the LeRoy Oaks Forest Preserve. GPS coordinates: 41 55.259 N / 88 20.874 W

Most of the road crossings west of IL 47 have room for at least one car to park. Additional parking is available at the following areas:

To park at the Campton Township Community Center in Wasco, head west from St. Charles on IL 64. In Wasco turn right onto LaFox Road. Park in the lot on the left.

To park at the west end of the trail in Sycamore, take I-88 to DeKalb and exit north onto Peace Road. Follow Peace Road all the way to IL 64 and turn right. After passing through Sycamore, turn left onto Old State Road. The parking area is immediately on the right.

By public transportation: The Union Pacific West Metra line stops in Geneva about 5 miles southeast of the trailhead.

THE RIDE

First established in 1885 as a regional railroad between St. Paul, Minnesota, and the Iowa-Minnesota state line, the Chicago Great Western Railroad eventually linked Chicago, Minneapolis, Omaha, and Kansas City. The route—nicknamed the Corn Belt Route because it toured the most productive agricultural land within the Midwest—was mostly abandoned in 1968 when the railroad was merged with the Chicago and North Western Railway. Fortunately, long sections of the railroad in Illinois, Iowa, and Minnesota have been transformed into rail trails, including two sections in northern Illinois. In addition to the section described here, an 11.5-mile section of the railroad between Villa Park and West Chicago has been developed as a rail trail.

Starting in LeRoy Oaks Forest Preserve, the trail launches you into a large prairie fringed by woods and wetlands. After a sharp turn to the right, you'll arrive on the railroad right-of-way and then pass above Peck Road on an arched metal bridge. Initially, new housing developments peek through the woods now and then. As the developments multiply, you'll have little doubt that local home builders have done a brisk business in the past decade. Shortly after crossing another arched bridge over Hidden Oaks Road, the trail pulls alongside IL 64. As the trail follows IL 64, the woodland along the trail grows thin, reducing the shade but increasing the views. Briefly the trail plunges through one of those human-made ravines designed to make the railroad run level.

> **Bike Rentals**
>
> The Bike Rack: 2930 Campton Hills Dr., St. Charles; (630) 584-6588; located close to the trailhead

With all the development in the area, it's no surprise that traffic is more than a trickle on many local streets. Fortunately trail users hop over the busier roads on the handsome metal bridges, many with a graceful arch.

After passing through Wasco, the trail, which becomes asphalt for a stretch, temporarily breaks away from IL 64. Woodlands intermittently appear alongside the trail, as do marsh grasses and small ponds. Ferson Creek winds between the trail and the foot of the small bluffs rising on the right. Before the trail crosses IL 47 on an old train bridge, another small creek connects Ferson Creek with the wetlands on the left.

A bridge spans one of the small creeks on the west section of the Great Western Trail.

After crossing IL 47, the remaining 9.5 miles of the trail closely parallels IL 64. This is also where housing developments subside and agricultural land begins to dominate the scenery. Vegetation tends to be sparse as the path runs about 30 feet north of the highway; occasional stands of trees interrupt the shrubs and prairie grasses. The lack of dense greenery allows long views from atop the 12-foot-high railroad embankment.

Before and after you bisect the hamlet of Virgil, the trail crosses the arms of Virgil Ditch. In the little gathering of houses called Richardson, Friday and Saturday nights bring the roar of car engines at the Sycamore Speedway, located a few hundred feet north of the trail. The shaded picnic table at the end of the trail offers a place to take a breather before returning to the trail's starting point.

Great Western Trail: Kane and DeKalb Counties

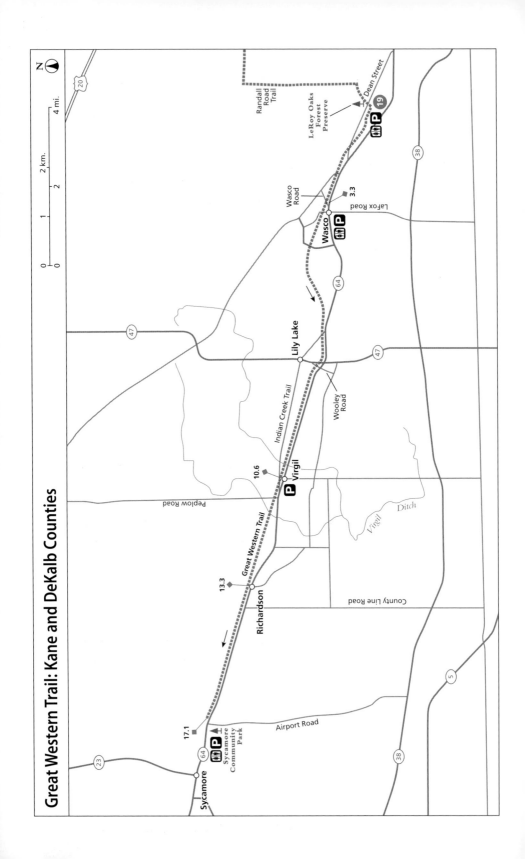

Those with energy to burn may consider a couple of tempting side trips. At the end of the trail, go 0.25 mile south on Airport Road to the entrance of Sycamore Community Park on the right. At the end of the 1-mile-long trail through the park, cyclists have the opportunity to follow an on-street bike route through Sycamore and into DeKalb.

Another side trip can be explored at the beginning of the Great Western Trail in St. Charles. Follow the trail north through LeRoy Oaks Forest Preserve and then continue north along Randall Road for a 7-mile connection to the Fox River Trail outside Elgin.

MILES AND DIRECTIONS

0.0 Start from LeRoy Oaks Forest Preserve.

3.3 Pass the trail parking area in Wasco.

10.6 Cross Indian Creek Road in Virgil.

13.3 Cross Old State Road in Richardson.

17.1 Arrive at the end of the trail outside of Sycamore.

RIDE INFORMATION

Local Events/Attractions

Midwest Museum of Natural History: Many animal specimens on display in exhibits focusing on different geographical areas; 425 West State St. (Highway 64), Sycamore; (815) 895-9777; www.mmnh.org.

Sycamore Speedway: Stock car and drag racing on Friday and Saturday nights since 1960; 50W086 Highway 64, Maple Park; (815) 895-5454; www.sycamorespeedway.com.

Restaurants

Cup of Joy Café: Located 1 block off the trail in Wasco; 40W450 Highway 64, St. Charles; (630) 377-9569.

Niko's Lodge Bar and Grill: Chicken, salads, and sandwiches in lodge setting; a stone's throw from the trail; 41W379 Highway 64, Wasco; (630) 443-8000; http://nikoslodge.com.

Restrooms

Start: Public restrooms and water are available at the Great Western Trail parking area.

Mile 3.4: Campton Township Community Center has restrooms.

Mile 17.1: Sycamore Community Park has restrooms and water (just south of the Airport Road trailhead).

Maps

USGS Elburn, Geneva, Maple Park, and Sycamore

DeLorme: Illinois Atlas and Gazetteer: Pages 27 and 28

Kane & Northern Kendall Counties Bicycle Map; Kane County Division of Transportation; www.co.kane.il.us/dot/com/publications

Illinois Prairie Path: Aurora and Elgin Branches

These two connected branches of the Illinois Prairie Path take you through a suburban landscape that is largely residential, sometimes industrial, and often feels more remote than it actually is. As the route cuts through a number of forest preserves, the dense trailside greenery falls away and majestic views of wetlands and prairie open up in front of you. At roughly the route's halfway mark, budget some time for checking out the shops and restaurants in Wheaton.

Start: Veterans Memorial Island Park, just north of Aurora

Length: 27.2 miles one way

Approximate riding time: 3 hours

Best bike: Road, hybrid, or mountain bike

Terrain and trail surface: The trail surface is asphalt for the first mile or so, crushed gravel surface for the remainder.

Traffic and hazards: The trail crosses a few busy streets; use caution while crossing these. Be mindful of other trail users, particularly on the busier sections of this trail.

Things to see: Woodland, wetland, prairie, Fox River, Blackwell Forest Preserve, Aurora, Wheaton, Pratts Wayne Woods Forest Preserve, St. James Farm, Timber Ridge Forest Preserve

Wheelchair access: The trail is wheelchair accessible.

Getting there: By car: From I-88 north of Aurora, head south on IL 31 (Lincoln Street). Turn left at Illinois Avenue. Park at Veterans Memorial Island Park on the right. From the island, catch the trail by heading to the east shore of the Fox River and following the path left. GPS coordinates: 41 46.209 N / 88 18.537 W

To park at the Eola Road parking area, head south from I-88 on IL 59. Turn right onto Diehl Road and then left onto Eola Road. Park on the right.

To park at the Winfield Road parking area, head north from I-88 on Winfield Road. Parking is on the left.

Wheaton contains many side streets where you can park at no cost near the trail. To park on Lincoln Avenue, go north on Main Street from

Roosevelt Road. Turn left onto Lincoln Avenue and look for parking as you get near the trail.

To park at the corner of County Farm and Geneva Roads, head west from I-355 on IL 64. Turn left onto County Farm Road. Park at the northwest corner of the intersection with Geneva Road.

To park at the Army Trail Road parking area, head south on IL 59 from I-90. Turn right onto Army Trail Road.

To park at the Raymond Street parking area, located at the north end of the route, head south on IL 59 from I-90. Turn right onto US 20 (Lake Street) and then left onto Raymond Street. Park on the right.

By public transportation: The Aurora stop on the BNSF Metra line is across the street from the south end of the trail in Aurora. The Wheaton stop on the Union Pacific West Metra line is a couple blocks east of the trail. In Elgin, the National Street station on the Milwaukee District West line is less than a mile north of the north end of the trail.

THE RIDE

In future years the area where this route starts will look much different. The city of Aurora is developing an ambitious riverside park that will contain a large outdoor performance venue, a wetland area where Indian Creek enters the Fox River, and a graceful curving bridge that connects to an island in the river and the opposite shore. The park will occupy the riverbank between Veterans Memorial Island Park and downtown Aurora. With or without the new park, downtown Aurora deserves a visit either at the beginning or the end of your trip.

The Fox River accompanies this route for just a brief moment as the path heads away from downtown Aurora and then climbs the wooded river bluff. At the top of the bluff, cross IL 25 (Aurora Avenue) and then catch the trail as it runs left off Hankes Avenue.

As you proceed, the greenery alongside the trail toggles between dense stands of trees and thick shrubbery. New residential developments proliferate, and this is where the trail shares a right-of-way with multiple power lines that crackle and hum overhead. After you cross Farnsworth Avenue, the shrubbery disappears briefly and a big grassy wetland opens on the left. A small collection of mowed hiking trails wind through the nearby prairie.

After this prairie-wetland oasis, you're quickly brought back to a heavily developed suburban reality as you pass an electrical substation and an office park and mount a pedestrian bridge over a busy highway. If you have kids along, they'll likely want to blow some money at Odyssey Fun World, an amped-up arcade with rides, games, and laser tag. (Look for the back parking area on the right after passing under I-88.)

In Warrenville the trail shoots across the West Branch of the DuPage River and then enters an attractive slice of Blackwell Forest Preserve. While accompanying Butterfield Road, you'll pass the St. James Farm, once a private estate but now owned by the DuPage County Forest Preserve District. The farm's brick barns, arena, and trails focus on equestrian activities.

The route toward downtown Wheaton offers densely wooded terrain, well-kept backyards, and crossings of low-traffic roads. You may also notice that this stretch of trail is well used by local residents. Proof of this path's popularity is demonstrated by home owners posting HOUSE FOR SALE signs along the path.

After passing the main stem of the Prairie Path in Wheaton and following a long pedestrian bridge over multiple railroad tracks, the path curves left as it

Expect to see wetlands galore on the Illinois Prairie Path near Pratts Wayne Forest Preserve.

Illinois Prairie Path: Aurora and Elgin Branches

reaches a bench overlooking a wetland called Lincoln Marsh. At the corner of Geneva and County Farm Roads, a spur trail on the right leads to Kline Creek Farm, another farm operated by the county park system. Continuing ahead, the landscape grows wooded, lush, and dense. Again the path crosses the West Branch of the DuPage River. Near where the Great Western Trail intersects the Prairie Path on the right, you'll encounter wetlands with ponds and stands of cattails. Patches of wetland continue—intermixed with residential developments and industrial areas—as the trail shoots straight northwest.

Bike Shop

Midwest Cyclery: 117 Front St., Wheaton; (630) 668-2424; www.midwestcyclery.com; located next to the Prairie Path Main Stem

Soon you'll arrive at Pratts Wayne Forest Preserve, a generous-size natural area that contains prairies, sprawling wetlands, and a collection of fishing ponds. As you enter the forest preserve, thick woods and a dense, leafy canopy turn the trail into a shadowy tunnel. The wooden railings and the wide treeless swath of marshland and wet prairie mark the spot where Norton Creek passes under the trail. Soon the cattails on the right give way to open water, much of it covered in algae. On the far side of the open water, look for waterbirds perched on fallen logs. Underneath another set of wooden railings, Brewster Creek passes under the path.

The final several miles of the path take you past former and current gravel mining operations and chunks of farmland. The trail ends at the Fox River Trail. Taking the Fox River Trail right brings you to Elgin and eventually to the Wisconsin border along the Prairie Trail. Turning left takes you back to Aurora.

MILES AND DIRECTIONS

0.0 Start from Island Park in Aurora.

4.4 Cross Eola Road.

8.2 Pass through Warrenville before riding through Blackwell Forest Preserve.

13.2 Pass the main stem of the Illinois Prairie Path in Wheaton.

15.7 Pass the Geneva Spur of the Illinois Prairie Path.

19.6 Cross IL 64.

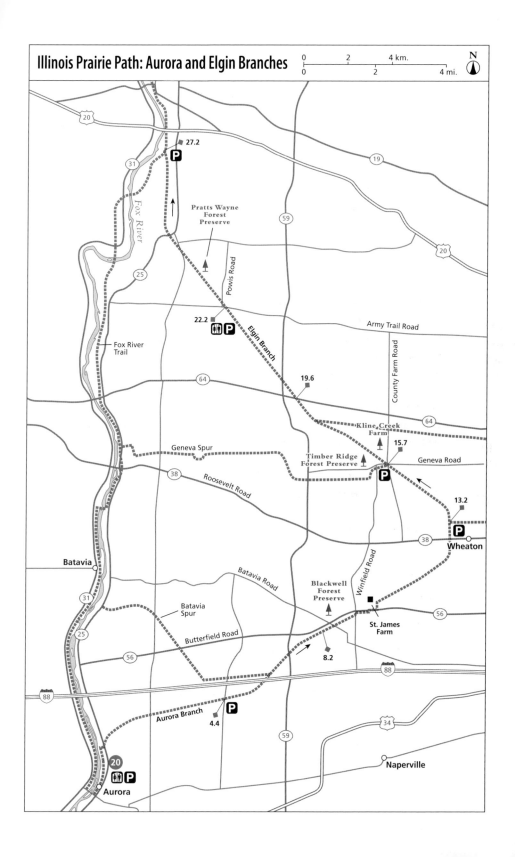

Illinois Prairie Path: Aurora and Elgin Branches

0 — 2 — 4 km.
0 — 2 — 4 mi.

N

20

31

27.2 P

Pratts Wayne
Forest
Preserve

Fox River

25

Powis Road

59

19

20

Army Trail Road

22.2 P

Elgin Branch

Fox River
Trail

64

19.6

County Farm Road

Kline Creek
Farm

64

Geneva Spur

Timber Ridge
Forest Preserve

15.7

Geneva Road

P

38

Roosevelt Road

13.2

P

Wheaton

38

Batavia

31

Batavia
Spur

Batavia Road

Blackwell
Forest
Preserve

Winfield Road

56

25

Butterfield Road

St. James
Farm

56

8.2

88

88

Aurora Branch

4.4 P

59

34

20

P

Aurora

Naperville

22.2 Cross Army Trail Road before arriving in Pratts Wayne Forest Preserve.

27.2 Arrive at the end of the trail and the junction with the Fox River Trail.

RIDE INFORMATION

Local Events/Attractions

Aurora Regional Fire Museum: Vintage firefighting equipment; located across the street from the trailhead in downtown Aurora; 53 North Broadway, Aurora; (630) 892-1572; www.auroraregionalfiremuseum.org.

Blackwell Forest Preserve: Boat rentals, campground, and lots of trails; Butterfield Road, just west of Winfield Road; (630) 933-7200; www.dupageforest .com.

Kline Creek Farm: Living-history farm with animals, education programs, and a visitor center; 1 mile south of North Avenue (IL 64); (630) 876-5900; www .dupageforest.com/education/klinecreek.html.

St. James Farm: Equestrian facilities; trails for hiking and riding; open seasonally on weekends; Butterfield Road east of Blackwell Forest Preserve, Wheaton; (630) 933-7200; www.dupageforest.com.

Restaurants

La Quinta de Los Reyes: Live music; courtyard area; located next to the trailhead in Aurora; 36 East New York St., Aurora; (630) 859-4000; http://laquinta delosreyesaurora.com.

Pad Thai Etc. Restaurant: Basic Thai offerings; located on the Prairie Path Main Stem in Wheaton; 563 West Liberty Dr., Wheaton; (630) 653-5337.

Restrooms

Start: There are public restrooms and water at Veterans Memorial Island Park.
Mile 8.2: There are restrooms in front of the Warrenville city offices.
Mile 22.2: Restrooms and water are available at the Army Trail Road parking area.

Maps

USGS Aurora North, Elgin, Geneva, Naperville, and West Chicago
DeLorme: Illinois Atlas and Gazetteer: Pages 20 and 28

Illinois Prairie Path: Main Stem

The Illinois Prairie Path, one of the first rail trails in the nation, runs along the route of the former Chicago, Aurora, and Elgin Railway, an electric railroad line that carried commuters and freight between Chicago and its western suburbs. Stretching from Wheaton to Maywood, the main stem of the Prairie Path takes you through wooded parks and greenways and offers a taste of a handful of communities that grew up alongside this route.

Start: In Elmer J. Hoffman Park on the east side of Wheaton

Length: 13.4 miles one way

Approximate riding time: 1.5 hours

Best bike: Road or hybrid bike

Terrain and trail surface: The trail is crushed gravel for the 9.4-mile-long DuPage County section, and it's asphalt for most of the 4-mile-long Cook County section.

Traffic and hazards: Sections of this trail can get busy; be mindful of other trail users. Watch for broken glass on the paved sections. The trail crosses a few streets with very heavy traffic. Waiting to cross sometimes requires patience.

Things to see: Parks, residential neighborhoods, and downtown areas in Villa Park, Wheaton, Maywood, Berkeley, Elmhurst, and Lombard

Wheelchair access: The trail is wheelchair accessible.

Getting there: By car: From I-355 head west on Roosevelt Road (IL 38). Turn right onto Lorraine Street. Turn left onto Hill Avenue and right onto Prospect Avenue. Park at Elmer J. Hoffman Park and catch the trail just north of the parking area. GPS coordinates: 41 52.244 N / 88 5.116 W

In DuPage County, parking is available in all the communities along the trail. On weekends most leased parking spaces near the Metra stations are free, as are most metered parking spaces. Farther east in Cook County, the path runs through residential areas where free parking is often available.

To park at the trailside parking area in Lombard, head north on Westmore Avenue from IL 38 (Roosevelt Road). The parking lot is on the left.

To park at the trailside parking lot in Elmhurst, head north from IL 38 (Roosevelt Road) on York Road. Turn left onto Madison Street and then right onto Spring Road.

By public transportation: Take the Metra's Union Pacific West line to either the Wheaton or College Avenue stop. The trail runs alongside the tracks. In Lombard and Villa Park, catch trains on the same Metra line several blocks north of the trail.

THE RIDE

Before heading east on the trail, consider taking the 1.5-mile trip west along the path into downtown Wheaton, where restaurants, bars, and shops line the streets. Along the way you'll pass Wheaton College, which contains a museum focusing on the school's most famous alumnus, the evangelist Billy Graham. The trail also passes a large Romanesque-style courthouse built in 1896 that is now on the National Register of Historic Places. The building, topped off by a large clock tower, was recently remodeled and now contains high-priced condos. The west side of Wheaton is where the Prairie Path splits into two main branches; one goes to Aurora, the other to Elgin.

Heading east on the path, you'll encounter another pleasant downtown area in Glen Ellyn. Smaller than Wheaton, Glen Ellyn also has a collection of shops and restaurants within sight of the trail. On the way out of Glen Ellyn, the trail passes through a little ravine before shooting under I-355. In Lombard a leafy residential atmosphere predominates as the trail crosses numerous side streets.

The trail is accompanied by an attractive greenway as it proceeds through Villa Park, the next town along the route. At Ardmore Street you'll sweep past an old Prairie-style train depot built with river rock in 1910. Just ahead, another former depot contains a museum with a few small exhibits focusing on local rail history, including the electric railroad that operated on these tracks. The depot was built in 1929 of cut stone and stucco with wood trim. The station has large windows, most notably on the east end, which was designed to house a pharmacy. Inside you'll learn that this rail line stopped

Bike Shop

Midwest Cyclery: 117 Front St., Wheaton; (630) 668-2424; www.midwestcyclery .com; located next to the trail

This grand old courthouse sits a block south of the trail in Wheaton.

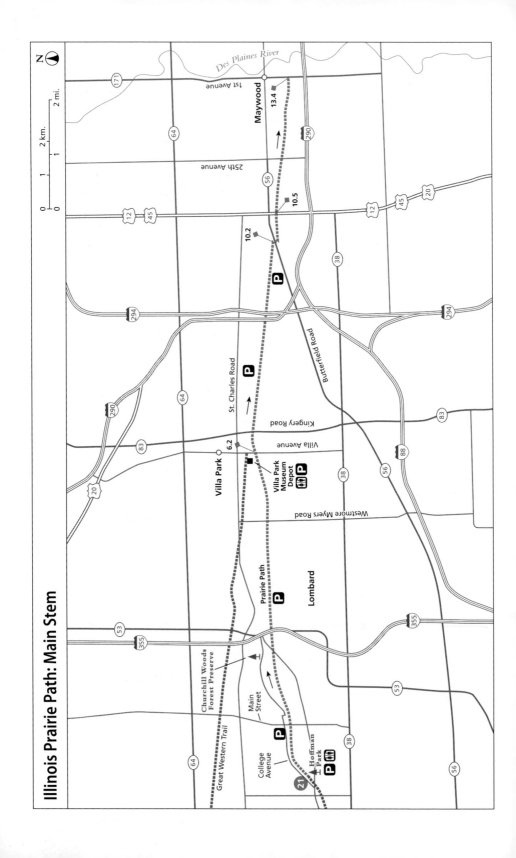

Illinois Prairie Path: Main Stem

service in the late 1950s and that the line was abandoned altogether in 1961. Signs near the museum point to the eastern terminus of the Great Western Trail, which starts just 1 block north.

In Elmhurst the many patches of trailside greenery will likely catch your eye. Well-tended flower gardens decorate the residential backyards along the path, and cottonwood, sumac, and oaks occasionally conspire to create a tunnel of trees that encloses the trail. Near Spring Road community volunteers maintain a swath of restored prairie thick with such plants as milkweed, baby's breath, compass plants, shooting star, and goldenrod.

Passing under I-290 and I-294 signals your departure from DuPage County and your entry into Cook County. In Berkeley the path again runs through a wide greenway sprinkled with picnic tables, playgrounds, and ball diamonds. After a brief on-street section of the trail in the community of Hillside, small industrial facilities multiply. For the remainder of the path through Bellwood and the much larger town of Maywood, residential neighborhoods with modest, well-kept homes intermingle with industrial districts. Through much of this area, the path shares the route with a power line right-of-way.

MILES AND DIRECTIONS

0.0 Start from Elmer J. Hoffman Park outside of Wheaton.

6.2 Pass the Villa Park Museum.

10.2 Cross IL 56 and keep straight ahead on Forest Avenue.

10.3 Turn left onto Warren Avenue.

10.5 Cross Mannheim Road and resume traveling on the Prairie Path.

13.4 Arrive at First Avenue, the end of the trail.

RIDE INFORMATION

Local Events/Attractions
Elmhurst Art Museum: Nice collection of contemporary art; 150 Cottage Hill Ave., Elmhurst; (630) 834-0202; www.elmhurstartmuseum.org.
York Theatre: An impressive Spanish-style film theater first opened in 1924; the pipe organ is played before some shows; 150 North York Rd., Elmhurst; (630) 834-0675.

Restaurants

Dairy Queen: Ice cream only; look for the vintage neon sign a few blocks north of the trail on Main Street in Lombard; 205 South Main St., Lombard; (630) 627-6364.

Pad Thai Etc. Restaurant: Basic Thai offerings; right on the trail in Wheaton; 563 West Liberty Dr., Wheaton; (630) 653-5337.

Roberto's Ristorante and Pizzeria: Slightly upscale, classic Italian food and thin-crust pizzas; located next to the trail; 483 Spring Rd., Elmhurst; (630) 279-8474; www.robertosristorante.net.

Restrooms

Start: There are public restrooms and water at Elmer J. Hoffman Park.
Mile 6.2: Water and restrooms are available at the Villa Park Museum.

Maps

USGS Elmhurst, River Forest, and Wheaton
DeLorme: Illinois Atlas and Gazetteer: Pages 28 and 29

Plano Loop

This ride takes you on a tour of the gently rolling rural landscape just beyond Aurora at the western edge of Kane and Kendall Counties. Mixed in with the farmland are plenty of woods and grassland; there are streams and small bluffs; there are parks and animal pastures. Near the end of the ride, you'll see some historic architecture in the old railroad town of Plano. Before returning to the starting point on the bank of the Fox River, the final mile takes you within striking distance of the Farnsworth House, an icon of twentieth-century residential architecture.

Start: Start at the Fox View picnic area at Silver Springs State Fish and Wildlife Area. Silver Springs is located in Kendall County, about 50 miles southwest of Chicago.

Length: 37.6 miles

Approximate riding time: 3 hours

Best bike: Road bike

Terrain: The terrain is composed of gently rolling woodland and farmland alongside the Fox River and a couple arms of Rock Creek.

Traffic and hazards: Watch for traffic on Galena Road and Fox Road. Otherwise, these roads are pretty quiet. A handful of roads on the route are not identified with signs at intersections (each instance of this is identified in the Miles and Directions). Despite the occasional lack of road signs, navigation should be clear. One stretch of Jericho Road has a pretty rough surface. At mile 20.6, you'll encounter a stretch of gravel road that is about 0.5 mile long.

Things to see: Prairie, woodland, farmland, forest preserves, Plano, Fox River, creeks, and small bluffs

Getting there: From Chicago, follow I-55 south until reaching exit 261, where you'll take Highway 126 southwest. Turn right onto Highway 47 in Yorkville and then turn left onto West Fox Road. Follow West Fox Road to Silver Springs State Fish and Wildlife Area. Continue past the first entrance that leads to the concession area on the right. Take the second entrance on the right to the Fox View picnic area. Follow the one-way park road and look for signs for the picnic area. GPS coordinates: 41 38.033 N / 88 31.842 W

THE RIDE

Silver Springs State Fish and Wildlife Area, located on the shore of the Fox River about 15 miles downstream from Aurora, serves as a perfect staging area for this ride. The park is named for an artesian well in the park that seeps from the ground all year long. Plenty of picnickers and anglers come to the park during the warmer months, as do hikers who come to explore the park's trails and have a look-see at the spring that bubbles up on the east side of the park. (The spring is a 0.5-mile hike from the Fox View picnic area where the ride begins. From the boat launch follow the wide trail to the right alongside the Fox River. After the pond, take the trail to the right.)

Start the ride by climbing a small river bluff out of the park and hopping on Fox Road as it cuts through farm fields and passes a newly sprouted housing

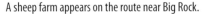

A sheep farm appears on the route near Big Rock.

development. On the aptly named Highpoint Road, the pavement takes you nearly 100 feet up over the course of about 1.5 miles. After turning onto Budd Road, you'll have 20- to 30-mile views of expansive farmland, patches of woodland, and the southern section of Silver Springs' parkland. About 1 mile later, the views vanish as the road takes you down into thick bottomland woods near the crossing of Hollenbeck Creek.

After passing through the village of Millbrook and then crossing the Fox River, check out the small riverside picnic area at the first turnoff on the right. (Staying to the right brings you to an old latticed bridge—now a pedestrian bridge—over the Fox River. The bridge provides a peaceful spot to linger and enjoy views of the densely wooded banks upriver.) From the shore of the Fox River, you'll climb and quickly descend a small bluff. This is a fine stretch of road: Now and then, the woodland opens on the right offering views of the river valley. Immediately after turning onto Burr Oak Road, you're greeted with another short climb.

Starting on Burr Oak Road and continuing for the next 10 miles, you'll be pedaling parallel to Little Rock Creek as it flows toward the Fox River. Attentive riders will catch glimpses of Little Rock Creek on the right as it bends, curves, and zigzags through the wooded terrain sprinkled with new ranchettes and old farmhouses. The left side of the road, in contrast, is uninterrupted farmland that seems to extend all the way to the Iowa border.

Instead of cows or horses in the pasture at the corner of Jericho and Hinckley Roads, you'll see white pillows of curls on four legs roaming the field and bleating. (The sheep will likely approach you if you stand by the fence and do not look like a wolf.) After skipping over the West Branch of Rock Creek and sweeping past a stately old brick farmhouse on the left, Hinckley Road takes you on a winding route into the village of Big Rock. South of Big Rock, it's a very short detour to Big Rock Forest Preserve, a former gravel mine that now contains a collection of hiking trails that run through woodland and prairies, and around a reservoir. South of the park, you'll pass through a checkerboard of open farmland before pulling up alongside Rock Creek's grassy floodplain.

With little warning or fanfare, you'll land on the residential streets of Plano on mile 33 of the ride. On Plano's sleepy downtown strip, watch for the former First State Bank, which looks like it was carved from a single giant block of limestone. Across the street, an old train depot built in 1913 still serves Amtrak passengers. At the corner of Main Street and West Street sits the former Plano Hotel, built in 1868 in an Italianate style. The two-story brick structure served as a hotel until the 1940s.

The town probably hasn't changed significantly since it was inhabited by its most famous resident, Cyrus McCormick, the inventor of the mechanical reaper. McCormick developed the final version of the horse-drawn grain harvester in 1834—after his father spent decades working on prototypes. Historians say the move from hand harvesting to McCormick's reaper allowed farmers to more than double their crop size. In 1839, McCormick left Plano for Chicago, founded a company called International Harvester, and began producing a variety of farm implements. (After merging with a company called Case, the International Harvester brand name is around still and continues to be one of the world's largest manufacturers of agricultural machinery.)

Bike Shop

Pedal and Spoke Limited: 157 South Lincoln Ave., Aurora; (815) 469-3534

The final leg of the journey takes you past Maramech Nature Preserve, located on Griswold Springs Road next to Big Rock Creek. As you cross Big Rock Creek, there's a large mound on the right called Maramech Hill that is part of the preserve. The hill has been a gathering spot since the first humans arrived in the area. Archaeological excavations revealed that the hill was a residence for Indians in these parts for thousands of years.

At River Road, a quick side trip takes you to the Farnsworth House, a famous house designed by the celebrated skyscraper architect Ludwig Mies van der Rohe, who lived and worked in Chicago for part of his career. The unadorned one-story house was built from glass and steel—the same materials that Mies van der Rohe used in his skyscrapers. Architecture fans likely will be enthralled by this 1951 structure that sits on the bank of the Fox River: The house's glass walls are particularly striking in the way they seem to allow a commingling of the indoors and outdoors. On several unfortunate occasions, the outdoors/indoors line was blurred a bit too much when floodwaters from the Fox River engulfed the house.

After crossing the Fox River, you'll enter Silver Springs again and take an enjoyable spin through bottomland woods and past a few ponds as you return to the Fox View picnic area where the ride started.

MILES AND DIRECTIONS

0.0 From the Fox View picnic area, follow the one-way park road back up to Fox Road.

0.4 Turn left onto Fox Road. Stay on Fox Road as it curves to the right.

2.7 When Fox Road curves left, continue straight ahead on Highpoint Road.

4.0 Turn right onto Budd Road. There's no road sign identifying Budd Road, but you won't miss it because it's the first right on Highpoint Road.

6.8 Turn right onto Millbrook Road.

7.1 Turn left onto Fox River Drive in the hamlet of Millbrook, and then immediately turn right onto Whitfield Road.

8.1 Take a break at the sheltered picnic table at the Shuh Shuh Gah Canoe Launch. There are no road signs for it on Whitfield Road; it's the first right after crossing the Fox River. Also visit the pedestrian bridge down the gravel road to the right.

9.1 Turn right onto Millhurst Road.

10.2 Turn left onto Burr Oak Road. Burr Oak Road is unmarked; it's your first left on Millhurst Road.

12.3 Turn left onto Griswold Springs Road where Burr Oak Road ends. No road sign for Griswold Springs Road.

12.7 Turn right onto Sandy Bluff Road.

13.9 Turn right onto Frazier Road.

15.3 Turn left onto Creek Road. No sign for Creek Road—Creek Road starts at the end of Frazier Road.

18.6 Turn right onto Galena Road. Watch for traffic during the 0.3-mile ride on Galena Road.

18.9 Turn left onto Bushnell Road. No road sign; it's your first left on Galena Road.

20.2 Turn right onto McDermott Road. McDermott Road becomes Nelson Road as it curves left. Nelson Road has rough pavement and about 0.5 mile of gravel surface.

21.5 Turn left onto Jericho Road. The pavement is rough on stretches of Jericho Road.

22.7 Turn right onto Hinckley Road.

25.1 Turn right onto Rhodes Street.

26.4 Turn right onto Granart Road.

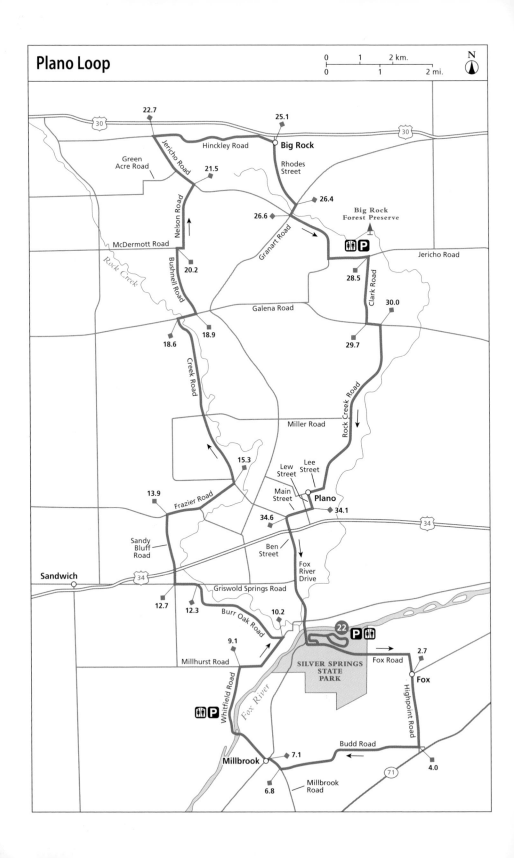

Plano Loop

0   1   2 km.

0   1   2 mi.

N

30

22.7

25.1

Hinckley Road

Big Rock

Green
Acre Road

Jericho Road

21.5

Rhodes
Street

30

26.4

Big Rock
Forest Preserve

26.6

Nelson Road

McDermott Road

Granart Road

Jericho Road

Rock Creek

20.2

Bushnell Road

Galena Road

28.5

Clark Road

30.0

18.6

18.9

29.7

Creek Road

Miller Road

Rock Creek Road

15.3

13.9

Frazier Road

Lew
Street

Lee
Street

Main
Street

Plano

34.1

34.6

34

Sandy
Bluff
Road

Ben
Street

Sandwich

34

Griswold Springs Road

Fox
River
Drive

12.7

12.3

Burr Oak Road

10.2

22

Fox Road

2.7

9.1

Millhurst Road

Whitfield Road

Fox River

SILVER SPRINGS
STATE PARK

Fox

Highpoint Road

Budd Road

71

4.0

7.1

Millbrook

6.8

Millbrook
Road

26.6 Turn left onto Jericho Road.

28.5 Before turning right onto Clark Road, you may want to take a spin through Big Rock Forest Preserve just 100 yards ahead on Jericho Road.

29.7 Turn left onto Galena Road. Watch for traffic; Galena Road is one of the busier roads on this route.

30.0 Turn right onto Rock Creek Road. Follow Rock Creek Road as it curves right and becomes East Lee Street in Plano.

33.8 Turn left onto Lew Street.

34.1 Before crossing the railroad tracks, turn right onto Main Street and enter Plano's downtown strip.

34.6 Turn left onto Ben Street. Outside of Plano, Ben Street becomes Fox River Road.

36.4 To reach the Farnsworth House, turn left onto River Road. The entrance is 0.25 mile ahead on the right.

36.9 Turn left onto Fox Road and then turn into the west entrance for Silver Springs State Park.

37.6 Follow the one-way park road to the Fox View picnic area where you started the ride.

RIDE INFORMATION

Local Events/Attractions

Farnsworth House: Located 0.25 mile off the route; all visitors must preregister for a tour; admission fee; 14520 River Rd., Plano; (630) 552-0052; www.farnsworthhouse.org.

Fox Valley Winery: A tasting room located several miles west of the route; 207 East Church St., Sandwich; (815) 786-3124; www.foxvalleywinery.com.

Lyon Farm Village: Contains a collection of local historic buildings and artifacts; located on Highway 71 east of Yorkville; (630) 553-6777; www.kchs.us/page2.htm.

Silver Springs State Fish and Wildlife Area: The concession stand on the east side of the park has food, snacks, and beverages; 13608 Fox Rd.; (630) 553-6297; http://dnr.state.il.us/lands/landmgt/parks/r2/silversp.htm.

Restaurants

Stone Fire Restaurant and Pub: 2075 Marketview Dr., Yorkville; (630) 553-4585; www.stonefiredine.com.

Restrooms

Start/finish: Restrooms and water are available in Fox View picnic area.

Mile 8.1: Restrooms and water are available at the Shuh Shuh Gah Canoe Launch.

Mile 28.5: Restrooms are available at the Big Rock Forest Preserve. Before turning right onto Clark Road, continue ahead for 100 yards on Jericho Road.

Maps

USGS 7.5" Big Rock quad, USGS 7.5" Newark quad, USGS Plano 7.5" quad
DeLorme: Illinois Atlas and Gazetteer: Page 27

Virgil Gilman Trail

This trail offers a perfect chance to get to know Aurora and its nearby residential and rural environs. West of the city, the trail repeatedly crosses Blackberry Creek and occasionally runs alongside its wooded banks. After crossing a new 100-yard-long trestle bridge over IL 56, you'll enter a stunning forest containing an example of a not-so-common geological feature.

Start: The Hill Avenue parking area east of Aurora

Length: 11.3 miles one way, with an option for extending the trip

Approximate riding time: 1 hour

Best bike: Road, hybrid, or mountain bike

Terrain and trail surface: The trail is paved and the terrain is flat.

Traffic and hazards: Watch for traffic—especially trucks—while following the brief on-street section.

Things to see: Aurora, Fox River, city parks, Blackberry Creek, Waubonsee Community College, prairie, woodland, and Blackberry Farm living-history museum

Wheelchair access: The trail is wheelchair accessible, but there is no sidewalk for a portion of the on-street section. This is also where there's a bit of heavy industry and truck traffic.

Getting there: By car: Head south on IL 31 from I-88. In downtown Aurora turn left onto Galena Boulevard. Continue on Galena Boulevard as the street curves right and becomes Hill Avenue. Look for the parking area on the right. GPS coordinates: 41 43.394 N / 88 17.045 W

To park at Copley Park, head south on IL 31 (Lake Street) from I-88. After passing Aurora's central downtown area, look for the park on the right.

To park at the Blackberry Farm parking area, head south on Orchard Road from I-88. Turn right onto Galena Boulevard and then left onto Barnes Road. There's a trailhead parking area on the right.

To park at the Merrill Road parking area at the west end of the trail, take I-88 west from Aurora. Exit at IL 56 and follow IL 56 to IL 47. Take IL 47 north to Bliss Road. Turn right onto Bliss Road and then left onto Merrill Road. Look for the parking area on the left.

By public transportation: The BNSF Metra line stops in Aurora a mile or so north of the trail.

THE RIDE

The first few miles of this trail offer an introduction to the modest leafy neighborhoods on the east side of Aurora. After an initial stretch where the trail traces an embankment that rises about 6 feet above the surrounding cropland and bottomland woods, residential neighborhoods take over. At 2.7 miles the trail crosses the Fox River on an old latticed train bridge. Before taking in fine views of the Fox from the high bridge, you may consider a side trip south on the 4.6-mile riverbank trail to the town of Oswego.

On the way to Oswego, this south section of the Fox River Trail passes through several parks, the best of which is a long, thin island in the river. While the river along this stretch is persistently eye-catching, the atmosphere is not terribly peaceful because the trail closely follows IL 25. Oswego contains a pleasant riverside park, as well as good dining options close to the trail.

Continuing west along the Virgil Gilman Trail, you'll duck under several bridges and skirt the edge of Copley Park. After passing the park, watch for trucks on Rathbone Street as the trail drops you off in the middle of a not-too-welcoming industrial area for a short on-street stretch.

Bike Shop

Mill Race Cyclery: 11 East State St., Geneva; (630) 232-2833

The beginning of the next section of the trail is marked by a handsome limestone sign and concrete benches. As the trail parallels a swath of bottomland woods, you will see occasional small ponds, some blanketed with algae. You'll also catch glimpses of the Aurora Country Club through the trees on the right. After crossing Orchard Road, look for waterbirds as the trail passes a lake and a couple more ponds. If you enjoy exploring grassland, turn left onto the trail near the ponds for a quick loop through the adjoining prairie and savanna.

After crossing Blackberry Creek on an old steel bridge, you'll arrive at Blackberry Farm Historic Village, a county park that offers kiddie rides, an arboretum, and several museum exhibits. One exhibit displays forty carriages, sleighs, and vintage commercial vehicles. Another exhibit contains a display of eleven late-Victorian-era stores, including a music shop, pharmacy, general store, photography shop, and toy store. The water park across the street is another popular stop for local families.

A mile or so west of Blackberry Farm, the ramp of a steel bridge spanning IL 56 gradually rises from the prairie in front of you. The 100-yard-long powder-blue trestle bridge recently replaced a flood-prone tunnel that went under the highway (the tunnel is still visible south of the bridge).

After crossing IL 56, the trail crosses Blackberry Creek again and then runs beside the creek as it cuts a straight course northwest. At Bliss Woods Forest Preserve, the path cuts through a lovely swath of state-protected woodland thick with sugar maple and basswood trees. In early spring you'll see flowers such as hepatica, bloodroot, and rue anemone. A sprinkling of houses appear on the right; on the left is a hill called an esker—a winding ridge of gravel deposited by a subglacial river. Crossing Bliss Road takes you into a grove of bottomland woods largely composed of oak and maple.

This new trail bridge over IL 56 replaces a flood-prone tunnel.

Virgil Gilman Trail

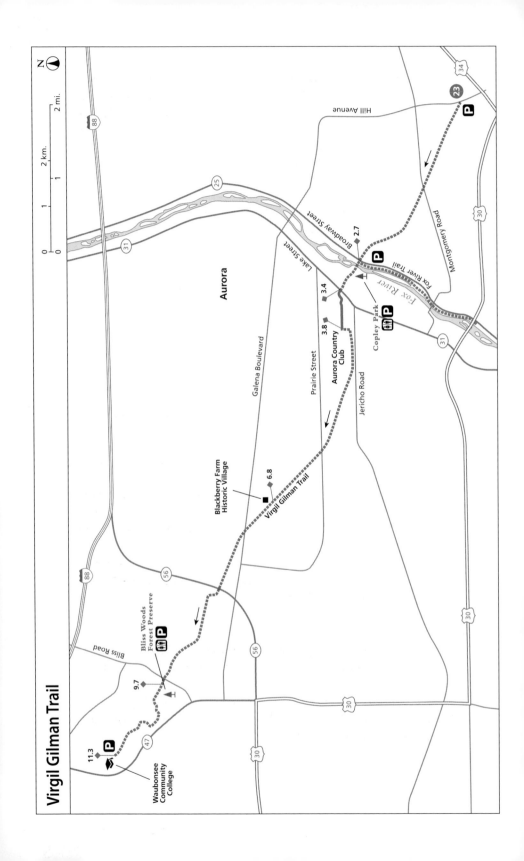

Just before crossing Blackberry Creek one last time, a spur trail on the right leads to a trailhead parking area. The final section of the Virgil Gilman Trail takes you through a large prairie on the campus of Waubonsee Community College. The college operates several campuses in the area, but this is the main one, open since 1967. If you feel like exploring the campus, you'll find a pleasant little pond behind the first set of buildings.

MILES AND DIRECTIONS

0.0 Start at the Hill Avenue parking area.

2.7 Cross the Fox River in Aurora.

3.4 Start brief on-street section by turning right onto Rathbone Street.

3.8 Turn left onto Terry Avenue.

3.9 Pick up the trail on the right.

6.8 Pass Blackberry Farm on the right.

9.7 Enter Bliss Woods Forest Preserve.

11.3 Arrive at the end of the trail at Waubonsee Community College.

RIDE INFORMATION

Local Events/Attractions
Aurora Regional Fire Museum: Vintage firefighting equipment; located in downtown Aurora, across the street from the trailhead for the Aurora Branch of the Prairie Path; 53 North Broadway, Aurora; (630) 892-1572; www.aurora regionalfiremuseum.org.

Blackberry Farm: A living-history museum featuring nineteenth-century exhibits and demonstrations; 100 South Barnes Rd., Aurora; (630) 892-1550; www.foxvalleyparkdistrict.org/?q=node/2.

Restaurants
La Quinta de Los Reyes: Live music and courtyard area in downtown Aurora; 36 East New York St., Aurora; (630) 859-4000; http:// laquintadelosreyesaurora .com.

Orchard Valley Restaurant: American food; located at the public golf course, fairly close to the trail; 2411 West Illinois Ave., Aurora; (630) 907-0600; http:// foxvalleyparkdistrict.org/?q=node/190.

Restrooms

Mile 3.4: There are public restrooms and water available at Copley Park.

Mile 5.6: Restrooms are available at the Orchard Road parking area.

Mile 9.7: Bliss Woods Forest Preserve has water and restrooms (follow the park road left after crossing Bliss Road).

Maps

USGS Aurora South and Sugar Grove

DeLorme: Illinois Atlas and Gazetteer: Pages 27 and 28

Waterfall Glen Trail

While following this winding trail through the diverse and sometimes rugged landscape at Waterfall Glen Forest Preserve, you'll encounter dense stands of oak and pine, a generous number of ponds and cattail marshes, a prairie, and a small waterfall. Just past the halfway point is an overlook of the Des Plaines River valley and the nearby community of Lemont.

Start: Begin the ride at the parking area on Northgate Road, west of Cass Avenue

Length: 9.3 miles

Approximate riding time: 1 hour

Best bike: A hybrid bike, a mountain bike, or a road bike with wider tires

Terrain and trail surface: Expect gently rolling terrain with occasional hills that will test your legs. The entire path is crushed limestone.

Traffic and hazards: This trail can get busy on the weekends. Keep an eye peeled for fellow trail users, particularly the young ones who may not be watching for bikes.

Things to see: Woodlands sprinkled with ponds, marshes, and small streams

Getting there: From Chicago, take I-55 south to exit 273A, Cass Avenue. Drive 0.2 mile and turn right onto Northgate Road, just beyond the Waterfall Glen Forest Preserve information building. Less than 100 yards up on the right is the parking lot and trailhead. GPS coordinates: 41 43.517 N / 87 58.449 W

In addition to the trailhead, you can park at Bluff Road parking area. From I-55, follow South Cass Avenue until it turns left and becomes Bluff Road. The parking area is on the right. To reach the Lemont Road parking area, head south from I-55 on Lemont Road (exit 271A). The parking area is on the left.

THE RIDE

Waterfall Glen surrounds Argonne National Laboratory, one of the U.S. Department of Energy's largest research facilities. Operated by the University of Chicago, Argonne and its previous incarnations have been involved in high-level national research, including the Manhattan Project. In more recent years, much of the research has been focusing on extremely bright X-ray beams. While circling Argonne Laboratory, you won't see any of the laboratory's buildings, but you will see plenty of ponds, wetlands, woods, and probably some wildlife such as deer, waterbirds, and hawks.

After saddling up at the trailhead, the first mile takes you across three roads before reaching the pristine 91st Street Marsh. At the marsh, swallows

The waterfall at Waterfall Glen Forest Preserve was built by the Civilian Conservation Corps from local limestone.

twirl above the open water. Stands of cattails gather at the edges of the water; pine and oak grow on the banks. Beyond the marsh, the trail passes under a canopy of arthritic oak and maple branches before leading you into a fragrant plantation of red, jack, and white pine. In the 1950s, Argonne planted pine trees to help with erosion control and to serve as a buffer against the surrounding community.

After passing the first parking area at about 3 miles into the ride, follow the Rocky Glen Trail to the right. This trail takes you down a steep wooded bluff to a 5-foot waterfall along Sawmill Creek. Oddly, Waterfall Glen actually was not named after this or any other waterfall. Rather, the name honors Seymour "Bud" Waterfall, who served as an early president of the county's forest preserve board. To further complicate matters, you should know that this waterfall is about

Bike Shop

Richard's Bicycles: This cycle shop has been around for more than a century; 11933 South Harlem Ave., Palos Heights; (708) 448-4601.

as natural as the plastic deer that Illinoisans love to stick on their lawns: The Civilian Conservation Corps built this waterfall in the 1930s using limestone from the preserve. During the late nineteenth century, three quarries in Waterfall Glen produced high-quality limestone. (Waterfall Glen provided the limestone for one of the most famous structures in Chicago—the Water Tower, built in 1869 at Chicago and Michigan Avenues.)

Back up the bluff, the trail traces the top edge of the 80-foot-deep ravine containing the creek. The sides of the ravine are blanketed with black and white oak, and bitternut and shagbark hickories. Near the electrical switching station, several concrete-and-stone building foundations from the early 1910s sit beside the trail. The foundations are remnants of a plant nursery the Chicago parks system once operated here.

Just ahead, you'll encounter a spot offering expansive views of a valley containing the Des Plaines River and the Chicago Sanitary and Ship Canal. The rising bluff on the opposite side of the river hosts the small community of Lemont.

People who take pleasure in wide-open spaces will enjoy the next stretch as the path gradually climbs about 100 feet into Poverty Prairie and Savanna, named for an abundant local plant called poverty-oat grass. The low horizons of the prairie offer an ideal spot for the model airplane airfield that sits near Bluff Road.

The remainder of the trail wiggles between large, dramatic oaks and several marshy areas. Following Tear-Thumb Marsh, the trail passes more planta-

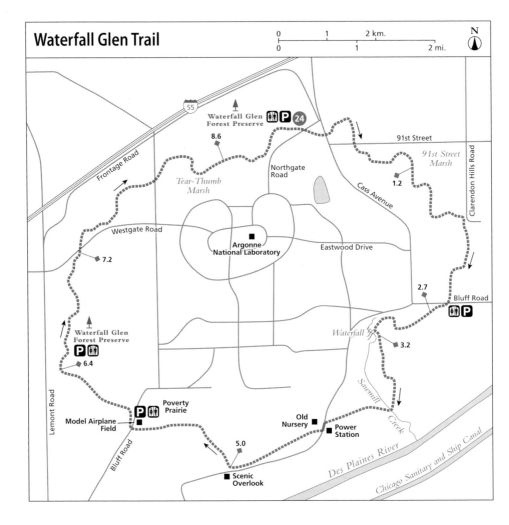

Waterfall Glen Trail

tions of pine and a swath of wetlands sometimes visible from the trail. A small bridge takes you over Sawmill Creek before arriving back at the parking lot.

MILES AND DIRECTIONS

- **0.0** Follow the spur trail from the parking area to the main loop trail. On the main trail, turn left for a clockwise loop.

- **2.9** Turn right onto the Rocky Glen Trail, which doubles as a gravel service road. One hundred feet ahead on the Rocky Glen Trail, turn left to follow a 0.2-mile trail down a ravine to Sawmill Creek.

4.9 Before turning right, continue ahead to the scenic overlook.

9.3 Return to the parking area where the ride started.

RIDE INFORMATION

Local Events/Attractions
Brookfield Zoo: Contains a huge variety of animals from all over the world; 3300 Golf Rd., Brookfield; (708) 688-8000; www.brookfieldzoo.com.
Morton Arboretum: Admirers of woody vegetation will be thrilled with this place; 4100 Highway 53, Lisle; (630) 968-0074; www.mortonarb.org.

Restaurants
Cornerstone Restaurant: Basic menu; close to the trail; 8025 South Cass Ave., Darien; (630) 960-1600.
Gordon Biersch Brewery: Part of a national chain of breweries; full menu; 639 East Boughton Rd., Bolingbrook; (630) 739-6036.
Joy Yee's Noodles: Local chain with a wide-ranging menu touching on many types of Asian food; 1163 East Ogden Ave., Naperville; (630) 579-6800.

Restrooms
Start/finish: Restrooms and water are available at the trailhead.
Mile 2.7: Restrooms and water are available at the Bluff Road parking area.
Mile 5.7: Restrooms are available at the model airplane field.
Mile 6.4: Restrooms are located at the Lemont Road parking area.

Maps
USGS 7.5" Sag Bridge quad, USGS 7.5" Romeoville quad
DeLorme: Illinois Atlas and Gazetteer: Page 28
Waterfall Glen trail maps are available at the information board in the parking area and on the DuPage County Forest Preserve District website: www.dupageforest.com/preserve.aspx?id=4224.

North Chicagoland and Wisconsin

As you start to explore the northern part of Chicagoland on a bicycle, a few things quickly stand out. First, you'll see the area is jam-packed with scenic destinations. The many miles of Lake Michigan shoreline, great parks, and interesting towns invite visitors to linger. Also of interest to cyclists—hills! Each of the road rides in this region serve up those landforms—typically elusive in Chicagoland—in various sizes and shapes. The Barrington Loop offers a fine collection of wooded hills and plenty of rural ambience in a location not terribly far from the city. Just 35 miles north of Barrington, on the Walworth/Racine Counties Loop, the rolling Wisconsin terrain is occasionally interrupted by tsunami-size hills, the largest of which actually hosts a ski resort.

A rolling pastoral landscape dominates the Walworth/Racine Counties Loop. See Ride 33.

The water tower at Fort Sheridan is a historic landmark on the North Shore. See Ride 30.

Two-wheeled explorers are missing some of the best riding in the area if they haven't journeyed down the Robert McClory Trail, the Des Plaines River Trail, and Prairie Trail. Since all three trails run parallel, there are options for jumping from one to another for the sake of creating a longer trip. The Des Plaines River Trail delivers the most natural beauty as it passes through about ten forest preserves within the Des Plaines River Valley. The Prairie Trail offers plenty of natural beauty, too, but fewer parks and more of a remote atmosphere. Paralleling the Lake Michigan shoreline to the east, the Robert McClory Trail runs through a string of bustling north shore communities where you can take a break in a coffee shop or sit down for a fine meal.

If your goal is to get away from the hubbub, the Long Prairie and Stone Bridge Trails, the Woodstock Loop, and the aforementioned Walworth/Racine Counties Loop all offer perfect options. Each of these rides takes you to the outer edges of the region where towns are few and the landscape expansive. On the Woodstock Loop, you will see the most charming town square in the Midwest.

If a shorter ride is on the agenda, be sure to check out the stunning patchwork of wetlands, small hills, creeks, and woods at Moraine Hills State Park. The centerpiece of the park, Lake Defiance, is one of only a handful of glacially created lakes in the area that has remained undeveloped. Just 20 miles northwest of Moraine Hills is another enjoyable short ride. This one takes you up steep bluffs and through a few small towns as you circle Geneva Lake. You'll quickly be won over by the historic structures and the inviting parks that appear along the way.

Short rides, long rides, urban or rural—you'll find plenty of great options to get your cycling fix in this part of Chicagoland.

Barrington Loop

Given the bustle of the surrounding suburban landscape, the rural character of this ride seems unlikely. As you encounter the oak-covered hills, sprawling marsh-lands, and farms mixed in with a scattering of often-palatial houses, you'll find yourself congratulating the local residents who fought to preserve the area's rural charm.

Start: Lions Park, located on the shore of the Fox River in Fox River Grove

Length: 28.9 miles

Approximate riding time: 2–3 hours

Best bike: Road bike

Terrain: The terrain is rolling and sometimes hilly.

Traffic and hazards: The two short stretches on Lake-Cook Road tend to be busy. Approach these sections of roadway with care.

Things to see: Woodland, prairie, wetlands, forest preserves, rural residential areas, and hills

Getting there: By car: Take I-90 northwest of Chicago to Barrington Road and head north. In Barrington, turn left onto Northwest Highway (US 14). Turn left onto Algonquin Road and then turn right onto River Road. Park in Lions Park at the end of the road. **By public transportation:** The ride starts 0.5 mile from the Fox River Grove Metra station on the Union Pacific District Northwest Metra line. From the Metra station, take Lincoln Avenue left (southwest). Turn right onto Beachway Drive, left onto Millard Avenue, and right onto River Road. Start from Lions Park on the right. GPS coordinates: 42 11.825 N / 88 13.705 W

THE RIDE

When Chicago businessmen and their families began coming to Barrington after World War I, they were attracted to the rural setting and saw the poten-tial to create a genteel atmosphere in the Chicago suburbs. They transformed old farms into estates and established numerous horse farms and riding facilities. Many houses were built to mimic English countryside manors or, in some bizarre cases, fortified castles from medieval England. Reinforcing this carefully cultivated air of English gentry, the area is sometimes referred to as "the Barringtons" because five local communities have "Barrington" in their names.

The first part of the ride takes you over the wooded bluffs that rise along the Fox River. Hills that line the opposite shore of the Fox occasionally peek through the trees while you're passing over the high point of the bluff. Descending to the river's edge, you'll follow a wavy ribbon of asphalt that parallels the 150-yard-wide waterway. River homes with big porches and inviting yards line the sides of the river.

Leaving the river behind, you'll make a short but steep climb back up the bluff. Spring Creek Road takes you through a landscape of cropland, wooded spots, various types of farms, and a small cemetery dating from 1842.

Remnants from Barrington's farming history appear regularly on this ride.

Lake-Cook Road marks the beginning of Spring Creek Valley Forest Preserve—4,000 acres of densely tangled woodland, tranquil prairie, and reedy marshes active with birds. Signs along the road indicate efforts to rid the area of invasive plants and restore the native landscape. Interrupting the savannas and wetlands are oak- and hickory-laden hills—some of which may prompt you to drop into the granny gear while climbing. Mixed in with the woods and open space are horse farms, scattered houses, and the occasional lavish estate.

Before you turn onto Otis Road, a vast marshland with acres of cattails and open water is cradled by the landscape on the left. More wetlands and a sprinkling of little lakes accompany the route into the village of Barrington.

Given the tony atmosphere of Barrington, one would not guess it was the location of the final shoot-out between the FBI and the notorious gangster "Baby Face" Nelson. During the 1934 shoot-out, two FBI agents were killed; Nelson died a short time later from seventeen bullet wounds.

Soon after Barrington, the route cuts through the links at the Barrington Country Club and then passes the Grigsby Prairie, a swath of grassland managed by local citizens. Near the end of the ride, along the rolling wooded hills of Plum Tree Road, you'll pass an enormous mansion-castle (you may expect to see archers standing guard on its turrets). Returning to Lions Park, take some time to relax on the shore of the Fox River before heading home.

Bike Shops

Prairie Trail Bike Shop: Located on the Prairie Trail; 315 Railroad St., Algonquin; (847) 658-1154

Village CycleSport: 203 West Northwest Hwy., Barrington; (847) 382-9200; http://villagecyclesport.com

MILES AND DIRECTIONS

0.0 From Lions Park, head south (away from the Fox River) on River Road.

0.3 Turn right onto Algonquin Road, then follow it left through a sharp turn. Stay right on Algonquin Road at the junction with Old Hunt Road and Plum Tree Road. At Haegers Bend Road, Algonquin Road becomes River Drive.

4.3 Turn left onto SR 62/Algonquin Road. This road is typically very busy; use care riding along this stretch or consider walking your bike on the sidewalk for this 2-block stretch.

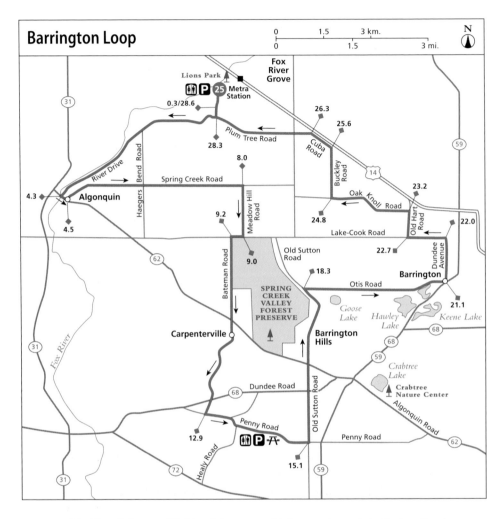

Barrington Loop

0   1.5   3 km.

0   1.5   3 mi.

N

Fox River Grove

Lions Park

P 25 Metra Station

0.3/28.6

31

26.3

25.6

Plum Tree Road

28.3

Cuba Road

8.0

59

Buckley Road

14

River Drive

Bend Road

Spring Creek Road

23.2

Haegers

4.3

Algonquin

Oak Knoll Road

Meadow Hill Road

9.2

24.8

Old Hart Road

4.5

Lake-Cook Road

22.0

62

22.7

Dundee Avenue

Bateman Road

9.0

Old Sutton Road

Barrington

18.3

Otis Road

31

Fox River

SPRING CREEK VALLEY FOREST PRESERVE

Goose Lake

Hawley Lake

21.1

Keene Lake

68

Carpenterville

Barrington Hills

68

59

Crabtree Lake

Crabtree Nature Center

Dundee Road

Old Sutton Road

Algonquin Road

68

12.9

Penny Road

P

Penny Road

62

72

Healy Road

15.1

59

31

4.5 Turn left onto Highland Avenue, which soon turns into Spring Creek Road.

8.0 Turn right onto Meadow Hill Road (watch closely for a somewhat hidden street sign).

9.0 Turn right onto Lake-Cook Road (stay close to the shoulder on this busy road).

9.2 Turn left onto Bateman Road.

12.9 Turn left onto Penny Road. Bear right at the slightly confusing intersection of Penny Road and Healy Road. The Penny Road Pond picnic area is the only forest preserve picnic area you'll encounter.

15.1 Turn left onto Old Sutton Road.

18.3 Turn right onto Otis Road.

21.1 Turn left onto Dundee Avenue (access downtown Barrington by turning right onto Station Avenue).

22.0 Turn left onto Lake-Cook Road.

22.7 Turn right onto Old Hart Road (the next street after Hart Road).

23.2 Turn left onto Oak Knoll Road.

24.8 Turn right onto Buckley Road.

25.6 Where Buckley Road ends, turn left onto Cuba Road (no street sign). On Cuba Road immediately turn right onto West Cuba Road (no street sign).

26.3 Bear left onto Plum Tree Road.

28.3 Turn right onto Algonquin Road.

28.6 Turn left onto River Road.

28.9 Return to Lions Park.

RIDE INFORMATION

Local Events/Attractions

Crabtree Nature Center: Features some of the best hiking trails in the area; 3 Stover Rd. (enter on Palatine Road, between Barrington Road and Algonquin Road), Barrington; (847) 381-6592.

Goebbert's Pumpkin and Farm Market: Large market with a cafe; 40 West Higgins Rd., South Barrington; (847) 428-6727; www.pumpkinfarms.com /SBarrington.html.

Lake County Discovery Museum: Impressive local museum contains largest postcard collection in the world; 27277 Forest Preserve Dr., Wauconda; (847) 968-3400; www.lcfpd.org/.

Restaurants

Barrington Chocolate and Ice Cream Shop: Also sells homemade fudge and pie; close to the route; 140 South Cook St., Barrington; (847) 381-9973; www .barringtonchocolate.com.

Egg Harbor Cafe: Local chain serves up breakfast and lunch; 210 South Cook St., Barrington; (847) 304-4033; www.eggharborcafe.com.

Millrose Restaurant: Steak, seafood, and sandwiches; 45 South Barrington Rd., South Barrington; (847) 382-7673; www.millroserestaurant.com.

Port Edward Restaurant: Seafood and steak; dining areas overlook the Fox River; 20 West Algonquin Rd., Algonquin; (847) 658-5441; www.portedward.com.

Restrooms

Start/finish: Portable toilets in Lions Park.

Mile 5.4: Presidential Park has restrooms and water.

Mile 14.4: Penny Road Pond picnic area has a portable toilet.

Mile 22.0: The Starbucks in Barrington has restrooms.

Maps

USGS: Barrington quad, Crystal Lake quad, Streamwood quad

DeLorme: Illinois Atlas & Gazetteer: Page 20

Single file, please

It's no surprise that road bikers from around the region are lured to Barrington's wooded hills, scenic farmland, and quiet roads. Unfortunately, this perceived proliferation of bright Spandex and carbon fiber bicycles has peeved some of the locals. In 2008 the Village of Barrington Hills passed an ordinance requiring that cyclists ride single file on municipal roads. So, when riding in Barrington Hills, which includes the entire south section of this ride, you have to follow-the-leader. Sure, it's a pain when you want to chat with fellow riders, but it's better than getting a traffic ticket. In passing this ordinance, Barrington Hills joined with a handful of other local communities that have similar laws. While many of these communities may not be enforcing the law, Barrington Hills claims it will.

Des Plaines River Trail

If you like riparian landscapes, you'll love the Des Plaines River Trail as it winds alongside tree-laden riverbanks, through dense bottomland woods, alongside ponds, and over footbridges. Quiet oak savannas and many acres of tallgrass prairie thick with goldenrod, asters, and big bluestem prairie grass decorate the trail borders. Spanning nearly the entire length of Lake County, the trail gives visitors an extended encounter with this attractive river and the surrounding— mostly wet—landscape.

Start: Half Day Forest Preserve in southeast Lake County near Vernon Hills

Length: 24.8 miles one way

Approximate riding time: 2–3 hours

Best bike: Hybrid or road bike

Terrain and trail surface: The trail is crushed gravel and the terrain is mostly flat.

Traffic and hazards: There are many trail junctions along the way, but the plentiful trail signs make navigation easy. Thanks to careful planning, the trail runs under most of the busy roads. Occasionally, the rising river swallows up these underpasses. The county posts signs during flooding, in which case you cross the road at street level instead.

Things to see: Des Plaines River, numerous forest preserves, bottomland woods, prairie, savanna, lakes, ponds

Wheelchair access: Both the trail and the parking areas are wheelchair accessible.

Getting there: By car: Several miles north of where I-294 and I-94 converge, exit I-94 at Half Day Road and head west. At IL 21 (Milwaukee Avenue) turn right. The entrance is on the right. GPS coordinates: 42 13.036 N / 87 56.069 W

To reach the IL 60 parking area, exit I-94 at IL 60 and head west. Park on the left just across the river.

To park at Old School Forest Preserve, exit I-94 at IL 176 and head west. Turn left onto St. Mary's Road. The entrance to the preserve is on the left.

To access the trail from Independence Grove Forest Preserve, exit I-94 at IL 137 and drive west. The preserve is on the right.

To reach the Kilbourn Road parking area, exit I-94 at IL 132 and drive east. Turn left onto Kilbourn Road; the parking area is on the left.

To reach the Wadsworth Road parking area from the south, exit I-94 at IL 132 and drive east. Turn left onto IL 21 (Milwaukee Avenue). Turn left again onto US 41 and then right onto Wadsworth Road. Parking is on the right.

To park at Van Patten Woods Forest Preserve, exit I-94 at IL 173 and drive east; the entrance is on the left.

To park at the Russell Road parking area, exit I-94 at Russell Road and head east. The parking area is on the right.

By public transportation: The Milwaukee District/North Metra line stops in Libertyville less than 1 mile from the Des Plaines River Trail. The route from the train station to the trail runs along quiet streets and has paths and sidewalks along the way. Just north of where the train crosses IL 21, turn right onto Appley Avenue and then left onto Oak Spring Road. The trail crosses the road after you pass Minear Lake on the left.

THE RIDE

Given all the development in the area surrounding the Des Plaines River, it may come as a surprise to see how much nature lines the river. Indeed, the many forest preserves that accompany the Des Plaines River in Lake and Cook Counties serve as the longest greenway in the Chicago region. In Lake County no fewer than ten forest preserves lie along a continuous path within the Des Plaines River Valley as it runs from Vernon Hills to the Wisconsin border. (To the south in Cook County, the Des Plaines River Trail runs for about another 20 miles or so—although not continuously.)

In addition to the many benefits these greenways provide for humans, ecologists will attest to the advantages of long, extended natural areas for local plants and animals too. Plants and animals tend to be healthier when they are not cut off from one another and are part of a larger gene pool. Animals also are more likely to thrive if they have room to move around and don't have to cross busy roads regularly.

As you start heading north along the trail from Half Day Forest Preserve, you'll immediately encounter one of many footbridges along the trail. This footbridge sits in an especially attractive setting: Half Day Forest Preserve is on one side and Wright Woods Forest Preserve is on the other. Across the bridge, spur trails spin off in various directions through the dense bottomlands of Wright Woods. Before the trail takes you beneath IL 60, you'll cross two more foot-bridges and pass through bottomland woods alongside the river and stretches of prairie that butt against a sprinkling of light industry on the left.

The next stretch of trail threads its way through two attractive forest pre-serves. The first preserve, MacArthur Woods, offers a mix of savanna and wood-land. Among the hickories, maples, and oaks, look for birds such as brown creeper, red-shouldered hawks, and pileated woodpeckers. The next forest pre-serve, Old School, takes you through a great expanse of prairie decorated with goldenrod, heath and sky-blue asters, and big bluestem prairie grass.

The prairie at Old School Forest Preserve gradually slopes down in the direction you're traveling—toward the Des Plaines River. Even though devel-

Prairie and wetlands figure prominently along much of the Des Plaines River Trail.

opment exists on both sides of the pathway, it's off in the distance and you don't feel cramped. Getting closer to the river, the path curls to the right and passes a housing development and thick bottomland woods and then brushes against a pond before heading under IL 176 and the North Shore Bike Path. (The North Shore Bike Path shadows IL 176 for 7.5 miles between Mundelein to the west and Lake Bluff to the east. In Lake Bluff you can connect with the Robert McClory Trail.)

Continuing north, the trail winds through groves of maple, hickory, and oak before cutting through marshland that hosts a scattering of ponds. After you cross Oak Spring Road, a small lake appears over the embankment on the left. Like many of the lakes and ponds along the river, this lake—called Minear Lake—was created by a former gravel mining operation. Up ahead, a sign points up the bluff to Adler Park, which contains picnicking areas and a Frisbee golf course. At Independence Grove Forest Preserve, the trail mounts a hill that allows an expansive view of the 1,110-acre preserve and the 6 miles of trails that wrap around the 115-acre lake (also a former gravel pit).

Bike Shop

Smart Cycling: 2300 Lehigh Ave., Suite 100, Glenview; (847) 998-0200

North of Independence Grove, the trail winds through prairie, savanna, and woodland and then weaves through a power line right-of-way before passing under IL 120. For the next 3.5 miles, between encounters with five busy roads, the trail runs intermittently alongside the river and through bottomland woods. Just before the Washington Street underpass, the roller coasters at Six Flags Great America Amusement Park appear above the trees to the west.

For those intrigued with floodplain forests and wet prairies, the next 4 miles after US 41 offer a special treat. First the trail mounts a raised bed and cuts through an area with dozens of little ponds surrounded by dense stands of elm, hickory, and maple trees. Beyond this very wet woodland, the trail skirts the edge of a pleasant expanse of water fringed by willows and cottonwood. The body of water seems to be a lake but is actually one of the pools of the river. After the pool, the trail swings left into open grassy wetlands, where you'll see groves of enormous oaks, a string of ponds to the left, and large spreads of cattails and wet prairie. The trail winds through more stunning wetlands, open prairie, and groves of oak after crossing Wadsworth Road. Traffic sounds come from US 41, which parallels the trail.

Before reaching the end of the trail, you'll encounter Sterling Lake—a former gravel pit that is now an attractive lake fringed by grassland and savanna.

Des Plaines River Trail

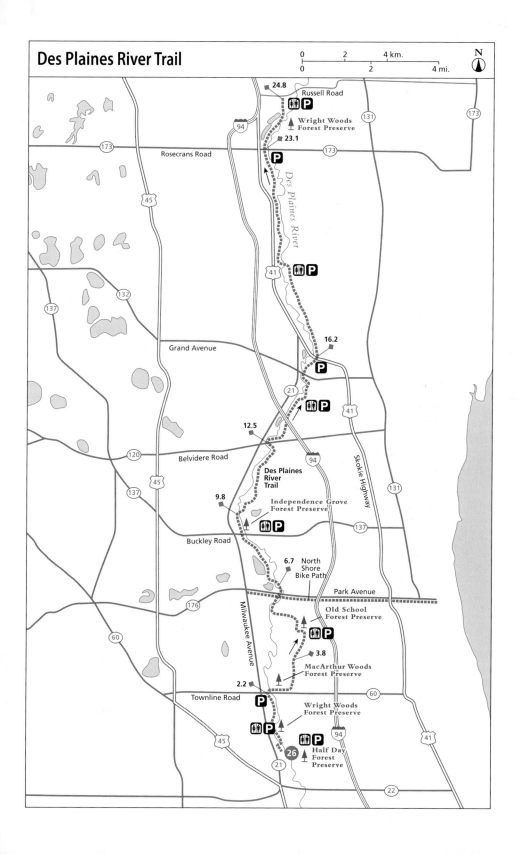

0   2   4 km.

0   2   4 mi.

N

24.8 Russell Road

Wright Woods
Forest Preserve

23.1

Des Plaines River

173

94

41

16.2

21

12.5

94

Des Plaines
River
Trail

9.8

Independence Grove
Forest Preserve

Belvidere Road

Buckley Road

6.7 North
Shore
Bike Path

Park Avenue

Old School
Forest Preserve

3.8

MacArthur Woods
Forest Preserve

2.2

Townline Road

Wright Woods
Forest Preserve

26

Half Day
Forest
Preserve

Milwaukee Avenue

Skokie Highway

Grand Avenue

Rosecrans Road

173

131

173

131

137

132

45

45

120

137

176

60

45

41

94

60

137

22

21

North of Sterling Lake the path runs through more prairie and savanna before hitting the Russell Road parking area at the end of the trail.

MILES AND DIRECTIONS

0.0   Start from Half Day Forest Preserve.

2.2   Cross a footbridge after passing the access to the Vernon Hills Bike Trail.

3.8   Go through a tunnel under the railroad tracks on the way to Old School Forest Preserve.

6.7   Cross a footbridge just north of IL 176.

9.8   Arrive at Independence Grove Forest Preserve.

12.5   Pass under IL 120.

14.3   Before passing under Washington Street, look west for a glimpse of Six Flags Great America theme park.

16.2   Cross US 41.

20.3   Cross Wadsworth Road.

23.1   Cross IL 173 and enter Van Patten Woods.

24.8   Arrive at the end of the trail at the Russell Road parking area.

RIDE INFORMATION

Local Events/Attractions

Lake County Discovery Museum: Nifty exhibits focusing on local history; museum contains the largest postcard collection in the world; 27277 Forest Preserve Dr., Wauconda; (847) 968-3400; www.lcfpd.org/discovery_museum. **Offshore:** Paddling shop located close to the Des Plaines River; rentals available; put in and take out at one of the many canoe launches on this stretch of river; 701 North Milwaukee Ave., # 348, Vernon Hills; (847) 362-4880; www .offshore-chicago.com.

Restaurants

Flatlanders Restaurant and Brewery: Good food; several regular and seasonal beers brewed on-site; located about 1 mile south of the trailhead; 200 Village Green, Lincolnshire; (847) 821-1234; www.flatlanders.com.

Restrooms

Start: Find restrooms and water at Half Day Forest Preserve.

Mile 5.1: Restrooms and water are available at Old School Forest Preserve.

Mile 9.8: Restrooms and water are available at Independence Grove Forest Preserves.

Mile 14.5: Growe Park has restrooms and water.

Mile 20.3: Restrooms are available north of Wadsworth Road.

Mile 24.8: Restroom and water are available at the north trailhead at Russell Road.

Maps

USGS Libertyville, Wadsworth, and Wheeling

DeLorme: Illinois Atlas and Gazetteer: Pages 20 and 21

Map boards are located along the trail; paper maps are sometimes available at the boards or visit www.lcfpd.org/ docs/map_22079.pdf.

Lake Geneva Loop

While circling Geneva Lake, you'll begin to understand why the captains of Chicago industry built their summer homes on the shoreline of this postcard-perfect lake in southeastern Wisconsin. The lake's wooded bluffs, the quaint lakeside towns, and swanky resorts continue to draw people from Chicago and Milwaukee. Most of the action on this ride takes place on the northern shore of the lake as you pedal through towns, past beaches, and along the shore of Lake Como. This is also where you'll come across the glorious Yerkes Observatory.

Start: Start at Edgewater Park located on the Geneva Lake shoreline in Williams Bay, located about 85 miles northwest of Chicago

Length: 20.2 miles

Approximate riding time: 2 hours

Best bike: Road bike

Terrain: Expect a mix of flat and rolling terrain, as well as a few big hills.

Traffic and hazards: Lakeshore Drive is not a particularly quiet road, but, typically, a good-size shoulder offers plenty of room for riding.

Things to see: Lake Geneva (the town and the lake), bluffs, Yerkes Observatory, Williams Bay, Fontana, Lake Como

Getting there: Take I-90/94 west, proceeding along I-94 as it splits off northward. Exit I-94 at Highway 173 (Rosecrans Road). Follow Highway 173 west until reaching US 12. Turn right onto US 12 and follow it into Wisconsin to Highway 50. Turn left onto Highway 50. After passing through the town of Lake Geneva, turn left onto Geneva Street toward Williams Bay. Park in one of the many spaces in Edgewater Park on the left. GPS coordinates: 42 34.722 N / 88 32.1 W

THE RIDE

Lake Geneva, once known as the Hamptons of the Midwest, became a popular resort destination following the Great Chicago Fire of 1871 when wealthy Chicago families built opulent summer homes on the shore of the lake. Industrialists with household names like Maytag, Swift, Wrigley, and Morton each built outsize estates. After the turn of the century, a number of clubs, youth camps, and upscale subdivisions started squeezing in between the sprawling estates. Even Chicago gangsters developed a fondness for the lake and its resorts catering to beachgoers, golfers, and sailing enthusiasts. Hugh Hefner raised Lake Geneva's profile by building a Playboy Club here.

While the mansions remain, the lake no longer carries the exclusive cachet it once did. Expensive resorts and clubs still operate on the shoreline, but now you also can find affordable restaurants and accommodations—as well as tiresome stores selling nifty stuff for tourists. (Officially, the town is called Lake Geneva, and the lake is called Geneva Lake. In practice, both names are used for the lake.) Many visitors to Geneva Lake come to gawk at the huge estates from the deck of a tour boat, or they opt for a closer look by following the extraordinary walking path that circumnavigates the entire lake.

Located on a bluff above Geneva Lake, the Yerkes Observatory served as an important astronomical research center in the early twentieth century.

In the early days, Chicago passengers would catch a train from Chicago to Geneva Lake. When arriving in the town of Williams Bay, passengers would disembark and waiting boats would take them to their shore-side estates. Now, the former train stop in Williams Bay is part of a wetlands nature preserve, complete with hiking trails. Across the street from the preserve is Edgewater Park, where this ride begins.

Leaving the beach and the small marina in Edgewater Park, you'll start off with a small climb up to Cedar Point, a well-groomed residential area containing one of the oldest housing subdivisions in the nation—built in 1923. This stretch of wooded lakeshore hosted the summer home of Andy of the "Amos and Andy" radio show. Also, four generations of the Schwinn family (of bicycle manufacturing fame) spent summers at a house formerly on this stretch of shoreline. It feels like the sort of neighborhood where a private security guard may suddenly pull up in a golf cart to ask where you're going.

The deluxe vacation homes immediately disappear after you take a short hop north to Lake Como. Lake Como is a smaller lake lined with modest homes and cottages. After 2 miles of perfect cycling on this smooth, quiet road that follows the shore, you'll trundle your way up a steep, lung-busting climb on McDonald Road. Soon, the rolling and wooded terrain gives way to a flat residential neighborhood within the town of Lake Geneva.

After crossing Main Street—brimming with shops—you'll pass the distinctive Prairie-style Lake Geneva Public Library building, built by a protégé of Frank Lloyd Wright. Also on the right is the Riviera Ballroom, constructed on a short pier on Geneva Lake by the Civilian Conservation Corps in the 1920s. Private parties and city events take place in the ballroom upstairs while the ground level offers an assortment of snack and knickknack shops. A fountain with an angel decorates the front of the building; tour boats dock at the back.

Wrigley Drive threads its way between the lake on the right and Flat Iron Park on the left. In the park stands a bronze statue of the cartoon figure Andy Gump, whose creator, Sidney Smith, lived on the lake. According to the plaque, Andy Gump was the first daily cartoon strip in the *Chicago Tribune*. The park also contains a gazebo, as well as a statue of the Three Graces—Joy, Charm, and Beauty are depicted as lithe young maidens.

After leaving the town behind, you'll pass Stone Manor, the largest and perhaps the most distinctive mansion on the lake. Built for about $1 million in 1901 by a Chicago real-estate investor, the four-floor, fifty-room Italianate palace was transformed into a private girls' school in the 1930s. In recent years, it was divided into condos, with a swimming pool plopped on the roof. Nearby on this stretch of shoreline is Maytag Point, named after the washing-machine manufacturer who once owned a house there.

When South Lakeshore Drive drops down to the shore of Geneva Lake, take a careful look at the seven-acre Ceylon Lagoon in Bigfoot Beach State Park on the left. Believe it or not, the lagoon, created by the Maytag family, is actually a small replica of Geneva Lake. While the banks of the lagoon changed slightly over the years, it retains the basic shape of the lake. The Maytag family and other local landowners sold this land to the state for the creation of the park in the 1940s and '50s. The park's namesake is Chief Maunk-suck—"Big Foot" in English—who lived in the area from the late 1700s until 1836, when

Bike Shop

RRB Cycles Lake Geneva: 629 Williams Street (Hwy. 120), Lake Geneva, Wisconsin; (262) 248-2588; http://rrbcyclesusa .com

he and his group of Potawatomis were kicked out and forced to move to Lawrence, Kansas. Downtown Fontana, on the west side of Geneva Lake, contains a bronze, life-size statue depicting a somber Chief Big Foot as he looks toward the lake for the last time before departing for Kansas.

Ready for a hearty climb back up the bluff? Let's hope so. For the next mile, the road climbs steadily with occasional steep spots. Halfway up the bluff, you'll pass the Geneva Inn, a newer resort perched on the bluff above the lake.

During the next 7.5 miles, with the lake out of view, you'll find yourself admiring a series of attractive yards and gardens and a handful of well-kept historic homes. The lake comes back into view briefly at a small roadside turnout with a sign commemorating the Badger State's first 4-H club. Hills and woods prevail as you draw near to the Abbey Springs Golf Course and the South Shore Club. Back at the shoreline in the town of Fontana, the road squeezes between a sprawling marina on the left and a wide sandy public beach on the right.

On the other side of Fontana, get ready for a long, curving, and punishingly steep climb on Lakeshore Drive. At the top of the bluff, the landscape flattens and becomes gently rolling as you pass George Williams College, originally a YMCA college that moved from Chicago to this location in the 1930s. In 1992 the college merged into Aurora University, based in Aurora, Illinois.

On the way back to Williams Bay, take a short detour to explore the grounds of the Yerkes Observatory, which contains the largest refractor telescope in the world. (The two main types of telescopes are reflecting telescopes, which use mirrors to gather light, and refracting telescopes, which use lenses to gather light. Most modern research telescopes are the reflecting variety.) The Yerkes telescope, built by the University of Chicago in 1897, is considered one of the great scientific instruments of the late Victorian age. The Romanesque-style

Lake Geneva Loop

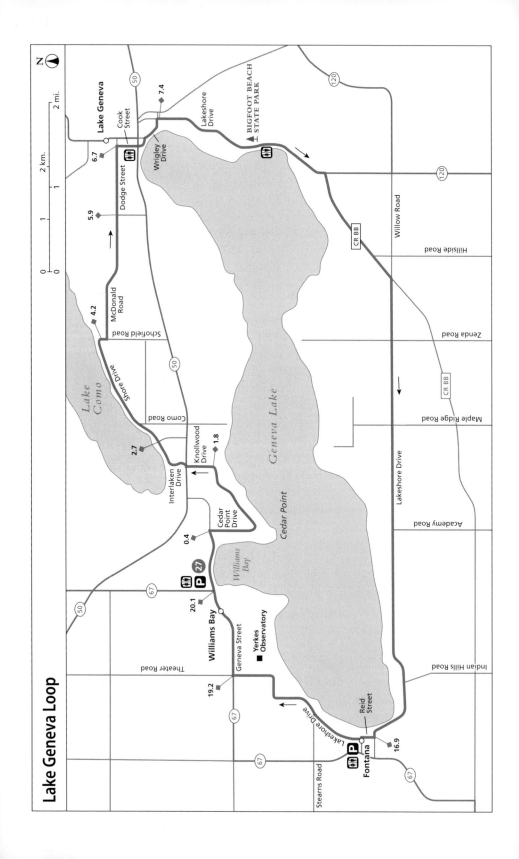

observatory is topped off with a 90-foot-diameter dome (the largest observatory dome ever built) and two smaller domes that, altogether, give the structure the feel of a castle or palace. In 2006 the university handed over the observatory to a nonprofit organization that maintains the facility as an astronomy education center. The parklike grounds of the observatory offer a place to relax before returning to the starting point down the hill at Edgewater Park.

MILES AND DIRECTIONS

0.0 From Edgewater Park in Williams Bay, head to the right on Geneva Street.

0.4 Turn right onto Cedar Point Drive. Stay on Cedar Point Drive as it curves left. Keep straight ahead as Cedar Point Drive becomes Lakeshore Drive.

1.8 Turn left onto Knollwood Drive. Cross Highway 50 and continue straight ahead on Interlaken Drive.

2.6 Take Interlaken Drive to the left (follow the sign for Chalet Parking) just after the tennis courts and before it dead-ends at the pool. Continue ahead as Interlaken Drive becomes West End Drive.

2.7 Turn left onto Shore Drive.

4.2 Turn right onto Schofield Road and then immediately turn left onto McDonald Road.

5.9 Turn left at Forest Street, which becomes Dodge Street as it curves to the right.

6.7 Turn right onto Cook Street. After crossing Main Street (Highway 50), Cook Street becomes Wrigley Drive. Stay on Wrigley Drive until it curves to the left and becomes Campbell Street.

7.4 Turn right onto South Lakeshore Drive. Stay on South Lakeshore Drive all the way to Fontana.

16.9 In Fontana, turn right onto Reid Street.

17.0 Turn left onto Kinzie Avenue and then immediately turn right onto Lakeshore Drive. Continue ahead as Lakeshore Drive takes a couple of turns and then becomes Fontana Road.

19.2 Turn right onto Geneva Street (Highway 67). The entrance to Yerkes Observatory is just 100 yards ahead on the right. Take a loop through grounds.

20.1 Keep straight ahead on Geneva Street as Highway 67 (Elkhorn Road) turns left.

20.2 Return to the parking area where you started at Edgewater Park.

Take a hike

Given the exclusive atmosphere at Geneva Lake, many people are surprised to learn that there's a public footpath circumnavigating the entire lake. The path runs along the shore and cuts through many dozens of carefully landscaped yards. While not all landowners have been happy with the path, they've been legally obligated to leave their gates open since a court decision in the 1970s granted the public a "right of passage." The court made its decision because the pathway existed before home owners bought their property. Indeed, before European settlers arrived in the area, the local Potawatomi Indians regularly used a narrow shoreline trail around Geneva Lake. Many signs are posted asking you to stay on the path. While walking through people's yards may feel strange at first, this feeling diminishes once you see the nice walkways installed by some home owners.

The north shore of the lake offers some of the best opportunities for gawking at historic homes and their carefully crafted gardens. A good place to start hiking (sorry, no bicycles allowed) is from the park in back of the Lake Geneva Public Library. Going counterclockwise from Lake Geneva, it's a 7-mile hike to Williams Bay and a 10-mile hike to Fontana. Some people schedule their hike so that they can pick up a tour boat in Williams Bay or Fontana for a lift back to Lake Geneva. On the way, you'll see a host of opulent homes. One major landmark is Wadsworth Hall, a stately redbrick mansion from 1905 with six fluted columns in front. Also on this stretch of shoreline is a home that was intended to look like Frank Lloyd Wright's famous house, Fallingwater.

RIDE INFORMATION

Local Events/Attractions

Geneva Lake Shore Path: A 20.2-mile footpath that circles the lake; the path on the north side of the lake is the most scenic and passes the greatest number of historic mansions; pick up the trail in any of the towns; walking guides can be purchased at local stores; www.genevalakewest.com/path.php.

Lake Geneva Cruise Line: Docks at the Riviera Ballroom and stops in towns around the lake; 812 Wrigley Dr., Lake Geneva, Wisconsin; (800) 558-5911 or (262) 248-6206; www.gageboats.com.

Yerkes Observatory: Open every Saturday for free public tours; contains exhibits and small shops; 373 West Geneva St., Williams Bay, Wisconsin; (262) 245-5555, ext. 832; http://astro.uchicago.edu/yerkes.

Restaurants

Harpoon Willies Bar and Grill: Bar food affordably priced; located next to starting point; 10 East Geneva St., Williams Bay, Wisconsin; (262) 245-6906; www.harpoonwillies.com.

Egg Harbor Café: Local chain serving good diner fare; 827 Main St., Lake Geneva, Wisconsin; (262) 248-1207; www.eggharborcafe.com.

Restrooms

Start/finish: Restrooms and water are available in Edgewater Park, where the ride begins.

Mile 7.0: The Riviera Ballroom has restrooms and water.

Mile 9.0: Bigfoot Beach State Park has restrooms and water.

Mile 16.9: The bathhouse at the beach in Fontana has restrooms, water, and concessions.

Maps

DeLorme: Wisconsin Atlas and Gazetteer: Page 94
Milwaukee and Southeast Wisconsin Bike Map, Little Transport Press; 4401 Grand Avenue, Minneapolis, Minnesota; www.littletransport.com
USGS 7.5" Lake Geneva quad, USGS 7.5" Walworth quad

Long Prairie and Stone Bridge Trails

As you travel from one side of Boone County to the other on the Long Prairie Trail, you'll encounter small winding creeks, a few small railroad towns, and plenty of open space. Leaving Boone County launches you on the Stone Bridge Trail, where the greenery grows thick and the landscape becomes more rolling. Toward the end of the route, a short trip off-trail brings you to a picturesque landmark—an old double-arched limestone bridge straddling a rocky creek.

Start: County Line Road parking area, located about 5 miles west of Harvard

Length: 20.4 miles one way

Approximate riding time: 2 hours

Best bike: Road or hybrid bike

Terrain and trail surface: The terrain is mostly flat. The trail is asphalt on the 15.1-mile Long Prairie Trail, and is crushed gravel on the 5.3-mile Stone Bridge Trail.

Traffic and hazards: Some sections leave trail users fairly exposed to sun and wind.

Things to see: Creeks, farmland, woodland, Capron, Poplar Grove, Caledonia, and an old double-arched limestone bridge

Wheelchair access: The route is wheelchair accessible.

Getting there: By car: From I-90 west of Elgin, exit north onto US 20. In Marengo turn right onto IL 23. South of Harvard turn left onto US 14 and left again onto IL 173. Turn right onto County Line Road. The parking area is on the left. GPS coordinates: 42 24.493 N / 88 42.931 W

Parking lots are provided in all three villages along the route:

To park in Poplar Grove, head west on IL 173 from Harvard. Turn left onto State Street and look for the trail as it crosses the road.

To park in Caledonia, head west on IL 173 from Harvard. Turn left onto Front Street.

To park at the Roland Olson Forest Preserve, head east on Belvidere Road from IL 251. Turn left onto Atwood Road.

THE RIDE

The route of the Long Prairie Trail originally served a railroad that the Kenosha, Rockford, and Rock Island Railroad Company started operating in 1858. The company that built the railroad soon sold it to the Chicago and Northwestern Railroad, which maintained it as an active line for nearly a century. As the story goes, the railroad was abandoned when a train crossing Beaverton Road (trail mile 5.6) derailed, leaving behind a torn-up railbed, broken ties, and twisted tracks. In lieu of making costly repairs, the railroad was mothballed. A gouge in the railbed remains today.

As you start toward Capron from the trailhead, the route immediately reaches across an arm of Picasaw Creek. Not far ahead, Picasaw Creek brushes against the trail in a couple of spots, resulting in lush greenery and grassy wet-lands fringed with willows. When the number of big oaks leaning over the trail starts to dwindle, you're allowed glimpses of horse pastures and the gently roll-ing agricultural landscape of the surrounding area.

The small town of Capron has been adorned with several different names. Originally called Helgesaw in honor of the many Scandinavians in the area, it was later renamed Long Prairie due to a sizable swath of nearby prairie. Then, like so many other towns in Illinois, it acquired the name of a manager with the local railroad.

South of Capron the trail hugs IL 173 for 2.5 miles. This largely unshaded strip of trail follows a small embankment and crosses a couple of minor streams. Look for Queen Anne's lace, black-eyed Susans, and goldenrod growing along-side the trail. On the way into Poplar Grove, the trail crosses Beaver Creek and then follows a 10-foot embankment above the surrounding landscape. Poplar Grove announces its arrival with a grain elevator and big storage silos alongside the trail.

After Caledonia, oak-hickory woods grow thick and the landscape becomes more textured. In one spot the trail mounts an embankment 30 feet high; in another, 35-foot-high ravines rise up on the sides of the trail. When the greenery opens, farms appear in the distance, but rarely are there structures near the trail. The lack of nearby development, combined with a small number of trail users, lends the trail a distinctly remote feel.

Leaving Boone County and entering Winnebago County at about 11.5 miles signals the beginning of the Stone Bridge Trail. In Winnebago County the

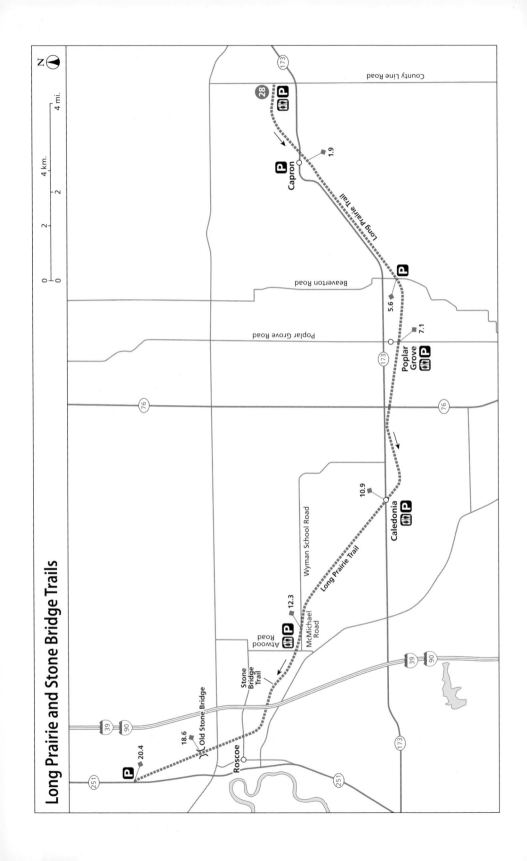

Long Prairie and Stone Bridge Trails

landscape becomes more rolling and wooded. Long views grow more frequent, and the ravines and embankments built for the railroad multiply.

As the trail passes over North Kinnikinnick Creek, the surrounding shrubs and grasses disguise the fact that you're high up on a bridge. The only features that give away your location are the wooded fencing on the sides of the trail and gurgle of the creek below. A walking path leads you on a series of switchbacks down the ravine to a wooden platform overlooking the creek, adjoining wetlands, and the namesake of the trail—

Bike Shop

Side by Side Cycles: 142 West Main St., Capron; (815) 569-2472; www.sidebyside cycle.com; rents bikes and dual trikes

a double-arched limestone bridge built in 1882. Local engineers say the bridge (now on the National Register of Historic Places) is unique for its date of construction and its design, which includes an internal drainage system.

For the final couple of miles, the railroad right-of-way carves a straight, level path through open savanna and prairie. Houses speckle the landscape. The views are wide, but shade is thin. Shortly after crossing the final bridge, which spans Dry Creek, you'll reach the parking area at the end of the trail.

MILES AND DIRECTIONS

0.0 Start at the trailhead parking area on County Line Road.

1.9 Pass through Capron.

5.6 Cross Beaverton Road.

7.1 Pass through Poplar Grove.

10.9 Pass through Caledonia.

12.3 Pass the Roland Olson Forest Preserve on the right.

18.6 Take the path on the right to visit Old Stone Bridge.

20.4 Arrive at the end of the trail at Rockton Road.

RIDE INFORMATION

Local Events/Attractions
Edwards Apple Orchard: A petting zoo, pony rides, and a store; locals come mostly for the pick-your-own apples; 7061 Centerville Rd., Poplar Grove; (815) 765-2234.

Restaurants

Trail Stop: Trailside ice-cream shop; 105 North State St., Poplar Grove; (815) 765-3799.

Restrooms

Start: There are public restrooms at the parking area on the east end of the trail.

Mile 7.1: Restrooms are available in Poplar Grove.

Mile 10.9: Restrooms are available in Caledonia.

Mile 12.4: Roland Olson Forest Preserve on CR 7 has water and restrooms.

Maps

USGS Belvidere, Belvidere North, Capron, and South Beloit

DeLorme: Illinois Atlas and Gazetteer: Pages 18 and 19

Illinois Bicycle Map, Region 2, Illinois Department of Transportation, www.dot .state.il.us/bikemap/state.html

Moraine Hills State Park Trail

When the last glacier receded from the landscape at Moraine Hills State Park nearly 16,000 years ago, it left behind a mosaic of marshes, prairies, bogs, hills, and streams, as well as the park's centerpiece, Lake Defiance. The landscape surrounding Lake Defiance is peppered with a series of moraines—mounds of dirt and gravel. While these glacially sculpted hills aren't huge by any measure, they offer a welcome retreat for nearby Chicagoans.

Start: At the Northern Woods parking area at Moraine Hills State Park

Length: 9.5 miles

Approximate riding time: 1 hour

Best bike: Mountain bike, hybrid bike, or road bike with wider tires

Terrain and trail surface: The crushed gravel trail snakes through a gently rolling terrain.

Traffic and hazards: Cyclists must follow the directional arrows on the trails; hikers may proceed in any direction. There are 800 acres of wetlands at Moraine Hills; be sure to bring mosquito repellent if the season warrants.

Things to see: Rolling woodland, wetlands, ponds, prairies, and the Fox River

Getting there: From Chicago, head north on I-94 until you reach Belvidere Road (Highway 120). Follow Belvidere Road west for 17 miles until reaching River Road. Turn left onto River Road and then turn left at the sign for the park. Proceed for 2 miles to the Northern Woods parking lot and picnic area. GPS coordinates: 42 19.496 N / 88 13.825 W

THE RIDE

Lake Defiance formed when a chunk of ice from a retreating glacier left a watery depression in the ground. Fed by a sprawling network of marshes, ponds, and old irrigation ditches within the park, Lake Defiance is one of the few glacial lakes in Illinois that has remained undeveloped and in a near-natural state. Another highlight of the park, also the result of retreating glaciers, are the moraines, which develop when an ice sheet stops in its tracks and the idling glacier acts as a sort of conveyor belt, depositing gravel and rock at its edges and sides. The wooded hills and ridges at Moraine Hills serve as records of where glaciers stood still during their retreat.

While wetlands and rolling glacial hills are the dominant features at Moraine Hills, the park also contains attractive wooded areas, prairies and savannas decorated with wildflowers, and a stretch of the wide and shallow Fox River. Throughout the ride, you'll notice that the landscape is constantly changing, and this is especially true during the first few miles.

Starting from the Northern Woods parking area, the trail climbs a small hill through dense stands of oak and hickory (two of the most common trees found in the park are shagbark hickory and white oak). Coming down the hill, a sprawling cattail marsh extends to the left and Tomahawk Lake opens up on the right. Without delay, the trail rises again, granting more views of the enormous marsh.

Glacial handiwork created a lake, wetlands, and a collection of small hills at Moraine Hills State Park.

As the landscape flattens, the trail winds past one of the sheltered benches that are widely spaced along the length of the trail. After skirting the edge of more marshland, the trail begins 0.5 mile of twisting and turning through prairies, savannas, and wooded stretches, occasionally offering glimpses of Leatherleaf Bog and patches of open water. Before reaching Junction B, the trail meanders through a wet prairie decorated with stands of cattails. Uncommon flowers such as lady's slippers can be found in the park's wet areas such as this one. Along this segment of the trail and elsewhere in the park, you'll see the drainage ditches created by farmers who unsuccessfully attempted to draw off the water from this exceptionally soggy landscape.

Bike Shop

Wally's Bike Haven: Located several miles north of the park entrance; 2908 Highway 120, McHenry; (815) 385-4642

From Junction B, the trail begins a clockwise loop around Lake Defiance. To the left is Leatherleaf Bog, a state-dedicated natural area, which features a floating mat of sphagnum moss and leatherleaf, a shrub that keeps its leaves all year round. After passing the entrance to the park office and cutting through a swath of prairie, the trail mounts a moraine overlooking forty-eight-acre Lake Defiance. Soon you'll roller-coaster over a series of small wooded hills that sit alongside Lake Defiance and its accompanying wetlands. Now and then, a steep hill will get your heart pumping (many of the steep sections are paved to prevent erosion).

Getting closer to the Fox River, the trail tunnels under River Road and then enters another sprawling marsh scattered with sedge grasses, moisture-loving trees, and patches of open water. On warm summer days, anglers and picnickers line the banks of the Fox River near the 4-foot-high McHenry Dam. First built in 1907, the dam was reconstructed in 1934 by the Civilian Conservation Corps. In 1939 the state acquired the dam and some of the surrounding property—the kernel of what would eventually become this 1,690-acre state park.

Before returning to the main section of the park and the North Woods parking area, you'll explore more of the wetland landscape on a levee alongside the Fox River and a series of open marshes. Moving away from the river, the trail ascends a couple of small hills overlooking the large wetland along the River Road. Whip out your field glasses for possible glimpses of sandhill cranes, great egrets, and various waterbirds taking a migratory pit stop. On the second hill, take the trail branching left, which leads to a viewing platform overlooking Black Tern Marsh. Like the rest of the park, the final mile or so back to the parking area offers no shortage of wetlands and winding pathways.

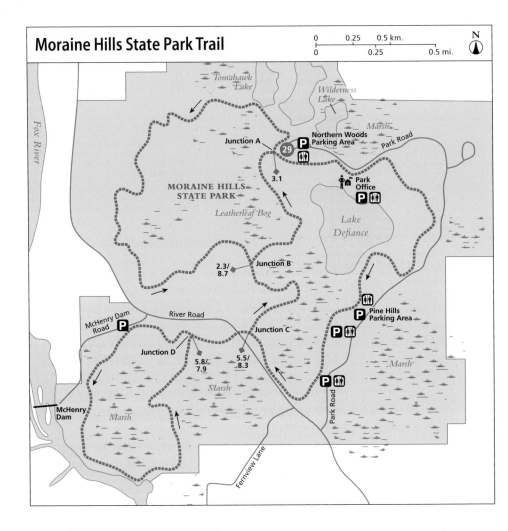

Moraine Hills State Park Trail

0   0.25   0.5 km.

0   0.25   0.5 mi.

N

Tomahawk Lake

Wilderness Lake

Marsh

Junction A

Northern Woods Parking Area

29

Park Road

Fox River

3.1

Park Office

MORAINE HILLS STATE PARK

Leatherleaf Bog

Lake Defiance

2.3/ 8.7

Junction B

McHenry Dam Road

River Road

Junction C

Pine Hills Parking Area

Junction D

5.8/ 7.9

5.5/ 8.3

Marsh

McHenry Dam

Marsh

Marsh

Park Road

Fernview Lane

MILES AND DIRECTIONS

0.0   The Northern Woods parking area offers flush toilets, water, and plenty of picnic tables. Catch the access trail left of the restrooms. Follow the arrows by turning right onto the Leatherleaf Bog Trail, and then turn left when you reach the intersection for the Opossum Run picnic area.

2.3   Turn left at Junction B.

3.1   Turn right at Junction A.

4.6 The Pine Hills parking area has restrooms and water. There are a number of parking areas along this stretch of trail. Each is well marked, and each offers drinking water and pit toilets.

5.5 Turn left at Junction C and pass though the tunnel under River Road.

5.8 Turn right at Junction D.

6.6 Pay a visit to the Fox River and McHenry Dam by following the picnicking/parking area to the right.

7.9 Turn right at Junction D.

8.3 Turn left at Junction C.

8.7 Turn right at Junction B.

9.5 Turn left at Junction A and return to the Northern Woods parking area.

RIDE INFORMATION

Local Events/Attractions
The Illinois Railway Museum: Railway artifacts, dozens of railcars on display, and opportunities for riding old trains; 7000 Olson Rd., Union; (815) 923-4000; www.irm.org.
Lake County Discovery Museum: Great local museum; contains largest postcard collection in the world; 27277 Forest Preserve Drive, Wauconda; (847) 968-3400; www.lcfpd.org.
Moraine Hills State Park: In the nature center/park office, pick up a brochure for the 0.5-mile interpretive trail along the Lake Defiance boardwalk; 1510 South River Rd., McHenry; (815) 385-1624; http://dnr.state.il.us.

Restaurants
Plum Garden: Cantonese food located in McHenry very close to the park; 3917 West Main St., McHenry; (815) 385-1530.
Port Edward Restaurant: Mostly seafood; pricey dinner menu; lunches much more affordable; 20 West Algonquin Rd., Algonquin; (847) 658-5441.

Restrooms
Start/finish: Restrooms and water are available at the Northern Woods Parking area.

Mile 4.6: Restrooms are available at the Pine Hills parking area.

Mile 6.6: Restrooms are available at the McHenry Dam picnic area.

Mile 7.0: The final couple miles of trail run by a handful of parking areas, many of which offer restrooms.

Maps

DeLorme: Illinois Atlas and Gazetteer: Page 20

Moraine Hills State Park trail map, http://dnr.state.il.us/lands/Landmgt/parks /r2/morhills.htm

USGS 7.5" Wauconda, Illinois quad

North Shore Loop

If you're like many cyclists, sometimes the momentum behind a bike ride is generated wholly by the desire to find a scenic spot to relax and enjoy the lunch you packed along. This ride offers a great choice of picnicking spots, including roadside prairies, bluffs above Lake Michigan, and several sprawling forest preserves. In addition to the many parks along the way, the second half of the ride takes you through the picturesque campus of Lake Forest College and the historic grounds of Fort Sheridan.

Start: The Glencoe Metra station at the corner of Park Avenue and Green Bay Road in Glencoe

Length: 35.4 miles

Approximate riding time: 3 hours

Best bike: Road or hybrid bike

Terrain and trail surface: The first half of the ride is flat; the second half is gently rolling.

Traffic and hazards: St. Marys Road has steady traffic, but there's an adequate shoulder for riding. While the traffic on most of these roads is minimal, many North Shore residents have an affinity for buying the largest cars available. Larger cars not only take up more road space but also render cyclists less visible.

Things to see: Lake Michigan; Wright Woods, Half Day, and Old School forest preserves; municipal parks; Lake Forest College; Fort Sheridan; Lake Bluff; Ravinia Park, Glencoe, Highland Park

Getting there: By car: From Chicago, take I-94 north to the Dundee Road exit. Head east on Dundee Road and then take a right onto Green Bay Road. Park at or near the Glencoe Metra station on the left. **By public transportation:** Take the Union Pacific North Metra line to the Glencoe station, where the ride starts. GPS coordinates: 42 8.059 N / 87 45.476 W

THE RIDE

While the communities of Chicago's North Shore generally aren't regarded as places rich with historic attractions, a few intriguing old landmarks do exist. One of these is Fort Sheridan, an army base established in 1887 at the urging of local businessmen so that troops could respond quickly to labor protests in Chicago. Though troops from Fort Sheridan would respond to labor unrest only once (in 1894 during the Pullman strike), it was a busy place while it served as a training and administrative center from the Spanish-American War through World War II, when over 500,000 military men and women were processed at the fort. The centerpiece of the fort is a 227-foot-tall water tower, originally the tallest structure in the Chicago area. It was shortened by 60 feet in 1940 because of structural problems. The long, squat row of buildings on each side of the tower served as troop barracks.

Lake Forest College's main campus area is dominated by Young Hall, built in 1878.

On the way to Fort Sheridan, the first half of the route passes by a series of large wooded parks that invite you to take a break and have a look around. The Heller Nature Center on Ridge Road is the first of these: It features a short network of trails that wind through oak-hickory forests, tallgrass prairie, and wetlands. On St. Marys Road, you'll encounter three county-owned forest preserves situated along the Des Plaines River. Wright Woods contains several miles of crushed gravel trails and hundreds of acres of thick bottomland woods along the river. Farther north, you'll pass savanna and stands of hickories, maples, and oaks at MacArthur Woods and eventually come to Old School Forest Preserve, offering more woodland and open prairie.

Just north of Wright Woods Forest Preserve sits a large modern home that belonged to Adlai Stevenson. Born and raised in Bloomington-Normal, Illinois, Stevenson served as Illinois governor, U.S. representative to the United Nations, and two-time presidential candidate. Stevenson didn't linger at this house frequently, but he reportedly enjoyed visiting and used it for entertaining guests such as Eleanor Roosevelt and John F. Kennedy. The Stevenson home is not a museum and is typically open only for special events. Several information panels in front of the house provide some background on Stevenson and the home.

After the bustle of Rockland Road, you'll arrive in the sleepy North Shore community of Lake Bluff. At Sunrise Park, pull up to one of the benches perched on a bluff above our inland sea. The park, located in a tony residential neighborhood, includes a sandy beach at the foot of the bluff.

The winding route of Sheridan Road cuts through the leafy campus of Lake Forest College. The college's stately buildings are surrounded by a series of enticing wooded ravines that bisect much of the area. Young Hall, a yellow brick building built in 1878, dominates the central campus. Behind Young Hall sits Hotchkiss Hall, a red stone structure with small elegant spires.

Bike Shop

Higher Gear: 1874 Sheridan Rd., Highland Park; (847) 433-2453; www.highergear chicago.com

A few miles south of Lake Forest College, you'll enter the gates of Fort Sheridan to see the hundred or so solidly built and well-maintained administration buildings and houses. The buildings, set within grassy lawns and among patches of woodland, were constructed between 1889 and 1910 of blond-colored bricks made of clay mined from nearby lakefront bluffs. After the base closed in 1993, an extensive environmental cleanup campaign was needed before transforming it into a residential development. An Army Reserve base continues to occupy some of the land, but the majority of it is now privately owned.

Continuing south along Sheridan Road, the landscape is peppered with deep wooded gullies. The thirty or so V-shaped ravines along the North Shore were carved by streams as they twisted from the higher flat ground to the lower level of the lake. While most of the ravines can only be admired from afar, there's one spot along the route where you can explore them more fully. At Moraine Park on Sheridan Road, stairs lead down into a ravine where two streams converge and flow into the lake. Visitors can follow the stone walkway alongside the stream all the way to the beach.

Back on Sheridan Road, you'll soon arrive in the busy downtown area of Highland Park. After passing Ravinia Park, the long-standing outdoor music venue, you'll soon arrive back at the Glencoe Metra station, where the ride began.

MILES AND DIRECTIONS

0.0 Head northwest on Green Bay Road.

2.3 Turn left onto Clavey Road.

3.8 Turn right onto Ridge Road.

4.8 Turn right onto Old Deerfield Road.

4.9 Turn left onto Richfield Road.

5.3 Turn right onto Ridge Road.

6.6 Turn left onto Churchill Lane, which changes to Tennyson Lane as it curves right. Tennyson Lane becomes Ridge Road north of Half Day Road.

8.5 Turn left onto Old Mill Road. Continue straight ahead on the pedestrian bridge when Old Mill curves left and becomes Milburne Road. Follow the trail straight ahead to resume the route on Old Mill Road.

10.7 Old Mill Road becomes Fork Drive as it curves to the right. As Fork Road curves right, it becomes Bowling Green Drive.

11.5 Turn left onto Old Barn Lane.

11.6 Turn left onto Everett Road. Everett Road becomes St. Marys Road as it curves right.

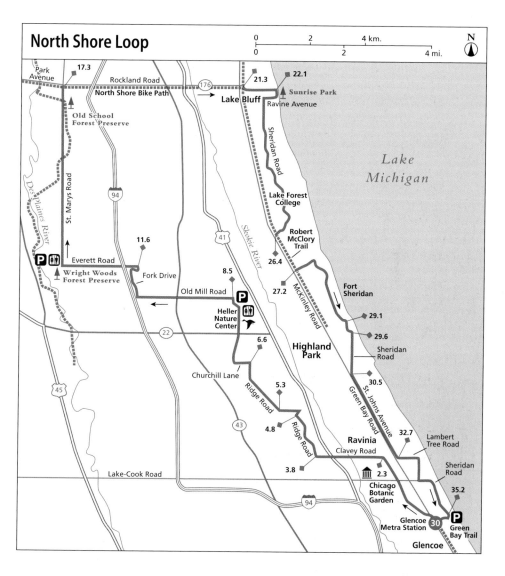

North Shore Loop

16.7 Side trip: Consider taking a 1.6-mile lap around the Old School Forest Preserve—you won't regret it.

17.3 Turn right onto the bike path that parallels Park Avenue/SR 176. This street soon becomes Rockland Road.

21.3 After passing under the train tracks, stay left at two successive trail junctions, and cross the bridge over West Scranton Avenue. Heading north on Sheridan Avenue, turn right onto East Scranton Avenue.

22.1 Turn right onto Sunrise Avenue. Jog right at Prospect Avenue and continue south on Sunrise Avenue.

22.4 Turn right onto Ravine Avenue.

22.7 Turn left onto Moffet Road. Continue south as Moffet Road merges with Sheridan Road.

26.4 At McCormick Drive, hop on the Robert McClory Trail as it parallels Sheridan Road on the right.

27.2 Turn left onto Simonds Way.

27.5 Turn left onto Leonard Wood North. Continue ahead on Leonard Wood North as it becomes Patten Road.

29.1 Turn left onto Walker Avenue.

29.3 Turn right onto Oak Street.

29.5 Turn left onto Edgecliff Drive.

29.6 Turn right onto Sheridan Road.

30.5 In downtown Highland Park, turn right onto Central Avenue, then immediately turn left onto St. Johns Avenue.

32.7 Bear left onto Lambert Tree Road as St. Johns Avenue ends. Merge onto Sheridan Road.

35.2 Turn right onto Park Avenue.

35.4 Arrive back at the Glencoe Metra station.

RIDE INFORMATION

Local Events/Attractions
Chicago Botanic Garden: The garden is free, but there's a fee for parking; 1000 Lake Cook Rd., Glencoe; (847) 835-5440; www.chicagobotanic.org.
Heller Nature Center: Large wooded park with trails; 2821 Ridge Rd., Highland Park; (847) 433-6901; www.pdhp.org.
Ravinia Music Festival: Hosts live concerts all summer long; lawn seats are a great deal; 418 Sheridan Rd., Highland Park; (847) 266-5000; www.ravinia.org.

Restaurants
Bluffington's Cafe: Good sandwiches and salads; 113 East Scranton Ave., Lake Bluff; (847) 295-3344.

The Perfect Blend: Inviting coffeehouse in downtown Highland Park; 491 Central Ave., Highland Park; (847) 266-1667.

The Silo: Known for its deep-dish pizzas; 625 Rockland Rd., Lake Bluff; (847) 234-6660; www.silopizza.com.

Yummy Bowl: Chinese and Thai cuisine; 1908 Sheridan Rd., Highland Park; (847) 266-8880.

Restrooms

Start/finish: Glencoe Metra station has restrooms.

Mile 13.3: Wright Woods Forest Preserve offers restrooms and water.

Mile 16.7: Old School Forest Preserve has restrooms and water.

Mile 29.8: Moraine Park has restrooms.

Maps

USGS: Highland Park quad, Libertyville quad, Waukegan quad, Wheeling quad
DeLorme: Illinois Atlas & Gazetteer: Page 29

31

Prairie and Hebron Trails

As the Prairie Trail spans nearly the entire north–south length of McHenry County, it shoots past some of the most scenic spots within northeast Illinois. In between towns such as Crystal Lake, McHenry, Ringwood, and Richmond, the trail takes you through stunning natural areas at Sterne's Woods, Glacial Park, and Nippersink North Branch Conservation Area. After finishing the Prairie Trail, the route heads west for 6.7 miles along the Hebron Trail.

Start: In Algonquin, located in southeast McHenry County

Length: 30.9 miles one way

Approximate riding time: 2–3 hours

Best bike: Road bike; a hybrid or mountain bike can work if riding a shorter distance.

Terrain and trail surface: Flat terrain dominates. The trail is asphalt between Algonquin and Ringwood, and is crushed gravel north of Ringwood.

Traffic and hazards: Watch for traffic at busy street crossings. Use caution while following the short on-street section in Crystal Lake. Keep your eyes peeled for bike trail signs that guide you through McHenry. Occasional sections leave trail users fully exposed to wind and sun.

Things to see: Sterne's Woods, Glacial Park, Nippersink North Branch Conservation Area, Crystal Lake, McHenry, Ringwood, and Richmond

Wheelchair access: The trail is wheelchair accessible, but the entire route north of Ringwood is crushed gravel.

Getting there: By car: From I-90 west of the Fox River, head north on IL 31. In Algonquin turn left onto Algonquin Road. Turn right onto Meyer Drive and then take a left into the Algonquin Road Trail access parking area. During winter, when this trailhead parking area is closed, use one of the parking areas listed below. GPS coordinates: 42 10.373 N / 88 18.093 W

To reach the Main Street parking area in Crystal Lake, head north on IL 31. Turn left at James Rakow Road and then right onto Pyott Road.

Turn left onto Berkshire Drive and then immediately right onto Eastgate Avenue.

To park at Veteran Acres Park, head north on IL 31. Turn left onto IL 176 and then right onto Lorraine Drive.

To access the trail at Petersen Park, head north on IL 31. North of McHenry turn left onto McCullom Lake Road and left again onto Petersen Park Road.

To park at the Glacial Park parking area, head north on IL 31 from McHenry. North of Ringwood turn left onto Harts Road. The parking area is on the right.

To park at the Nippersink North Branch Park parking area, head west on IL 173 from I-94. After passing Richmond, turn right onto Keystone Road. The parking area is on the right.

To park in Hebron, keep heading west on IL 173 and turn right onto Seaman Road. The parking area is on the right.

By public transportation: The Crystal Lake Metra station on the Union Pacific/Northwest Line is less than 1 mile from the Veteran Acres parking area. The McHenry station on the same Metra line is just 1 block from the Prairie Trail in McHenry.

THE RIDE

Starting from the south end of the Prairie Trail, the trip between Algonquin and Crystal Lake leads you through a landscape once dominated by gravel mining operations. In many spots residential developments have been built on top of the former gravel pits. But not all the gravel mining is gone: As you pass the long conveyer belts and industrial buildings that are part of an active gravel mining operation, look for a couple of small creeks flowing on either side of the trail. On the way into Crystal Lake, the path passes Lake of the Hills Airport and accompanies Main Street, which is fairly busy.

Once you've left the bustle of Crystal Lake behind and completed the 1-mile-long on-street section of the route, Sterne's Woods will take you by surprise. The trail wriggles like a snake over steep hills and underneath arthritic limbs of big oak trees. Even though this hilly section is brief, those on bicycles should ride the steep, curving downhill sections with care—wipeouts are frequent at the bottom of these steep hills. A tiny stream runs through a small ravine on the right; benches along the path invite you to sit down to admire the hills and fragrant groves of pine.

Continuing north toward McHenry, the trail shadows a set of railroad tracks through a wide-open landscape that leans strongly toward agriculture.

Not far from the Wisconsin border, the Prairie Trail ducks under an old wooden bridge.

The gently rolling terrain contains patches of wetlands. After passing through McHenry, the trail brushes against Petersen Park, which contains a number of fine picnicking spots on the shore of McCullom Lake. If you're a fan of small-town architecture from the early twentieth century, turn left at Bernard Mill Road in Ringwood to visit an eye-catching post office just 1 block off the trail.

For those with an interest in learning the ways that glaciers sculpted the landscape in northeastern Illinois, be sure to visit Glacial Park, which you'll encounter at 19.2 miles. The park is chock-full of kames—essentially mounds—which are formed when glacial meltwater deposits heaps of sand and gravel in depressions in the ice or at the edge of the glacier. The bog and marshes at the park also offer a visual link to the area's geologic past. These wetlands began to take shape

Bike Shop

The Bike Rack: 2930 Campton Hills Dr., St. Charles; (630) 584-6588

when large chunks of ice detached from a receding glacier: As ice melted, a pond formed in the depression; eventually vegetation overtook the pond. More than 5 miles of hiking trails allow you to explore the kames, dry and wet prairie, woodland, and a creek.

Between Glacial Park and Richmond, the gently rolling terrain surrounding the trail contains swaths of attractive wetland. In some spots, ravines rise up on the sides of the trail, but most often you're granted long views of the surrounding landscape. On the way into Richmond, duck under a one-hundred-year-old wooden railroad bridge. The main drag in Richmond is lined with a collection of buildings from the turn of the twentieth century containing a small assortment of shops focused on items such as jewelry, handmade crafts, and antiques. Further explorations of the village will reveal attractively restored Victorian homes and several Sears Catalog homes.

After Richmond you'll cross the North Branch of Nippersink Creek and then encounter more sprawling wetlands. One-third mile before the end of the Prairie Trail, turn left onto the crushed gravel path that leads into Nippersink North Branch Conservation Area. This winding trail runs through many acres of rolling terrain covered with restored prairie and stands of hardwood. You'll cross the Nippersink North Branch again as it winds through the prairie.

The first mile or so on the Hebron Trail is dominated by cropland with patches of intermittent woodland alongside the trail. After a very short on-street section, you'll know you're approaching wetlands when you hear the uneven honking of sandhill cranes, a large gray bird that is a rare sight in Illinois. Streets Lake offers a trailside viewing platform where you can survey a collec-

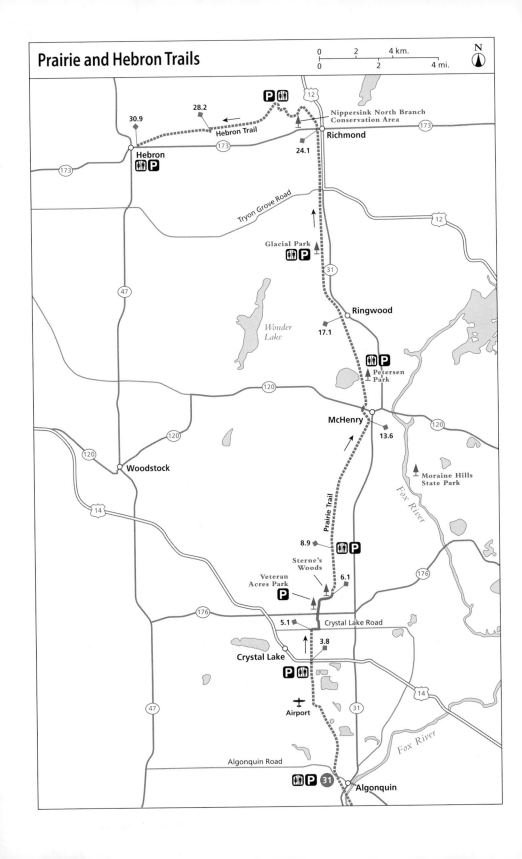

Prairie and Hebron Trails

N

0   2   4 km.
0   2   4 mi.

28.2

30.9

P 🚻

12

← Hebron Trail

Nippersink North Branch
Conservation Area

173

Hebron

🚻 **P**

173

24.1

Richmond

Tryon Grove Road

12

47

Glacial Park

🚻 **P**

31

Ringwood

17.1

Wonder
Lake

🚻 **P**

Petersen
Park

120

McHenry

13.6

120

120

120

Woodstock

Fox River

Moraine Hills
State Park

14

8.9

🚻 **P**

Prairie Trail

176

Sterne's
Woods

6.1

Veteran
Acres Park

P

176

5.1

Crystal Lake Road

3.8

Crystal Lake

P 🚻

14

31

Airport

47

Fox River

Algonquin Road

🚻 **P** **31**

Algonquin

tion of muskrat lodges, big stands of sedge grasses and cattails, and rafts of waterbirds. The trail ends at the edge of the tiny town of Hebron.

MILES AND DIRECTIONS

0.0 Start heading north from the Algonquin Road trailhead.

3.8 Pass the Main Street trailhead in Crystal Lake.

5.1 Start the 1.0-mile-long on-street section by turning right onto Crystal Lake Avenue. This road is busy; take the sidewalk on the left side of the road if necessary.

5.4 Turn left onto East Street.

5.7 Turn right onto Glenn Avenue.

5.9 Turn right onto Terra Cotta Avenue.

6.0 Turn left onto Lorraine Drive.

6.1 Resume the Prairie Trail from the parking area.

8.9 Cross Edgewood Road.

13.6 Cross IL 120 in McHenry.

17.1 Pass through Ringwood.

24.1 Leave the Prairie Trail and start the Hebron Trail by turning left into the Nippersink North Branch Park.

28.2 Take a short jog to the left on Lange Road and then regain the trail on the right.

30.9 Arrive at the end of the trail in Hebron.

RIDE INFORMATION

Local Events/Attractions

Lake Geneva: A charming—if somewhat touristy—town situated on a beautiful lake just across the Wisconsin border about 10 miles north of the trail. For information contact the Walworth County Visitors Bureau, 9 West Walworth St., P.O. Box 1015, Elkhorn, WI 53121; (262) 723-3980; www.visitwalworth county.com.

North Wall: An indoor climbing facility alongside the trail in Crystal Lake; 824 South Main St., Suite 106, Crystal Lake; (815) 356-6855; www.climbnorthwall .com.

Royal Oak Orchard: In addition to the orchard, there's a bakery, a gift shop, and a restaurant; located west of Hebron; 15908 Hebron Rd., Harvard; (815) 648-4141; www.royaloakfarmorchard.com.

Restaurants

Doyle's Pub and Eatery: Located in the former mill in Richmond; 5604 Mill St., Richmond; (815) 678-3623; http://doylespubrocks.com.

JW Plateks Restaurant and Brewery: Serves bar food and microbrews; 8609 US 12, Richmond; (815) 678-4078; www.plateks.com.

Wild Orchid Thai Bistro: Located across Main Street from the trail in Crystal Lake; 6000 Northwest Hwy, Crystal Lake; (815) 788-0633; www.wildorchidthai bistro.com.

Restrooms

Start: Restrooms are available at the Algonquin Road trail access.

Mile 3.8: Restrooms and water are available at the Main Street parking area in Crystal Lake.

Mile 7.6: Restrooms and water are available at the Hillside Road parking area.

Mile 14.7: Restrooms and water are available at Petersen Park.

Mile 19.2: Restrooms and water are available Glacial Park parking area.

Mile 25.6: Nippersink North Branch parking area has restrooms and water.

Mile 30.2: There's a restroom at the Seaman's Road parking area in Hebron.

Maps

USGS Crystal Lake, McHenry, Hebron, and Richmond
DeLorme: Illinois Atlas and Gazetteer: Pages 19 and 20

Robert McClory Trail

As this route runs from Fort Sheridan to the south edge of Kenosha, Wisconsin, you'll see the nation's largest Navy training center, parks such as Lyons Woods Forest Preserve, and the far north shore towns of North Chicago, Waukegan, and Zion.

Start: The north parking lot at the Fort Sheridan Metra station, located at Old Elm and Sheridan Roads

Length: 22.8 miles one way

Approximate riding time: 2 hours

Best bike: Road bike or hybrid bike

Terrain and trail surface: The terrain is flat. The trail is crushed gravel with occasional paved sections.

Traffic and hazards: Be ready for stretches where trail users are fully exposed. Watch for cars pulling in and out of parking spaces as the trail cuts through Metra station parking lots. The trail crosses busy roads in a number of places.

Things to see: Fort Sheridan; Lake Bluff; Kenosha, Wisconsin; Great Lakes Naval Training Center; Lyons Woods Forest Preserve; North Chicago; Waukegan; and Zion

Wheelchair access: The trail is wheelchair accessible.

Getting there: By car: From I-94 north of Chicago, head north on US 41 (the Skokie Highway). Turn right onto Old Elm Road. Park on the north side of Old Elm Road at the Fort Sheridan Metra station. (Bring quarters—you may have to feed the meters.) Catch the trail as it heads north from the parking lot. GPS coordinates: 42 13.109 N / 87 49.275 W

To park at the Lake Bluff station, take US 41 north from I-94. Turn right onto IL 176/Rockland Road. Turn left onto Sheridan Road and park in the station on the left.

In North Chicago and Waukegan, on-street parking options are frequently available alongside the trail. Follow Sheridan Road north and then take any major street west to reach the trail.

To park at Lyon Woods Forest Preserve, exit from I-94 on IL 120 heading east. Turn left onto Sheridan Road/IL 137 and look for the entrance to Lyons Woods on the left.

To park at Anderson Park, located at the northern end of the trail, take I-94 north into Wisconsin. Exit at 104th Street and head east. Turn left at 39th Avenue and then right onto 89th Street. Turn left onto 30th Avenue and then right onto 87th Place. Park in the lot between the high school and Anderson Park. Catch the trail heading south from the intersection of 30th Avenue and 89th Street.

By public transportation: Take a Union Pacific District North Metra train to the Fort Sheridan station. The Union Pacific North Line runs parallel to this entire route. The first 7.0 miles of the trail run next to four Metra stations. Continuing north, another five Metra stations are within 1 to 2 miles east of the trail.

THE RIDE

The first section of this trail is alternately wooded and grassy as the route parallels train tracks on one side and Sheridan Road on the other. After about 1 mile, you'll encounter a stately building that once housed Barat College. The college, which first opened in 1858 as a Catholic girls' school, was shuttered in 2005 and sold to a condominium developer.

Peeking through the trees on the right is Lake Forest High School, where the 1980 film *Ordinary People* was filmed. The school claims a handful of alumni involved in creative pursuits, such as the musician Andrew Bird, writer Dave Eggers, and actor Vince Vaughn.

Before arriving at the Lake Bluff Metra station, you'll see the North Shore Bike Path branching to the right alongside IL 176/Rockland Road. The North Shore Bike Path intersects the Des Plaines River Trail about 4 miles to the west.

Lake Bluff was one of the communities represented by the trail's namesake, Robert McClory, a Republican member of the U.S. House of Representatives for twenty years. The national spotlight shone on McClory when he served on the House Judiciary Committee and became a key figure in the impeachment proceedings against President Richard Nixon.

The next major landmark along the trail is the Great Lakes Naval Training Center, the largest military facility in Illinois and the largest Navy training center in the nation. The eighty-year-old naval base has more than 1,000 buildings throughout 1,600 acres. In the Great Lakes Metra station that sits alongside the trail, you'll likely see some train passengers sporting brush cuts and bright white sailor hats.

As the route follows a perfectly straight course through North Chicago, the trailside scenery offers a mix of industrial developments and working-class neighborhoods with modest homes. Vegetable gardens planted alongside the trail give a dash of vitality to the right-of-way that is mostly open, grassy, and treeless. Continuing through North Chicago and entering Waukegan reveals more of the bustling industry for which these North Shore cities are known.

As the pockets of industry retreat, suburban residential neighborhoods take over and several community parks appear alongside the trail. A few parks are situated near the shiny new Lake County Family YMCA in Waukegan. At about 13 miles into the trail, a sign marks the entrance to Lyons Woods Forest Preserve, which contains 3 miles of trails that wind through savanna, oak woodland, and restored prairie.

North of Lyons Woods, residential neighborhoods come and go; small parks offer a respite from the trail. The path gets lush and leafy before reaching Zion and then becomes open and grassy again once you've entered the city.

In Zion a few trails and bike lanes will allow you to explore this community founded in 1890 by Scottish faith healer John Alexander Dowie. The church owned the town's commercial establishments and had strict rules about what couldn't be sold in the stores. For example, the stores were forbidden from selling liquor, playing cards, pork, clams, and tan shoes, among other items. The community collapsed financially in 1939, and private individuals began acquiring the property that belonged to the church.

After entering the Badger State at Russell Road, all that remains is 3.5 miles to the trail's northern terminus in Kenosha, Wisconsin. As you travel these final few miles—now along the Kenosha County Bike Trail—the greenery becomes more prominent and housing developments fade. The trail ends at 89th Street, across the road from a patchwork of soccer fields at Anderson Park.

MILES AND DIRECTIONS

0.0 Start heading north on the trail from the Fort Sheridan Metra station.

4.4 Pass the Lake Bluff Metra station.

6.9 The trail leaves Sheridan Road and follows Commonwealth Avenue to the left.

10.1 The trail crosses Washington Street in Waukegan.

13.1 Pass Lyons Woods Forest Preserve on the right.

16.7 Cross IL 173 in Zion.

22.8 Arrive at the end of the trail in Kenosha, Wisconsin.

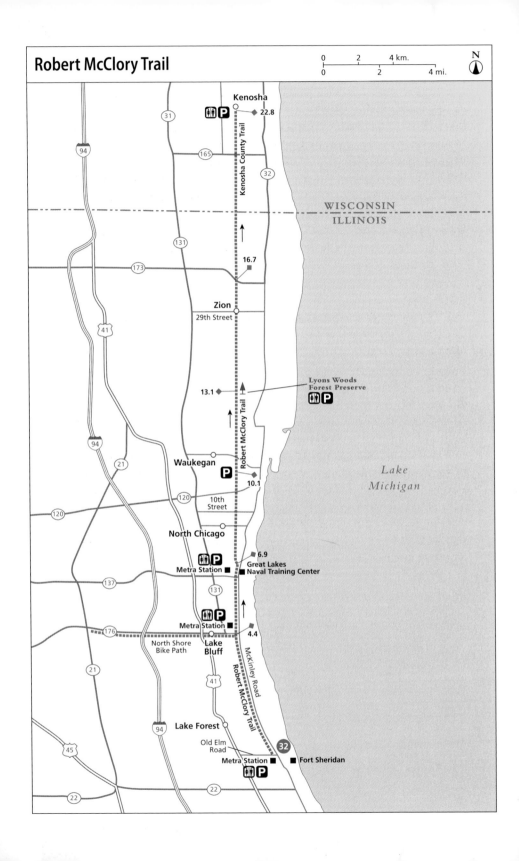

Robert McClory Trail

0   2   4 km.
0   2   4 mi.

N

Kenosha

31

Kenosha County Trail

22.8

165

32

WISCONSIN
ILLINOIS

94

131

173

16.7

Zion
29th Street

41

Lyons Woods
Forest Preserve

13.1

Robert McClory Trail

Waukegan

10.1

94

21

120

10th
Street

120

North Chicago

Lake
Michigan

6.9
Great Lakes
Naval Training Center

Metra Station

137

131

Metra Station

4.4

176

North Shore
Bike Path

Lake
Bluff

21

McKinley Road
Robert McClory Trail

41

94

Lake Forest

Old Elm
Road

32

45

Metra Station

■ **Fort Sheridan**

22

22

RIDE INFORMATION

Local Events/Attractions

Illinois Beach State Park: Popular among local beachgoers; quieter stretches of beach can be found south of the conference center; 701 North Point Dr., Winthrop Harbor; (847) 746-2845; www.dnr.illinois.gov

Green Bay Trail: On the south side of Highland Park; catch the Green Bay Trail heading south through Chicago's swankiest North Shore suburbs of Wilmette, Kenilworth, Winnetka, Glencoe, and Highland Park.

Shiloh House: Elegant twenty-five-room mansion built by Zion's founder, John Alexander Dowie; open for tours on weekends; 1300 Shiloh Blvd., Zion; (847) 746-2427; www.zionhs.com.

Restaurants

The Silo: Known for its deep-dish pizza; 625 Rockland Rd., Lake Bluff; (847) 234-6660; www.silopizza.com.

Bluffington's Cafe: Good sandwiches and salads; 113 East Scranton Ave., Lake Bluff; (847) 295-3344.

Restrooms

Start: There are public restrooms and water available at the Fort Sheridan Metra station.

Mile 4.4: Restrooms and water are available at the Lake Bluff Metra station.

Mile 6.9: Restrooms and water are available at the Great Lakes Metra station.

Mile 13.1: Restrooms and water are available at the Lyon Woods Forest Preserve (follow signs through the forest preserve for about 1 mile to the main entrance near the corner of Blanchard and Sheridan Roads).

Mile 22.8: Restrooms and water are available at Anderson Park at the northern end of the trail in Kenosha.

Maps

USGS Highland Park, Kenosha, Waukegan, and Zion
DeLorme: Illinois Atlas and Gazetteer: Page 21

Walworth/Racine Counties Loop

If you're looking for a long scenic ride at the outer edges of the Chicago region, this one is hard to beat. During nearly 60 miles of riding, the landscape and scenery never stay the same for long. Flat, rolling, or hilly—take your pick; you'll meet up with all of it. Quiet roads lead you through a landscape of oak-hickory woodlands, wetlands, and fields of hay and corn. In the village of East Troy, take a break in the historic town square. As icing on the cake, a handful of roads along the route are state-designated scenic roads.

Start: Begin the ride in the tiny town of Lyons, Wisconsin, located about 85 miles northwest of Chicago

Length: 58.1 miles

Approximate riding time: 4 hours

Best bike: Road bike

Terrain: It's a mix of flat, rolling, and hilly terrain, but is mostly rolling.

Traffic and hazards: Watch for tractors pulling heavy farm equipment. A charity biking event uses this route in early fall. The route is marked with a blue "N" and an arrow pointing the way. Don't expect the route described here to perfectly match the painted arrows.

Things to see: Oak-hickory woodlands, wetlands, the Fox River, assorted streams, fields of hay and corn, Rochester, Lyons, and East Troy

Getting there: Take I-90/94 west, proceeding along I-94 as it splits off northward. Exit I-94 at Highway 173 (Rosecrans Road). Follow Highway 173 west until reaching US 12. Turn right onto US 12. Highway 120 briefly joins with US 12 and then separates. Take Highway 120 north as it runs north to Springfield. Turn right onto Highway 36. In Lyons, turn right onto Mill Street, and then turn right again onto Railroad Street. Park in one of the spaces immediately on the left alongside the White River Trail. GPS coordinates: 42 39.118 N / 88 21.492 W

THE RIDE

After starting out from the parking area in Lyons, the first leg of the ride takes you through a setting dominated by cropland and sprinkled with barns, farmhouses, marshy spots, and shady nooks. When the road reaches higher ground, a scattering of sylvan hills are revealed in the distance to the south. On Bowers Road, wide-open farmland reigns. All is relatively flat until 9.5 miles into the ride when a steep ravine takes you on a thrill ride nearly 200 feet down. Zip-zip-whoo-whoo! When the roller coaster bottoms out, keep an eye out for loose gravel as the road curves and crosses Sugar Creek. If you have a granny gear, get ready to downshift for the big, lengthy climb out of the ravine—the steepest and longest hill you'll encounter all day. There will be at least a half-dozen times when you think you're approaching the top, and you realize you're seriously mistaken.

After making this arduous climb, you'll probably be greeted at the top by a herd of dairy cows watching you indifferently from a roadside pasture. Beyond the cows, you'll see broad views of a rolling landscape 30 miles to the north. Also, at the top of the hill, look to the right to see the western edge of the Alpine Valley Resort, which contains a hotel, a ski hill, and one of the largest performance amphitheaters in the nation. Alpine Valley has been a regular tour stop for major pop music stars since the venue opened in 1977. It was a sad occasion in 1990 when a helicopter containing the musician Stevie Ray Vaughn crashed into the resort's ski hill, killing Vaughn and four others.

Not far ahead, you'll arrive in East Troy's town square, where you can pull up a bench to enjoy the small downtown containing a handful of historic buildings. A brick bandstand built by the Works Progress Administration in the 1930s adorns the center of the grassy square. The most striking building on the square is the three-story cobblestone structure built in 1843 as a hotel and tavern (at the corner of Church Street and Main Street). Far more common on the East Coast, cobblestone buildings were built in this area for only thirty years, beginning in the 1840s. The cobblestones in this building, fairly uniform in size and shape, were laid in horizontal bands with mortar between them.

From East Troy to Rochester, the cropland continues, as do the swaths of woodland, occasional herds of grazing cattle, and views of far-off rolling hills. Outside of East Troy, the route passes a dam on Honey Creek and then follows a lovely road named after the creek. Getting closer to Rochester, you'll encounter a pleasing mix of woods and wetlands on Oak Knoll Road, which is designated as a Wisconsin Rustic Road—the state's program for preserving old and attractive roadways. Just ahead, the route takes you over the Fox River in Rochester. If you're familiar with the Fox as it flows through Chicago's far western suburbs, you'll barely recognize this much leaner upper section of the river. Case Eagle

A local artist has installed roadside sculpture along the route.

Park, on the outskirts of Rochester, offers access to the Fox and contains a nice stretch of a bike trail that runs toward Burlington.

On Sheard Avenue, you may be surprised when an 8-foot steel sculpture of a horse—made partly from rusted car bumpers—pops up from the side of this quiet rural road. The artwork is the creation of local artist Richard Arfsten, who lives on the road and makes his living creating art and painting barns. As Sheard Avenue becomes CR B (another state-designated rustic road), the landscape flattens and widens. Ag fields abound. On CR J, lush woodland returns in full force as you pass between the Burlington School Forest and the western edge of Richard Bong State Recreation Area. Cross the Fox River again and then enter the lovely sprawling wetlands of Karcher Marsh Wildlife Area.

Bike Shop

Bob's Pedal Pusher: Full-service bike shop; 466 South Pine St., Burlington, Wisconsin; (262) 763-7794

If you enjoy locally produced gourmet items, River Valley Kitchens at the corner of 400th Avenue and 60th Street deserves your attention. In addition to selling jars of canned vegetables mixed with spices and herbs, the store offers a great variety of homemade dips, sauces, and spreads containing many ingredients grown on-site. If you end up buying goodies here, fortunately, there's only about 10 miles left to ride with the added weight.

The final stretch of the ride frequently follows a series of Wisconsin Rustic Roads through dense stands of oak, maple, and hickory. Tree limbs often reach out over the road, and high spots allow you to admire the handiwork of local glaciers. After wrapping up the journey in the town of Lyons, reward your efforts with something sweet and chocolaty from the convenience store across the street from the parking area.

At some point during your visit to the area, you may want to take a jaunt along the White River Trail, which runs alongside the parking area in Lyons where this ride begins. This 11-mile trail shoots from Elkhorn to the outskirts of Burlington. If your time is limited on the trail, head west toward Elkhorn, where you'll encounter sections of rugged wooded terrain and a former train depot alongside the trail that has been turned into a cafe/antiques store.

MILES AND DIRECTIONS

0.0 Head west (left) on North Railroad Street.

0.1 Turn right onto Church Street.

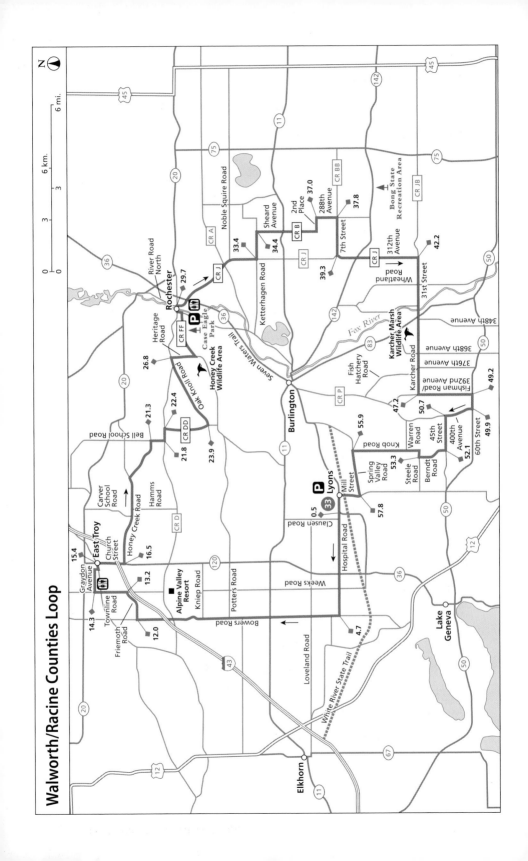

Walworth/Racine Counties Loop

0.2 Turn left onto Highway 36.

0.5 As Highway 36 veers left, stay to the right on Hospital Road.

4.7 Turn right onto Bowers Road.

12.0 Turn right onto Friemoth Road.

13.2 Turn left onto Townline Road. (On the way into East Troy, you'll pass a grocery store on the right.)

14.3 Turn right onto Graydon Avenue.

15.2 Turn right onto Beulah Road, and then quickly turn left onto Union Street.

15.4 Turn right onto Church Street (Highway 120). Stop in the East Troy town square. When leaving East Troy, continue heading south on Church Street (Highway 120).

16.5 Turn left onto Honey Creek Road.

21.3 Turn right onto Bell School Road.

21.8 Turn left onto CR D.

22.4 Turn right onto CR DD.

23.9 Turn left onto Oak Knoll Road.

26.5 Turn right onto CR D.

26.8 Turn right onto Heritage Road.

27.6 Turn left onto CR FF (Academy Road).

29.4 Turn left onto Front Street in Rochester.

29.5 Turn right onto CR D and cross the Fox River.

29.7 Turn right onto CR J.

33.4 Turn left onto Ketterhagen Road.

34.4 Turn right onto Sheard Avenue. Soon, Sheard Avenue becomes CR B. As CR B turns to the left, it becomes Second Place.

37.0 Turn right onto 288th Avenue.

37.8 Turn right onto CR BB (Seventh Street).

39.3 Turn left onto CR J (312th Avenue).

42.2 Turn right onto CR JB (31st Street). This road soon turns into Karcher Road.

47.2 Turn left onto Fishman Road (392nd Avenue).

49.2 Turn right onto 60th Street.

49.9 Turn right onto 400th Avenue (CR P).

50.7 Turn left onto 45th Street.

52.1 Turn right onto Berndt Road.

53.3 Turn right onto Steele Road, which soon curves to the left to become Knob Road.

55.9 Turn left onto Spring Valley Road.

57.8 Turn right onto Mill Street.

58.1 At Railroad Street, turn left and return to your starting location.

RIDE INFORMATION

Local Events/Attractions

East Troy Railroad Museum: Located just north of the town square on Church Street, East Troy, Wisconsin; (262) 642-3263; www.easttroyrr.org.

NAMI Racine Bike 'n Hike: Follows the route described here; starts in Waterford; held in September; 2300 DeKoven Ave., Racine, Wisconsin; (262) 637-0582; www.namiracine.org/bikenhike.

Restaurants

Gus's Drive-In: Located a few blocks off the town square in East Troy; classic fast food; 3131 Main St. (CR ES), East Troy, Wisconsin; (262) 642-2929.

Local Folks Bar and Grill: Standard diner fare with a bar; on the route; 39601 60th St., Burlington, Wisconsin; (262) 539-3200.

River Valley Kitchens: Serves sandwiches in addition to plenty of canned and packaged food; 39900 West 60th St., Burlington, Wisconsin; (262) 539-3555; www.rivervalleykitchens.com.

Restrooms

Start/finish: Restrooms and water are available in the small convenience store across the street. Be sure to buy something if you use the facilities.

Mile 13.8: On the way into East Troy, you'll pass a large community park that contains restrooms.

Mile 28.2: Restrooms and water are available at Case Eagle Park outside of Rochester.

Maps

DeLorme: Wisconsin Atlas and Gazetteer: Pages 94 and 95

Milwaukee and Southeast Wisconsin Bike Map, Little Transport Press; 4401 Grand Avenue, Minneapolis, Minnesota; www.littletransport.com

USGS 7.5" Burlington quad, USGS 7.5" East Troy quad, USGS Genoa City 7.5" quad, USGS Rochester 7.5" quad

Woodstock Loop

After a lap around Woodstock's celebrated town square, the route takes you through the rolling terrain of northern McHenry County. At Glacial Park, one of the most attractive parks in northern Illinois, you'll come across a fine picnicking spot at the edge of a gurgling creek that runs through a large grassland. On the return trip to Woodstock, the hills increase, as do long-range views of the surrounding landscape sprinkled with farms and houses.

Start: Parking area 1 block east of the Woodstock town square at Jefferson Street and Jackson Street

Length: 33.7 miles

Approximate riding time: 2–3 hours

Best bike: Road bike

Terrain and trail surface: Much of the ride is gently rolling. Hills do appear along the way, but none are steep.

Traffic and hazards: While traffic is minimal on most of these roads, use caution because cars tend to move briskly.

Things to see: Woodstock, farmland, wetlands, and quiet country roads

Getting there: By car: From I-90 northwest of Chicago, head north on SR 47. In Woodstock, turn left onto Calhoun Street, then turn right onto Jefferson Street. Park in the lot near the train tracks at the northwest corner of Jefferson Street and Jackson Street. **By public transportation:** The Union Pacific Northwest Metra line offers service from Chicago to Woodstock. From the train station, catch the route by heading 1 block east to Clay Street. GPS coordinates: 42 18.901 N / 88 26.736 W

THE RIDE

By all accounts, Woodstock has the most charming town square in the entire state. Hollywood reinforced this impression by shooting most of the 1993 film *Groundhog Day* in Woodstock's downtown area. The town square is composed of a leafy park and a bandstand surrounded by a series of Victorian buildings containing an assortment of restaurants and inviting shops focusing on antiques, art, handicrafts, and sweets. Visitors often stop at the galleries at the Old Courthouse Arts Center to see artwork by local and national artists. They also come to admire the historic opera house. Since it opened in 1890, the opera house has hosted luminaries one would hardly expect to appear in a small-town venue. The list includes speakers such as Jane Addams and Leo Tolstoy and actors like Paul Newman and Orson Welles.

After soaking up the atmosphere in downtown Woodstock, it's time to start meandering north through Woodstock's residential neighborhoods. The residential areas give way to farmland and open countryside upon reaching Queen Anne Road at mile 3. On Thompson Road, the gently rolling roadway drops into a shallow ravine to cross Nippersink Creek.

After grazing the shoreline of Wonder Lake and logging about a dozen miles of riding, don't miss the picnic area alongside Nippersink Creek at Glacial Park (turn right onto Keystone Road). For those with an interest in learning how glaciers sculpted the landscape in northeastern Illinois, Glacial Park is a geologic jewel. Rising in the distance, just beyond the big swath of prairie that

Nippersink Creek runs through a picnic area at Glacial Park.

borders the picnic area, is a series of glacially created mounds called kames. Kames are formed when glacial meltwater deposits large quantities of sand and gravel in depressions in the ice or at the edge of the glacier. The 100-foot-high Camelback Kame, located directly east, is said to have formed at the edge of a glacier as it receded some 15,500 years ago.

Glacial Park's bog and marshes also offer a link to the area's geologic past. These wetlands began to take shape when large chunks of ice detached from a receding glacier; as ice melted, a pond formed in the depression and, eventually, vegetation overtook the pond. Some visitors arrive at Glacial Park via the Prairie Trail, a 25-mile multiuse path that stretches from the Wisconsin border south to the town of Algonquin.

Bike Shop

Village Pedaler: 470 West Virginia St., Crystal Lake; (815) 459-1833; www.village pedaler.com

Now turning to the west, you'll make a gradual climb up Barnard Mill Road and then take in long views to the north as you follow Vander Karr Road. At SR 47, picnic shelters and a sign offering a rough sketch of Illinois history serve as a welcome for visitors from Wisconsin, which borders Illinois 3 miles north. Farms come and go as you turn onto Johnson Road and catch views of the wide, shallow valley containing Nippersink Creek to the east. The agricultural landscape is speckled with houses, silos, barns, and patches of woodland.

On St. Patrick Road, you'll pass a country church of the same name and an accompanying cemetery. If the season permits, an apple farm on this stretch of roadway invites you to select fruit from a roadside stand or straight from the tree. Returning to Woodstock on Rose Farm Road, the rolling, wooded terrain continues to offer long views of woodland and hills to the south. Closing in on Woodstock, a series of minor hills are mixed with a sprinkling of ponds. Once in the town, handsome wood-frame homes escort you back to the parking area.

MILES AND DIRECTIONS

0.0 From the parking lot at the corner of Jackson Street and Jefferson Street in Woodstock, head west on Jackson Street.

0.1 At the town square, turn right onto Benton Street. Continue ahead as Benton Street becomes Clay Street.

1.4 Keep straight ahead on Locust Street as Clay Street turns left.

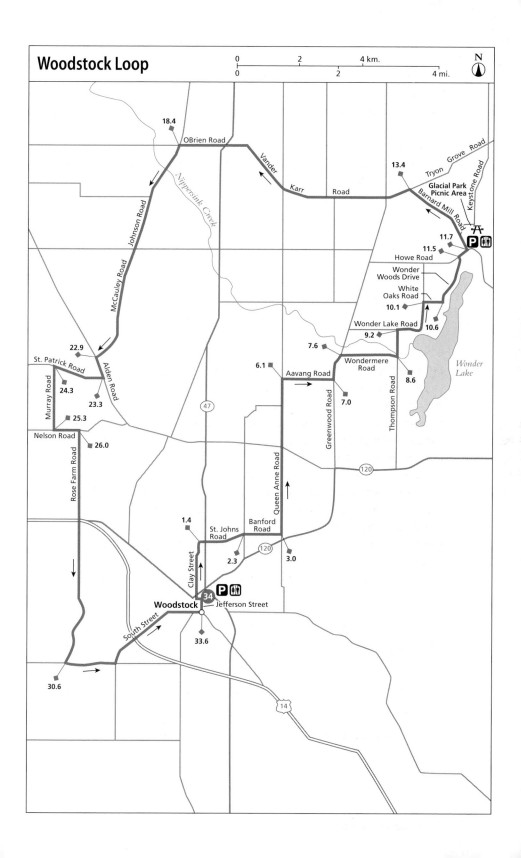

Woodstock Loop

0   2   4 km.
0   2   4 mi.

N

18.4
OBrien Road
Vander
Karr   Road
13.4
Tryon   Grove   Road
Keystone Road
Glacial Park
Picnic Area
Barnard Mill Road
Nippersink Creek
Johnson Road
11.7
11.5
Howe Road
Wonder
Woods Drive
White
Oaks Road
McCauley Road
10.1
10.6
Wonder Lake Road
9.2
7.6
Wondermere
Road
8.6
22.9
St. Patrick Road
6.1
Aavang Road
Wonder
Lake
Murray Road
24.3
Alden Road
23.3
7.0
Greenwood Road
Thompson Road
25.3
Nelson Road
26.0
Rose Farm Road
47
120
Queen Anne Road
1.4
St. Johns
Road
Banford
Road
2.3
120
3.0
P
34
Woodstock   Jefferson Street
Clay Street
33.6
South Street
30.6
14

1.5 Turn right onto SR 47/Seminary Road, then immediately turn left onto St. Johns Road.

2.3 Jog left onto Raffel Road, then immediately turn right onto Banford Road.

3.0 Turn left onto Queen Anne Road.

6.1 Turn right onto Aavang Road.

7.0 Turn left onto Greenwood Road.

7.6 Turn right onto Wondermere Road.

8.6 Turn left onto Thompson Road.

9.2 Turn right onto West Wonder Lake Road.

10.1 Turn right onto White Oaks Road.

10.6 Turn left onto Wonder Woods Drive.

11.5 Turn right onto Howe Road.

11.7 Turn left onto Barnard Mill Road.

12.0 **Side trip:** Take a brief side trip to the Glacial Park picnic area by turning right onto Keystone Road.

13.4 Turn left onto Tryon Grove Road. Continue ahead as Tryon Grove Road becomes Vander Karr Road. Vander Karr Road becomes OBrien Road after crossing SR 47.

18.4 Turn left onto Johnson Road, which soon becomes McCauley Road.

22.9 Turn left onto Alden Road.

23.3 Turn right onto St. Patrick Road.

24.3 Turn left onto Murray Road.

25.3 Turn left onto Nelson Road.

26.0 Turn right onto Rose Farm Road.

30.6 Turn left onto South Street (there is no sign identifying this road).

33.6 Turn left onto Jefferson Street.

33.7 Return to the parking area where the ride started.

RIDE INFORMATION

Local Events/Attractions

Lake Geneva: Charming—if somewhat touristy—town situated on a beautiful lake just across the Wisconsin border about 20 miles north of Woodstock; Walworth County Visitors Bureau, 9 West Walworth St., Elkhorn, Wisconsin; (262) 723-3980; www.visitwalworthcounty.com.

McHenry County Conservation District: Operates Glacial Park Conservation Area and the 25-mile Prairie Trail; 18410 US 14, Woodstock; (815) 338-6223; www.mccdistrict.org.

Royal Oak Orchard: In addition to the orchard, there's a bakery, gift shop, and restaurant; located west of Hebron; 15908 Hebron Rd., Harvard; (815) 648-4141; www.royaloakfarmorchard.com.

Woodstock: The city's website has a handy walking tour of the town square; 121 West Calhoun St., Woodstock; (815) 338-4300; www.woodstock-il.com.

Woodstock Farmers Market: Held in the town square Tuesday and Saturday mornings, May through October; www.woodstockfarmersmarket.org.

Restaurants

La Petite Creperie and Bistro: Crepes and wine on the town square; 115 North Johnson St., Woodstock; (815) 337-0765; www.lapetitecreperie.net.

Pirro's Restaurante: Traditional Italian menu, including a great selection of pizzas; 228 Main St., Woodstock; (815) 337-7341; http://pirrosrestaurante.com.

Accommodations

Bundling Board Inn: Affordable and close to downtown; 220 East South St., Woodstock; (815) 338-7054; www.bundlingboard.com.

Days Inn Woodstock: 990 Lake Ave., Woodstock; (815) 338-0629.

Restrooms

Mile 1.0: Olson Park has a portable toilet in the northwest corner of the park.
Mile 12.0: Restrooms are available at the Glacial Park picnic area.

Maps

USGS: Hebron quad, Marengo North quad, Richmond quad, Woodstock quad
DeLorme: Illinois Atlas & Gazetteer: Pages 19 and 20

Rides at a Glance

9–20 miles
24. Waterfall Glen Trail: 9.3 miles
29. Moraine Hills State Park Trail: 9.5 miles
23. Virgil Gilman Trail: 11.3 miles
18. Great Western Trail: DuPage County: 11.7 miles
21. Illinois Prairie Path: Main Stem: 13.4 miles
10. Joliet Area Trails Loop: 15.9 miles
19. Great Western Trail: Kane and DeKalb Counties: 17.1 miles
1. Beverly/Oak Lawn Loop: 17.9 miles
12. Oak Savannah/Prairie Duneland Trails: 19.7 miles

20–30 miles
7. I&M Canal/Centennial Trails: 20.1 miles
27. Lake Geneva Loop: 20.2 miles
28. Long Prairie and Stone Bridge Trails: 20.4 miles
16. Wauponsee Glacial Trail: 22.3 miles
9. Indiana Dunes/Porter County Loop: 22.4 miles
32. Robert McClory Trail: 22.8 miles
26. Des Plaines River Trail: 24.8 miles
15. Valparaiso Loop: 26.6 miles
13. Old Plank Road Trail: 26.5 miles
20. Illinois Prairie Path: Aurora and Elgin Branches: 27.2 miles
3. Chicago South Side Loop: 27.7 miles
25. Barrington Loop: 28.9 miles
2. Chicago Lakefront and Boulevard Loop: 29.6 miles

30–40 miles
5. Salt Creek Trail/Oak Park Loop: 30.2 miles
31. Prairie/Hebron Trails: 30.9 miles
11. LaPorte Loop: 32.3 miles
4. North Branch and Green Bay Trails Loop: 32.7 miles
17. Fox River Trail: 32.8 miles

34. Woodstock Loop: 33.7 miles

30. North Shore Loop: 35.4 miles

22. Plano Loop: 37.6 miles

40 miles and up

6. Cedar Lake Loop: 44.7 miles

33. Walworth/Racine Counties Loop: 58.1 miles

8. I&M Canal Trail: 61.9 miles

14. Southwest Michigan Loop: 67.7 miles

Regional Bicycle Clubs and Advocacy Groups

Active Transportation Alliance, 9 West Hubbard St., Suite 402, Chicago, Illinois 60654; (312) 427-3325; www.activetrans.org

Arlington Heights Bicycle Association, www.cyclearlington.com

Beverly Bicycle Club, www.beverlybikeclub.org

Bicycle Club of Lake County, P.O. Box 521, Libertyville, Illinois 60048; www.bikebclc.com

Bikeable Roads and Trails Supporters, The Conservation Foundation, 10S404 Knoch Knolls Road, Naperville, Illinois 60565; (630) 428-4500

Bike Psychos, P.O. Box 652; Oak Lawn, Illinois 60454; http://bikepsychos.org

Blue Island Bicycle Club, www.geocities.com/repto/BIBC.html

Calumet Crank Club, www.bicycling.org

Chicago Cycling Club, P.O. Box 1178, Chicago, Illinois 60690-1178; (773) 509-8093; www.chicagocyclingclub.org

Chicagoland Cycling Meetup Group, www.meetup.com/chicagoland-cycling

Citzens for Connecting Communities, P.O. Box 183, Hobart, Indiana 46342-0183; www.geocities.com/calumetcitizens

Cycling Sisters, http://cyclingsisters.org

Downers Grove Bicycle Club, 900 Ogden Ave, #261, Downers Grove, Illinois 60515; http://downersgrovebicycleclub.org

Elmhurst Bicycle Club, P.O. Box 902, Elmhurst, Illinois 60126; www.elmhurst bicycling.org

Evanston Bicycle Club, P.O. Box 1981, Evanston Illinois 60204-1981; www.evanstonbikeclub.org

Folks on Spokes, P.O. Box 763, Matteson, Illinois 60443; www.folksonspokes.com

Fox Valley Bicycle & Ski Club, P.O. Box 1073, Saint Charles, Illinois 60174-7073; www.fvbsc.org.

Greenway Planning Database, Chicago Area Trails, www.greenways.us

Joliet Bicycle Club, http://jolietbicycleclub.org

League of Illinois Bicyclists, 2550 Cheshire Dr., Aurora, Illinois 60504; (630) 978-0583; www.bikelib.org

Major Taylor Bike Club, P.O. Box 4812, Chicago, Illinois 60680; www.mtc3.org

McHenry County Bicycle Advocates, www.mcbicycleadvocates.org

McHenry County Bicycle Club, P.O. Box 917, Crystal Lake, Illinois 60039-0917; www.mchenrybicycleclub.org

Mount Prospect Bike Club, www.geocities.com/mpbccyclist

Naperville Bicycle Club, P.O. Box 150, Winfield, Illinois 60190; www.naperville bikeclub.com

Oak Park Cycle Club, P.O. Box 1488, Oak Park, Illinois 60304; www.oakpark cycleclub.org

Schaumburg Bicycle Club, P.O. Box 68353, Schaumburg, Illinois 60168-0353; www.schaumburgbicycleclub.org

Wheeling Wheelmen, P.O. Box 7304, Buffalo Grove, Illinois 60089-7304; (847) 520-5010; www.wheelmen.com

Windy City Cycle Club, 1658 North Milwaukee Ave., #171, Chicago, Illinois 60647; www.windycitycyclingclub.com

Index

About the Author

While researching *Best Bike Rides Chicago*, Ted Villaire learned two chief lessons: He learned that cyclists can find hills in the Chicago region if they know where to look, and he learned that eating stale trail mix for several consecutive days is harmful for one's morale. Villaire is the author of *60 Hikes within 60 Miles: Chicago, Best Rail Trails Illinois, Camping Illinois, Easy Hikes Close to Home: Chicago*, and *Road Biking Illinois*. He's a Chicago resident and a year-round cyclist who loves pedaling, paddling, camping, and hiking in the western Great Lakes region. His freelance articles have appeared in the *Chicago Tribune, Des Moines Register*, and *Rails to Trails* magazine, among many other publications. He's worked at a handful of local newspapers and nonprofits as a writer and editor, and now serves as the editorial manager for the Active Transportation Alliance, a local nonprofit that works on behalf of Chicagoland cyclists, pedestrians, and transit users. Villaire received a bachelor's degree from Aquinas College in Grand Rapids, Michigan, and a master's degree from DePaul University in Chicago. Get in touch with him and learn more about getting outside in Illinois by visiting www.tedvillaire.com.

FalconGuides publishes a wide array of useful guides to all of your favorite outdoor activities. Grab a guide, head outside, and start having fun!

Best Bike Rides® in the Midwest
Best Hikes Near Chicago
Best Rail Trails Illinois
Best Rail Trails Wisconsin
Camping Illinois
Hiking Indiana
Hiking Michigan
Hiking Wisconsin
Mountain Biking Michigan
Mountain Biking Wisconsin
Rails-to-Trails Wisconsin
Road Biking Illinois
Road Biking Michigan
Road Biking Minnesota
Road Biking Ohio
Road Biking Wisconsin